Evangelist
ALAN CRANE

Twelve Tremendous Themes

Twelve Tremendous Themes

By

EVANGELIST JOHN R. RICE, D.D., LITT.D.

Editor The Sword of the Lord. *Author* Prayer—Asking and Receiving; The Home—Courtship, Marriage, and Children; Power of Pentecost; Is Jesus God? When Skeletons Come Out of Their Closets; "And God Remembered . . ."; Bobbed Hair, Bossy Wives and Women Preachers; "What Must I Do to Be Saved?" The Coming Kingdom of Christ; What Is Wrong With the Movies? Bible Facts About Heaven; The Soul-Winner's Fire, etc.

WITH INTRODUCTION BY
REV. ROBERT G. LEE, D.D., LL.D., LITT.D.
Pastor, Bellevue Baptist Church
Memphis, Tennessee

SWORD OF THE LORD PUBLISHERS
WHEATON, ILLINOIS

10,000 copies, cloth, November, 1943
5,000 copies, paper, November, 1943
5,000 copies, cloth, October, 1946
5,000 copies, cloth, April, 1954

Printed in U. S. A.

Introduction

WITHOUT CLAIMING full agreement as to every iota of every statement, yet without taking issue with the author at any point, and with gratitude for the book with its alluring and alliterative title—"TWELVE TREMENDOUS THEMES"—I commend it as a worthy book which will be profitable for all to possess and propagate. I have read the manuscript with delight and with profit and with prayer that it will have a wide circulation. Such a book is needed and will, when read and preached, do unmeasurable good in this day of invertebrate theology, jelly-fish morality, India-rubber convictions, see-saw philosophy, scientific conceit—when some speak with breath strong with conjectural onions and foul with the garlic of critical contempt for Scriptural certainties.

This book is truth simply and pungently phrased. It sets forth conclusions clearly and concisely expressed. It is declaration saturated and foundationed with the Scriptures. It makes appeal wooingly and earnestly uttered. This book is real bread and meat for the strengthening of Christians, real milk for nourishing the Christian, honey for sweetening the Christian, fire for warming the Christian. Those who read it and lay hold of its truths will know that it is stimulation for the sluggard, stirring for the complacent, anchorage for the unstable, courage for the timid, insistence for the undecided.

This book honors God, honors the Christ who is God, honors the Holy Spirit, honors the church, honors the Gospel, warns the wicked, invites the sinner to accept Christ—and comforts all who believe the Bible to be the inspired, infallible, inerrant Word of God.

ROBERT G. LEE, D.D., LL.D., LITT.D.
Pastor, Bellevue Baptist Church
Memphis, Tennessee

Author's Foreword

THE AUTHOR, though an evangelist, has been for nine years the editor of the evangelistic Christian weekly, *The Sword of the Lord*. Along with evangelistic sermons are talks or messages to Christians. He has published many doctrinal Bible studies. In this book are collected twelve of the most important of these treatments of great Bible themes.

What man could please everybody in discussing all these great doctrines? This writter cannot. Nor is there space enough in one book to deal adequately with these great themes. Yet the reception accorded these studies when printed in *The Sword of the Lord* encourages us to believe that our heavenly Father will use them to help many to a more thorough understanding of these twelve great doctrines. Oh, to help men to know better their Bibles and thus to know better their Saviour and their God!

In Christ's dear name, yours,
JOHN R. RICE

Wheaton, Illinois
September, 1943

Preface to revised edition: 1954—

For eleven years this book has been greatly blessed of God. We are deeply grateful. Now with some changes and corrections, we send out the new edition, praying God's blessings upon it and all who read to learn more of the truth of God as taught in His wonderful book, the Bible.

Table of Contents

I

Verbal Inspiration

Or, How True Is the Bible?

"All scripture is given by inspiration of God, and is profitable for doctrine, for reproof, for correction, for instruction in righteousness."—II Tim. 3:16.

"For the prophecy came not in old time by the will of man: but holy men of God spake as they were moved by the Holy Ghost."—II Peter 1:21.

HOW TRUE is the Bible? What a queer question to ask! And yet there are people who claim to be Christians who believe that the Bible is partly true and partly false.

Some say that the Bible is inspired in the same sense that great literature is inspired, as the plays of Shakespeare or the poems of Tennyson and Browning. Such people sometimes say, "I know the Bible is inspired because it inspires me." Really they mean that the Bible is not the infallible Word of God but that it is a good inspiring book even though it has mistakes. Some say that God gave the general thought and left it to men to write it down so that of necessity there would be some slight errors. Some say that the New Testament is authoritative and true, but the Old Testament is imperfect and is simply a survival of primitive religious thinking. Some so-called scholars, who are not scholars enough to know what the Bible claims for itself nor the evidence that it is true, teach a so-called "progressive revelation" and say that none of the

Bible is reliable except the very words of Jesus, and they doubt many of the statements of the gospels. Many good men are deceived by these theorists and quote them. Some people say that the Bible *contains* the Word of God, that not all of it is the Word of God. If one must find for himself or depend upon some modernistic scholar to say just how much of the Bible is really the Word of God and authoritative, of course no two living men, on that plan, would perfectly agree as to what was true and what was not.

Some good men very foolishly say that the Bible is inspired and reliable for *religious* knowledge but is not necessarily true in scientific matters, or in history.

Great Saints Believed in Word-for-Word Inspiration

The greatest saints, Bible scholars, preachers and soul winners have believed the Bible to be the infallible, verbally-inspired Word of God.

My mother believed that the Bible was absolutely the Word of God, true in every particular. So did my father, a country Baptist preacher. And so, I feel sure, did the mothers and fathers of most of you who read these words. Devout Christians through the ages have accepted the Bible for what it claims to be, the very Word of God, true in every particular. And that is true of the most scholarly Christians, the greatest preachers, the Spirit-filled soul winners most greatly used of God through the centuries.

Charles H. Spurgeon prepared and signed with six of his brethren what he called "A Confession," and therein declared, "We . . . avow our firmest belief in the verbal inspiration of all Holy Scripture as originally given. To us, the Bible does not merely contain the Word of God, but is the Word of God. From beginning to end, we accept it, believe it, and continue to preach it. To us, the Old Testament is no less inspired than the New, the Book is an organic whole."

B. H. Carroll, a great Southern Baptist preacher, founder of the Southwestern Baptist Theological Seminary, certainly the greatest theologian Southern Baptists have had, said, "Any talk about revelation without inspiration of the words is fool's talk," and wrote a whole book (*Inspiration of the Bible*, Revell) to prove that the Bible was inspired word for word.

Moody and Torrey, greatest soul winners that America has seen, believed in the word-for-word inspiration of the Bible; and the Moody Bible Institute statement of faith still states that belief in verbal inspiration.

The Irish Baptist statement of faith avows belief in verbal or word-for-word inspiration of the Bible. So does the statement of faith of Wheaton College, the most prominent and influential Christian college in America; and the statements of faith of practically all the Bible institutes and many great seminaries.

Wesley, Finney, A. J. Gordon, Chapman, Sunday, the greatest of soul winners, believed, like Moody, Spurgeon and Torrey, in the word-for-word inspiration of the Bible.

The late Dr. I. M. Haldeman, pastor of the First Baptist Church of New York City, in his own trembling hand wrote me his profound conviction that God gave the very words and quoted Isaiah 51:16, "I have put my words in thy mouth," to prove it.

Dr. W. B. Riley and all the leaders of the World's Christian Fundamentals Association have believed in verbal or word-for-word inspiration of the Bible and have so declared themselves.

Dr. L. R. Scarborough, president of the Southwestern Baptist Theological Seminary and president of the Southern Baptist Convention, has declared his belief in verbal inspiration of the Bible (Introduction to B. H. Carroll's book, *Inspiration of the Bible*).

Bible Itself Explicitly Claims to Be the Infallible Word of God

Those who believe the Bible to be literally and infallibly the Word of God, reliable and exactly true in every detail, are in good company. They agree with the great saints of God throughout the ages.

Those who have foolish theories about mistakes and inaccuracies in the Bible deny the very Word of God itself. Either the Bible is what it claims to be, the eternal and infallible and perfect Word of God, or it is an imposture. The Bible claims perfection, claims that it is settled in Heaven, claims that it is true from the beginning, claims that it is made up of the very words of God, that even every jot and tittle was given by inspiration and will not pass away, claims that men will be judged by whether they take from or add to the very words of the Scripture. There are only two honest and intelligent positions to take: 1. That the Bible is what it claims to be, dictated by the mouth of God, the infallible and perfect Word of God that cannot be broken; 2. That the Bible is merely the work of men, claiming to be what it is not, that the Bible is false and not true, and with no binding authority on mankind, no direct and authoritative revelation from God.

However, on further investigation there will be found only one position for the person who is both spiritually honest and intelligent and that is that the Bible is all it claims to be, actually the Word of God, proving itself on every point as a miraculously inspired, divine revelation.

Notice what the Bible says about itself:

"The law of the Lord is perfect . . ."—Ps. 19:7.

"Forever, O Lord, thy word is settled in heaven."—Ps. 119:89.

"Thy word is true from the beginning; and every one of thy righteous judgments endureth for ever."—Ps. 119:160.

"The scripture cannot be broken."—John 10:35.

Notice that the above Scriptures plainly claim that the Bible is perfect (specifically the Old Testament and more specifically the law, including the Genesis account of creation, the flood, the countless miracles). These Scriptures claim that the Word of God is "true from the beginning," that is, from the very first word of Genesis. They claim that the Word of God is settled forever in Heaven, that is, that it is divine and eternal instead of being human and fallible and subject to being displaced by later findings of science. The Bible even claims that "the scripture cannot be broken" which is simply another way of saying it claims absolute infallibility.

Second Timothy 3:16 says, "All scripture is given by inspiration of God." And even in the American Standard Version which modernists quote here, it really means exactly the same thing. "Every scripture inspired of God is also profitable for teaching, for reproof," etc., simply means that all the writings or books in the canon of our Bible, being divinely inspired, are reliable and infallible for doctrine, for reproof, for correction, for instruction in righteousness. The best scholarship concedes that this is the meaning of the Greek text.

And II Peter 1:21 says:

"For the prophecy came not in old time by the will of man: but holy men of God spake as they were moved by the Holy Ghost."

The Bible was not written by men of their own choice nor from their own sources. But this is the way the Bible came: "holy men of God spake as they were moved by the Holy Ghost." That claims divine inspiration for everything in the Scriptures.

And notice particularly that this claim for supernatural revelation in II Timothy 3:16 and II Peter 1:21, is made primarily for the Old Testament which is usually attacked by modernists and unbelievers! The Genesis account of creation, the story of the flood, the plagues in Egypt, the miracles of crossing the Red Sea under Moses and crossing the flooded Jordan under Joshua, of the fall of Jericho and the conquest of Canaan, of the sun standing still in the heavens about the space of a day, of Jonah's being swallowed by the whale—all these accounts were written by holy men of God who spake as they were moved by the Holy Ghost.

Literally hundreds of times in the Bible the writers say that "The word of the Lord came to Moses and to Aaron, saying . . .," or "Thus saith the Lord," or "Moreover the word of the Lord came to me, saying . . .," or "For thus saith the

Lord God of Israel unto me," etc. I say *many hundreds of times;* as often as *scores of times in one book of the Bible,* such statements are given, CLAIMING TO GIVE DIRECT QUOTATION OF WORDS FROM THE MOUTH OF GOD! It is impossible to believe what the Bible says about itself and not accept it as the very Word of God, inspired word for word.

I. What We Mean by Verbal Inspiration

What did Spurgeon and Moody and Torrey and Carroll and Haldeman and Scarborough and the Bible institutes and multitudes of Christians mean—what do they mean when they say they believe in the "verbal inspiration" of the Bible? *Verbal* inspiration means *word* inspiration, from the Latin term for *word.* They mean that God gave the very words to the writers that they were to write down. God did not give the general thought and allow the human authors to put the thought in their own words. God did not simply leave them to search out the sources, talk with eye-witnesses, copy from old records and so write the Bible. God did not simply superintend the writings so that the writers would be kept from error. No, by verbal inspiration we mean that God gave the words in the Bible. Of course we do not mean that God gave the words in English as they are in our King James or Authorized Version of the Bible. We mean that God gave the words as the original writers wrote them down; the Old Testament writers writing generally in Hebrew, the New Testament writers writing in Greek. (Parts of Daniel were written in the Chaldaic language.) In the original manuscripts the very words were the words of God.

Of course copyists occasionally made mistakes in copying by hand the Scriptures. But we have so many hundreds of manuscripts of both the Old and New Testaments that by comparing them we find there is not over one word in ten thousand of the original manuscripts that cannot be reproduced as it was first given in the original languages. And so many earnest scholars have made so many careful translations of the Bible in our own language, through hundreds of years of time, that we can depend with confidence upon our English translations of the Bible.

Remember, however, that when we speak of verbal inspiration we mean that God gave the very words originally to the Bible writers, and as they put them down in the original manuscripts the very words were the words of God. That means that the Bible is the infallible Word of God, reliable in religion, reliable and perfectly accurate in science, infallibly correct in history, true in every particular. "The law of the Lord is perfect." "Forever, O Lord, thy word is settled in heaven." "Thy word is true from the beginning."

II. Indisputable Examples of Verbal Inspiration

Even a casual reading of the Bible shows some remarkable examples of verbal inspiration. Later we will prove that every word in the original Scriptures was dictated by God. But first let us give some outstanding examples.

1. The Ten Commandments were given by the voice of God speaking aloud from Mount Sinai. Exodus 20:1, preceding the Ten Commandments, says, "And God spake all these words, saying." Then in verse 22 in the same chapter we are told,

"And the Lord said unto Moses, Thus thou shalt say unto the children of Israel, Ye have seen that I have talked with you from heaven."

There cannot be any possible doubt that here, according to the Bible, we have the very words of God in the Ten Commandments.

2. Balaam's ass spake by verbal inspiration. Sometimes smart men try to insist that God gave the thought but that man put it in his own words. Or they claim that men were so exalted in spirit and so guarded by the Holy Spirit that they wrote without any physical miracle with fair accuracy. All this reasoning of man's wisdom falls away, however, when you consider how God used a donkey to give His message to Balaam. In Numbers 22:28–30 we are told how the Lord

opened the mouth of the ass and she spake to Balaam. That is a clear case of verbal or word-for-word inspiration since donkeys do not have words of their own. God gave the very words.

3. But God deals with men just as He does with donkeys in the matter of inspiration. The case of Caiaphas is very similar. In John 11:49-52 we read this remarkable passage:

"And one of them, named Caiaphas, being the high priest that same year, said unto them, Ye know nothing at all, nor consider that it is expedient for us, that one man should die for the people, and that the whole nation perish not. And this spake he not of himself: but being high priest that year, he prophesied that Jesus should die for that nation; and not for that nation only, but that also he should gather together in one the children of God that were scattered abroad."

Caiaphas was a wicked, unconverted man, helping to crucify Jesus. He was not exalted into a high state of spiritual perception. He was not speaking out of his own knowledge. In fact, we can be certain that Caiaphas meant something entirely different from what God meant. Caiaphas simply thought, "We had better kill Jesus and keep the nation from falling under the wrath of Rome so we priests can keep our jobs." But God meant it as a prophetic and verbally inspired statement of the blood atonement of Jesus for the sins of the whole world. Certainly and without any shadow of doubt or any other possible explanation, that was word-for-word inspiration. God gave the very words.

4. And God used this same kind of inspiration many times so that those who wrote it down word for word did not fully understand even what they said. They did not fully understand the thought God gave, they did not select the words but simply wrote down what God said, as is proven by I Peter 1:10-12.

"Of which salvation the prophets have inquired and searched diligently, who prophesied of the grace that should come unto you: searching what, or what manner of time the Spirit of Christ which was in them

*did signify, when it testified beforehand the sufferings of Christ, and the
glory that should follow. Unto whom it was revealed, that not unto
themselves, but unto us they did minister the things, which are now
reported unto you by them that have preached the gospel unto you with
the Holy Ghost sent down from heaven; which things the angels desire
to look into."*

Notice these very prophets "who prophesied of the grace
that should come unto you," inquired and searched diligently
into their own prophecies, into the Scriptures they themselves
had written, "searching what, or what manner of time the
Spirit of Christ which was in them did signify, when it testified
beforehand the sufferings of Christ, and the glory that should
follow." These prophets searched their own writings, earnestly
desiring to find out what the Holy Spirit meant when He,
the Holy Spirit, testified through their pen of the first and
second coming of Christ and such other matters written down
in the Bible!

These human writers of the Bible knew (vs. 12), had it revealed to them from God, that they were simply agents
ministering to us and not unto themselves the things which
the Holy Ghost gave them to write down.

It cannot possibly be said then, that the inspiration spoken
of here was anything but verbal or word-for-word inspiration.
They did not know what they were writing about when they
wrote. They did not understand even the thought in the mind
of God; how could they know what words to use? They did
not select either the thoughts or the words. They simply wrote
down what the Holy Spirit said write. And then they searched
and inquired diligently, trying to find out the meaning of the
Scripture which they had written. And so precious was the
Word of God thus inspired, so far beyond the possibility of
any human being giving it of himself, that even the angels
desire to look into these things!

Certainly then, verbal inspiration is plausible, nay, is absolutely essential in any reliable revelation from God.

III. Paul Says That Revelation Is Given "in the Words Which the Holy Ghost Teacheth"

The Bible so often claims word-for-word inspiration that it is only proven ignorance for a child of God not to know the Bible doctrine of inspiration. I will show you how Paul, Moses, Isaiah, Jeremiah, Ezekiel, David, John, and our Lord Jesus Christ all explicitly and expressly stated that God gave the very words of the Bible.

Some men have said, "We know that the Bible is inspired, but we do not know the method of inspiration." Well, one who does not know the method of divine inspiration simply has not read or does not believe the Bible, for the Bible leaves no doubt about how it was written.

In I Corinthians, chapter 2, Paul gives us detailed explanation about divine revelation. In verse 7 he declares:

"But we speak the wisdom of God in a mystery, even the hidden wisdom, which God ordained before the world unto our glory."

Divine revelation is about mysterious and hidden things of God that man cannot naturally know. Verses 9 and 10 continue:

"But as it is written, Eye hath not seen, nor ear heard, neither have entered into the heart of man, the things which God hath prepared for them that love him. But God hath revealed them unto us by his Spirit: for the Spirit searcheth all things, yea, the deep things of God."

The Holy Spirit is God's agent in getting the Bible written. The men who wrote down the things in the Bible did not write what eye had seen nor what ear had heard, neither what entered through natural sources into the heart of men, we are told. But the things written down in the Bible, all of them, "God hath revealed them unto us by his Spirit" (vs. 10). It is foolish then to give any credit to men who wrote the Bible because they were eye witnesses or as if they copied from other manuscripts or as if they got their information from others. No, the things in the Bible "God hath revealed them unto us by his Spirit." The Holy Spirit is the true Author of the Bible. Each Bible writer was directly inspired and wrote down what the Holy Spirit gave. Now the only remaining question is, how did he get the words to write down what God revealed?

The matter of the words in which the Bible was written is explained in verse 13 of that second chapter of I Corinthians:

"Which things also we speak, not in the words which man's wisdom teacheth, but which the Holy Ghost teacheth; comparing spiritual things with spiritual."

The Holy Spirit gave the *matter* of inspiration and then not relying on man's wisdom, the Holy Spirit taught the very *words* in which revelation was to be written down. The Bible was written "not in the words which man's wisdom teacheth, but which the Holy Ghost teacheth." And the Standard Version makes it even clearer, saying, "Not in words which man's wisdom teacheth, but which the Spirit teacheth; COMBINING SPIRITUAL THINGS WITH SPIRITUAL WORDS." The matter in the Bible is Spirit-given matter, revealed in every detail by the Holy Ghost. The words in the Bible are likewise spiritual words, that is, Spirit-given words. God could not say it plainer, the Holy Spirit dictated the very words in which divine revelation was given. The words of the Bible are God's words, not man's. In the original manuscripts the human authors simply wrote down the words that the Holy Spirit gave them. Sometimes they understood what they wrote. Sometimes they certainly did not understand and searched diligently in their own writings to see what the Holy Spirit meant by the things He said as we have seen from I Peter 1:10–12. THE WORDS ARE GOD'S WORDS!

The Slur of Modernists About "Mechanical Dictation"

Modernists and unbelievers always want to exalt man and belittle God. They make man's sins small so they can minimize the grace of God and the need for blood atonement. The constant tendency of modernism is to preach a great mankind and a little Christ. Even in their theories of inspiration, they want to exalt man and belittle the supernatural and miraculous element. So modernists love to deride what they call the "mechanical dictation" theory of inspiration. Nevertheless, according to the Scripture, God's method of inspiration is literally dictation of the very words.

But why slur dictation as "mechanical"? I am dictating this article just now after long, long months of study, after hours of prayer, with most carefully prepared thoughts and exactly selected words. I am earnestly, fervently, with the gravest concern, giving the very words to my stenographer. The thoughts are my thoughts, and not the stenographer's. The words are my words, not the stenographer's words. I am dictating the very words, and yet there is nothing mechanical about it. That term "mechanical dictation" is simply the slur of unbelievers at the miraculous exactness and perfection of God's divine revelation to man.

Why should any man not be proud to write down the very words of God? If Baruch wrote down the very words of Jeremiah, and Timothy the very words of Paul, how would Jeremiah and Paul be insulted to write down the words dictated by God?

The varying style in the books of the Bible is not the style respectively of various authors, but the style of the Holy Spirit adapted to God's own purpose. I have stenographers with varying qualifications. For certain types of work I select one stenographer. For other types of work I select another. I use them according to my own purpose. But the style is not the style of the stenographer, it is my own. The words are my words. Even so God Himself, having an infinite variety to choose from, chose such men as pleased Him, used the language that pleased Him in each case, but in each case dictated the very words.

Remember that the Bible never gives any significance to the fact that the literary style varies. That is the argument of unbelievers who hope to discredit the Bible. But all the styles in the Bible are God's styles! He gave the very words, "not in the words which man's wisdom teacheth, but which the Holy Ghost teacheth," says I Corinthians 2:13. Again I say, the words are the words of God, not the words of men. The Bible does teach that revelation came by word-for-word inspiration.

And why should it not be so? If I am so meticulously careful about the wording of this article, would the infinite God care less about His perfect Word, His revelation to all mankind to last forever? Since God could give the words, how foolish it is to suppose that He did not do that. If I am careful to give the very words and the punctuation, then surely a merciful, all-wise God would be equally careful, nay, many times more careful that His own thoughts and revelation to mankind be stated in divine words exactly according to His will. My stenographers do not always understand what they write down; so I could not trust them to select the words. The prophets of God did not fully understand what they wrote down and could not have put God's perfect thought in human words with any reliable accuracy.

IV. Moses Given the Law by Verbal Inspiration

The principle of verbal inspiration was given in I Corinthians 2:13. That verse alone ought to settle that all of God's divine revelation was given in the words "which the Holy Ghost teacheth." But to make the assurance doubly sure, let us follow through the Bible and see how various human authors of the Bible were given the very words of God.

The writings of Moses are attacked more often than any other part of the Bible as being not accurate, not scientifically true, or not historically correct. So-called scientists attack the Genesis account of creation. Modernists do not believe in these miracles: the flood, the plagues in Egypt, the crossing of the Red Sea, the manna which fell for forty years in the wilderness, etc. Ingersoll liked to talk about "the mistakes of Moses." Unbelievers cannot believe, they say, that God created the earth in six days. So those who with unbelieving, rebellious hearts criticize the first five books in the Bible, claim that it is not perfectly inspired; that it is made up of legends, that is, it is the work of many authors; that it contains many "survivals of primitive religious thinking." But we are not left in the dark about the method of inspiration of these books of Moses. In Exodus 24:3–8 we are told how Moses wrote down the books ascribed to him. Notice particularly the following phrases and sentences in that passage:

"And Moses came and told the people ALL THE WORDS OF THE LORD, and all the judgments: and all the people answered with one voice, and said, ALL THE WORDS WHICH THE LORD HATH SAID will we do. And Moses wrote ALL THE WORDS OF THE LORD . . .

"And he took the book of the covenant, and read in the audience of the people: and they said, ALL THAT THE LORD HATH SAID will we do . . .

". . . Behold the blood of the covenant, which the Lord hath made with you concerning ALL THESE WORDS."

It could not be more clearly stated that Moses told the people "ALL THE WORDS OF THE LORD," that the people agreed to follow "ALL THE WORDS WHICH THE LORD HATH SAID," and that when Moses wrote the book he wrote "ALL THE WORDS OF THE LORD." The covenant which God made with Israel was "concerning all these WORDS." What Moses wrote were the very words of the Lord. The Holy Spirit gave His revelation to Moses by verbal, or word-for-word inspiration. One who does not believe that Genesis or Exodus, for example, is inspired like the words of Jesus, is simply denying the plain statements of the Bible.

No wonder then that throughout the gospels Jesus referred continually to Genesis, quoting from it and confirming it repeatedly. Jesus believed in the Genesis account of creation of man (Matt. 19:4–6). He believed in the literal, miraculous destruction of Sodom and Gomorrah by fire from Heaven (Luke 17:28–32). He believed also the Genesis account of the flood (Luke 17:26, 27). The books of the law were written by

verbal inspiration and must be accepted as absolutely accurate by those who claim to believe the Bible at all and to be
followers of Christ. It is either verbal inspiration or rank infidelity. There is no intelligent and true middle ground.

Incidentally Jesus also expressly declared that Jonah was
three days and three nights in the belly of the whale just like
the book of Jonah says (Matt. 12:40). If you do not believe
that the events chronicled in the book of Jonah literally occurred, then you do not believe in the deity of Jesus Christ
nor in the inspiration of the book of Matthew where Jesus
approved the book of Jonah as correct.

V. Isaiah, Jeremiah, Ezekiel, All Claimed Word-for-Word Inspiration

In the prophecies of Isaiah we read again and again the
statement, "Thus saith the Lord," and what follows is given
as the very words of God in direct quotation. Did God dictate
to Isaiah the very words of His prophecies? That is the im-
plication throughout the book, and Isaiah 51:16 expressly
states it.

*"And I have put my words in thy mouth, and I have covered thee in
the shadow of mine hand, that I may plant the heavens, and lay the
foundations of the earth, and say unto Zion, Thou art my people."*

God says to Isaiah, "I have put my words in thy mouth."
The words are GOD'S WORDS. That is verbal inspiration,
word-for-word dictation of the Scripture.

However, there is a blessed thought further than this in the
verse. Not only did God put His words in the mouth of Isaiah,
but the whole nation Israel was specifically prepared that
through Jewish prophets the Word of God should be given
word for word. This agrees with Romans 9:4, 5.

*"Who are Israelites; to whom pertaineth the adoption, and the glory,
and the covenants, and the giving of the law, and the service of God,
and the promises; whose are the fathers, and of whom as concerning
the flesh Christ came, who is over all, God blessed for ever. Amen."*

God gave the covenant, the law, the promise and gave His

Son through the nation Israel. See again Romans 3:1, 2:
*"What advantage then hath the Jew? or what profit is there of cir-
cumcision? Much every way: chiefly, because that unto them were committed the oracles of God."*

Isaiah 51:16 says that God put His own words in the mouth
of Isaiah. But it says also that since all the Scripture came
from the pen of Jews, that God put His words in the mouth of
all these prophets who wrote and that all the Bible is verbally
inspired. If you carefully read the context, you will see that
is God's meaning.

To Jeremiah also God dictated the very words of His
prophecy. In Jeremiah 1:9 we are told how God spoke to the
timid prophet, promising word-for-word inspiration for his
prophecies.

*"Then the Lord put forth his hand, and touched my mouth. And the
Lord said unto me, Behold, I HAVE PUT MY WORDS IN THY
MOUTH."*

The words of Jeremiah's prophecies were the very words of
God. That is word-for-word inspiration. Those words of God
are the very words that are written down in our book of
Jeremiah, for Jeremiah 30:1, 2 says:

*"The word that came to Jeremiah from the Lord, saying, Thus
speaketh the Lord God of Israel, saying, Write thee all the words
that I have spoken unto thee in a book."*

And then verse 4 following says,

*"And these are the words that the Lord spake concerning Israel and
concerning Judah."*

Jeremiah wrote down the very words of God in a book.

God gave further prophecies to Jeremiah and so commanded him again in Jeremiah 36:2:

*"Take thee a roll of a book, and write therein ALL THE WORDS
that I have spoken unto thee against Israel, and against Judah, and
against all the nations, from the day I spake unto thee, from the days
of Josiah, even unto this day."*

The very details of the word-for-word dictation and the
way they were written down are told us in Jeremiah 36:4:

"Then Jeremiah called Baruch the son of Neriah: and Baruch

wrote from the mouth of Jeremiah ALL THE WORDS of the Lord, which he had spoken unto him, upon a roll of a book."

Thereafter Jeremiah called this roll which he had written "the words of the Lord" (Jer. 36:6).

That roll which Jeremiah had written containing the very words of God was cut with a penknife and burned up by the wicked king Jehoiakim (Jer. 36:21–23) and we are plainly told that

"Then took Jeremiah another roll, and gave it to Baruch the scribe, the son of Neriah; who wrote therein from the mouth of Jeremiah ALL THE WORDS of the book which Jehoiakim king of Judah had burned in the fire: and there were added besides unto them many like words"—Jer. 36:32.

The unbelief and rebellion of wicked men, Satan's effort to prevent our receiving the verbally inspired Word of God, came to nought, and now the book of Jeremiah in our Bible is made up of the very WORDS OF THE LORD as given to Jeremiah and as he dictated them to Baruch, the scribe who wrote down "the words of the Lord." God, the second time, directed His message to Jeremiah and Jeremiah dictated words to Baruch who wrote them down.

Ezekiel was also timid and hesitant when God called him to be a prophet. But God said,

"And thou shalt speak MY WORDS unto them, whether they will hear, or whether they will forbear: for they are most rebellious"— Ezek. 2:7.

And then as a symbol of direct verbal inspiration, God miraculously gave Ezekiel a roll of a book where were written lamentations and mourning and woe, and he was commanded to eat the roll and did so. Thus Ezekiel symbolized that the words which he should speak and write were literally the words of God, dictated by the Holy Spirit. God assured Ezekiel,

"But when I speak with thee, I will open thy mouth, and thou shalt say unto them, Thus saith the Lord God."—Ezek. 3:27.

The words of the Bible are God's words. Those who believe the Bible must believe in verbal inspiration. The only intelligent alternative is complete repudiation of the Bible—infidelity; and yet that, God knows, is not very intelligent.

If God used word-for-word inspiration in giving the prophecies of Isaiah, Jeremiah, and Ezekiel, it is equally evident that verbal inspiration is *the unchanging rule* in God's revelation; that God in the Bible always gives spiritual truth "not in the words which man's wisdom teacheth, but which the Holy Ghost teacheth" (I Cor. 2:13).

VI. David Wrote Psalms by Verbal Inspiration

The Psalms were inspired of God just like the rest of the Bible. In Acts 1:16 we are told:

"Men and brethren, this scripture must needs have been fulfilled, which the Holy Ghost by the mouth of David spake before concerning Judas . . ."

When David wrote or spoke the Psalms, we are told that it was simply the Holy Ghost speaking "by the mouth of David." The words were the words of the Holy Spirit.

In the "last words of David," we are told again, *"The Spirit of the Lord spake by me, and his word was in my tongue"* (II Sam. 23:2). It was God who was doing the speaking when David wrote those of the Psalms which are his.

Note particularly from these two Scriptures that the Holy Spirit did not *think* through David's brain, did not recall through David's memory, did not feel through David's heart, but the Holy Spirit *spoke* words through David's mouth and tongue! It was not the thoughts only, but the very words, which the Holy Spirit dictated.

That is why in the Psalms there could be so many revelations of the future which could not possibly have been foreseen by man. The twenty-second Psalm, for instance, gives many details concerning the death of Christ and His very words upon the cross. The second Psalm, the twenty-fourth, and many others give details concerning the second coming and the reign of Christ on earth when Christ shall come to Jerusalem and reign on David's throne. Such things David surely could not perfectly understand, and he could not be

trusted to supply the words for God's thoughts. The Psalms
are written, "not in the words which man's wisdom teacheth,
but which the Holy Ghost teacheth," and so with the rest of
the Bible.

VII. How Did Jesus Christ Regard the Inspiration of the Bible?

Jesus quoted from Moses, referred constantly to the Old
Testament, and always as if it were infallibly correct. But
that is not all; Jesus expressly stated that the very words of
the Scriptures were inspired.

For instance, when Jesus met Satan and was tempted in the
wilderness, He answered Satan's temptation with this Scripture from the Old Testament:

*"It is written, Man shall not live by bread alone, but by every word
that proceedeth out of the mouth of God."*—Matt. 4:4; Luke 4:4.

Jesus believed concerning the Bible that literally every
word "proceedeth out of the mouth of God." There is as
clear a statement of verbal or word-for-word inspiration as
it is possible to make.

Not only did Jesus say that the very words are inspired but
the very spelling and marking of the Scriptures, according
to Jesus, were likewise inspired. In Matthew 5:17, 18, Jesus
said:

*"Think not that I am come to destroy the law, or the prophets: I am
not come to destroy, but to fulfil. For verily I say unto you, Till heaven
and earth pass, one jot or one tittle shall in no wise pass from the law,
till all be fulfilled."*

Remember that Jesus was defending the Old Testament
which the critics and modernists usually attack and Jesus said
not only that the words would endure but that not even one
jot or one tittle, the least letter or marking, would pass away.
God not only gave the thoughts, not only gave the words, but
verily gave the jots and tittles as well! And remember that it
was Jesus Himself who was speaking and that what He said
applied particularly to the Old Testament and not only the
New!

VIII. Revelation Claims That the Whole Canon of Scripture Is Verbally Inspired

In the last chapter of the Bible a most solemn warning is given concerning the canon of Scripture. Men are warned not to add to the Scripture on penalty of being cursed with the plagues that are written in the Book. Men are warned not to take from the Scripture on penalty of losing the offered part in the book of life and the heavenly Jerusalem and the blessings promised the saints in the Bible. And now the remarkable thing is that these warnings specifically mention that they refer TO THE VERY WORDS of the Bible. Read Revelation 22:18, 19.

"For I testify unto every man that heareth THE WORDS of the prophecy of this book, If any man shall add unto these things, God shall add unto him the plagues that are written in this book: and if any man shall take away from the WORDS OF THE BOOK of this prophecy, God shall take away his part out of the book of life, and out of the holy city, and from the things which are written in this book."

God is emphasizing that He holds men to account for the very words of Scripture. Men dare not take from the words nor add to the words of the Bible. It will not do for men to change a thought, but it will not even do for men to change the words. THEY ARE GOD'S WORDS!

From Mount Sinai the thunderous voice of God spoke giving the Ten Commandments, and we are told that "God spake all these words." But that Scripture might fittingly be used about every word of holy writ. They are really the words of God. The only kind of inspiration which the Bible speaks of is verbal, or word-for-word inspiration.

Blessed Assurances From This Precious Doctrine

Since God gave the words, then we may believe what the Bible says. Another Scripture says, "Behold, a virgin shall conceive, and bear a son" (Isa. 7:14). Then we may know that God insists on the word *virgin*. It was not simply a young married woman who bore our Saviour; it was a virgin. On one word there hangs the deity of Christ! If Jesus were born of a young woman, not necessarily a virgin, then Jesus had a human father, His birth was not miraculous, and He was not the Son of God. The angel Gabriel based his claim that Jesus was "the Son of the highest" on the fact that the Holy Spirit should come upon Mary while she was still a virgin and the Saviour should be conceived (Luke 1:34, 35). Thank God, we can believe in the word-for-word inspiration of the Scriptures. When God says *virgin,* He means virgin, nothing more, nothing less, and He challenges men not to change it, to add to it, or take from the words. He promises, praise His name, that not a jot or tittle shall pass away since all are perfect, settled forever in Heaven, and true from the beginning.

Suppose in John 3:16 that God had given the general thought but had not dictated the word *whosoever.* Then my eternal soul would be in jeopardy because I trusted in that one word that God meant me and was willing to save me. Men dare not trifle with the very words of the Bible.

In those wonderful promises of salvation in John 3:16; John 5:24; John 6:47, suppose that the one word *everlasting* might be changed. Then what a woeful limitation of the blessedness of God's promise! Living ten years, a hundred years, a thousand years is not life enough. Jesus promised everlasting life. Thank God that the words are God's words! On any word of the Bible a lost sinner may rest his immortal soul in full assurance that God will back up the very words. They are His words, not man's. The Psalmist had sometime based his hope upon some single and blessed word in a promise of God, as I have done many times. So in Psalms 119:49 he cries out to God, "Remember the *word* unto thy servant, upon which thou hast caused me to hope."

There Could Be No Inspiration Without the Words

The truth is that men cannot think without words. Psychologists and educators know that there is a definite growth in the intellectual activity of a child as he begins to use words.

The mind cannot carry on consecutive, intelligent reasoning without words. One cannot have music without notes, cannot have arithmetic without figures, cannot have thoughts without words. One cannot have a revelation from God unless God Himself gives the words. No wonder that Dr. B. H. Carroll said that any talk about inspiration that does not include inspiration of the words is "fool's talk." It is not only fool's talk, it is infidel's talk, the talk of the wicked, rebellious, disbelieving, Christ-rejecting, sinful, carnal heart, for

"The natural man receiveth not the things of the Spirit of God: for they are foolishness unto him: neither can he know them, because they are spiritually discerned"—I Cor. 2:14.

Difficulties in the Bible

There may be some things about the Bible you cannot explain. But your ignorance is a sorry excuse for criticizing the blessed Word of God. Other men, more devout than you, more scholarly than you, older in experience than you, greater soul winners than you, have been able to believe in the Bible. Do not let your youth or your ignorance or your pride or your friendship for modernists and unbelievers lead you into the terrible sin of adding to or taking from the words of the Bible.

If space permitted, we could harmonize apparent differences in Scriptures which unbelievers use as an argument against verbal inspiration. For example, a careful study of the words in the inscription above the cross will show that each one of the gospels give a part of the inscription and gives that part absolutely accurately. But when they are combined together all four give an entire inscription, "This is Jesus of Nazareth, the King of the Jews."

I have considered prayerfully for years all the so-called contradictions alleged to be in the Bible, and little by little by faith and prayer and the Holy Spirit's leading and careful study of the Word of God I have found the apparent discrepancies and difficulties fade away. Those who do not believe the Bible are simply those who have not given it a chance to prove itself what it claims to be, the verbally inspired, infallible Word of God, true from the beginning, perfect, written "not in the words which man's wisdom teacheth, but which the Holy Ghost teacheth."

There are no difficulties in accepting the Bible as the verbally inspired Word of God that compare at all with the insurmountable, faith-destroying difficulties of those who compromise with modernism, deny the verbal inspiration of the Bible, and yet try to claim to be Christians and claim that the Bible is in some sense inspired! That road leads to infidelity and atheism. For in truth the honest inquirer must see that the Bible is either all it claims to be or it is a man-made system of lies, unreliable, scientifically false, historically inaccurate, religiously powerless.

But man-made and false, dear reader, the Bible cannot be. The Bible has proven itself. Its prophecies have come to pass in countless cases. Its promises have proven true to millions who trusted them. The God who revealed Himself in the Bible has revealed Himself through salvation to millions of believers. After all, dear reader, it is not the *Bible* that is on trial but the *reader* of the Bible. Let God's Word be true and every man a liar. The critics damn not the Bible but themselves. Unbelievers prove not their wisdom but their folly. Those who will not believe the Bible and trust the Christ of the Bible lose comfort day by day, lose assurance in the heart, lose the answer to their prayers, and God pity them, lose everlasting life and the joys of Heaven!

(This message available from the publishers in a 28-page pamphlet at 15¢, seven for $1.00.)

II

Scientific Accuracy of the Bible Proven

Bible Shows How Life Processes Are All Carried on by the Circulation of the Blood; How the World Is Round, A Ball Hung Out in Space, Rotating to Make Day and Night; That the Earth Is One Among Many Planets; A Divine Law That Species Produce Only "After Their Kind"; That the Bible Will Prove Itself to Every Honest Investigator, and Only Ignorant, Willful Fools Reject It

"O fools, and slow of heart to believe all that the prophets have spoken."—Luke 24:25.

THE BIBLE is infallibly correct. It is correct in science. It is accurate in history and in every other matter discussed.

Bob Ingersoll talked about, "the mistakes of Moses," and I have heard even friends of the Bible say, "The Bible is not a book of science." But infidels and timid Christians are both wrong in this matter. The Bible *is* a book of science. It plainly deals with many scientific matters. And wherever the Bible mentions matters of science, it does it with the absolute authority of the infallible Word of God. God made the world, and God made the Bible. So when God speaks in the Bible about the world which He made, He tells the exact truth. In fact, the Bible is the only absolutely scientific book in the world. All other books of science eventually are outgrown and found out of date and inaccurate. Now century after century finds the Bible still infallibly correct.

When Jesus rose from the dead, He walked on the road to Emmaus, unrecognized by the two sorrowing disciples who did not believe He had risen. Hear these words of our Saviour:

"Then he said unto them, O fools, and slow of heart to believe all that the prophets have spoken: ought not Christ to have suffered these things, and to enter into his glory? And beginning at Moses and all the prophets, he expounded unto them in all the scriptures the things concerning himself"—Luke 24:25–27.

Jesus says that one is a fool even to hesitate about believing all the Bible, all that the prophets have spoken! And He speaks here of all of the Old Testament, beginning with the writings of Moses, that is, beginning with Genesis. Of course, what He said here is equally true about the New Testament. However, most of the enemies of the Bible attack first the Old Testament. But Jesus says that any man is a fool who is slow to believe the Bible.

To strengthen the faith of Christians and to convince every honest doubter who may read this, I will give some examples of the absolute scientific accuracy of the Bible. The only reason anybody does not believe the Bible is that he has not honestly investigated it, has not given God's Word a chance to prove itself, as it will prove itself to every sincere, surrendered heart that intelligently investigates it.

I. "For the Life of the Flesh Is in the Blood"—Lev. 17:11

The Bible gives the most accurate, definite, brief statement of the use of the blood in the body, a statement which is absolutely scientific. Scientists have never been able to form a better statement. But the Bible made its scientific statement about 3,500 years ago, and science has only discovered the use of the blood in the last one hundred years!

Leviticus 17:11 says:

"For the life of the flesh is in the blood."

Leviticus 17:14 says:

"For it is the life of all flesh; the blood of it is for the life thereof: therefore I said unto the children of Israel, Ye shall eat the blood of no manner of flesh: for the life of all flesh is the blood thereof . . ."

And before that, Genesis 9:4 says:

"But flesh with the life thereof, which is the blood thereof, shall ye not eat."

The life is in the blood!

It is the blood that carries on all the life processes of the body.

It is the blood that absorbs the oxygen from the air in the lungs and carries this oxygen throughout the body.

It is the blood that collects the carbon dioxide and other wastes that are then discharged by the blood into the lungs, and breathed out of the body.

It is the blood that collects digested food, takes it from the little cilia in the intestines and distributes it to the various parts of the body.

It is the blood that causes growth, builds new cells, grows bone and flesh, stores fat, makes hair and nails.

It is the blood that feeds and supports all the organs of the body. If the blood supply be cut off from an arm, that arm will immediately begin to die and rot. If the blood be not sufficiently supplied to the scalp, the head becomes bald.

It is blood that repairs the body. The blood can make new bone and knit the break together. The blood can close wounds and grow new flesh, new skin, and even new nerves.

It is the blood which fights disease. We now know that infectious germs are destroyed by white corpuscles in the blood and the pus from a sore is simply white corpuscles that have been killed in this battle against the enemies of the body. *The life of the flesh is in the blood!* All nourishment, all growth, all repair of tissues, all the fight against disease within the body is carried on by the blood.

If the body is to be immunized against certain diseases, it is the blood which must make it immune.

If disease is about to overcome the body, often the only remedy is a transfusion of blood.

Certainly the Bible is exactly scientifically accurate when it says that "The life of the flesh is in the blood."

But remember that though the Bible has said so for about 3,500 years, the scientists are just now finding it out!

For example, in 1799, George Washington died, 155 years ago. This greatest man in America, one of the greatest in world's history, had a doctor called. The doctor bled Washington three times, and the last time took more than a quart of blood! From his sickness Washington might have recovered if he had had his blood. But the doctor, the scientist of his day, had not yet discovered what the Bible had been saying for many centuries. He did not know he was draining away the life of the father of his country into a bucket, when he took the blood from Washington's veins. He foolishly thought that most illnesses were caused by too much blood. And practically all the scientists of his day were agreed with that poor doctor.

William Harvey had discovered that the arteries contained blood instead of air about 1628 and thought that the blood circulated, but had not proven it. Practically nothing was known of the life-sustaining work of the blood until modern times.

Lister, who first proved the presence of germs and introduced the antiseptic system of modern surgery, died as recently as 1912. The scientists of George Washington's day did not know that the blood, which is the life of the flesh, must destroy germs.

Scientists have learned many things in the last century, but they have never yet caught up with the Bible. The Bible is absolutely scientifically accurate. The theory of a scientist may be out of date in ten years, though it be acclaimed from the housetops today. But the Word of God stands forever. "The law of the Lord is perfect" (Ps. 19:7).

So Jesus says that one who is slow to believe the Bible is a fool.

II. Bible Said World Is Round Centuries Before Scientists Discovered It

What a great hullabaloo there was among the scientists when some investigative and bold soul began to believe that the world was round, perhaps a planet rotating and revolving around the sun! The scientific thinkers of his day had the Roman Catholic Church bring all the pressure it could against Galileo for the startling "heresy." When Columbus said the world was round and that he could reach India by sailing westward, the scientific men of his day thought he was a crackpot and a fool. Only when Magellan's expedition sailed around the world was it generally believed that the earth was round.

And yet strangely enough, these scientific facts, now so generally accepted and proven, were stated in the Bible thousands of years ago. The Bible clearly teaches that the world is round.

Isaiah 40:22 says:

"It is he that sitteth upon the circle of the earth, and the inhabitants thereof are as grasshoppers; that stretcheth out the heavens as a curtain, and spreadeth them out as a tent to dwell in."

"THE CIRCLE OF THE EARTH." Or more literally, "the roundness of the earth."

It is true that Isaiah 11:12 mentions "the four corners of the earth." But the word *earth* there means primarily the land, and the four corners simply refer to the four directions, the extreme limits of land, when the Lord says that He shall "gather together the dispersed of Judah from the four corners of the earth" (Isa. 11:12). The Bible did not mean that the earth was flat with four corners any more than modern speakers and writers mean the earth is flat when they speak of "the four corners of the earth" or "the ends of the earth," figures of speech simply referring to the farthest extent of human habitations on the earth. The Bible never does say, never even intimates, that the earth is flat. No, the Bible through the centuries has plainly taught that the world is round.

III. The Bible Pictures the Earth Suspended in Space Before Scientists Discovered That Fact

Not only does the Bible picture the earth as round, but pictures it as a planet suspended in space, hung there by the hand of God! In Job 26:7 the Scripture says of God: "He stretcheth out the north over the empty place, *and hangeth the earth upon nothing.*"

It was God who stretched infinite space out beyond the empty space in the heavens which we may discern on a starry night by looking toward the north. And it was the same God who hung the earth upon nothing, and still holds it, a planet which turns on an invisible axis, a ball which travels in an intangible orbit about the sun, held in place only by the hands of God!

Down through the years timid church people have been browbeaten by the loud-voiced educators, the so-called scientists. How much wiser Christians would have been if they had taken the Bible from the beginning and believed every word of it. Then they would not have fallen into scientific error about this fundamental fact. The earth is a planet suspended in space, not a flat tableland supported by elephants or a giant turtle, with an underground river Styx and stables for the sun chariot, as the wise men of the earth, "the scientists" of their day, once believed!

IV. The Rotation of the Earth, a Ball Out in Space, Clearly Pictured by Jesus Christ

Was Jesus Christ a scientist? Yes, for it was He Himself who made the worlds (Heb. 1:2; Col. 1:16). So when Jesus made a statement involving scientific fact, that statement was always exactly and absolutely correct. And the Bible is the only infallible book of science in the world.

For example, in Luke 17:34–36 Jesus is discussing the time of His coming. There Jesus says:

"I tell you, in that night there shall be two men in one bed; the one shall be taken, and the other shall be left. Two women shall be grinding together; the one shall be taken, and the other left. Two men shall be in the field; the one shall be taken, and the other left."

When Jesus comes, He said, on part of the earth it will be night. Two men will be in one bed, and one will be taken and the other left (vs. 34). On part of the earth it will be morning, and two women will be grinding their meal for the day, and one will be taken and the other left (vs. 35). In some parts of the earth men will be working in the field in daytime, and one will be taken and the other left (vs. 36).

But Christ's coming will be like lightning. "As lightning cometh out of the east, and shineth even unto the west; so shall also the coming of the Son of man be" (Matt. 24: 27). It will be even "in the twinkling of an eye" (I Cor. 15:52), that Jesus will come to take away His own. And in that moment, it will be night on one part of the earth, morning on another part of the earth, and midday on another part of the earth, Jesus said. How can that be?

Why Jesus simply knew that the earth is round and revolves continually; that it is night on one part of the earth when it is day on another part of this round ball; and that the time, day or night, morning or evening, is simply determined by any given portion of the earth turning into the light of the sun on the east or away from it on the west. Christ's statement about His second coming was made in the light of all the scientific facts. Even the background of the Bible is absolutely scientifically accurate. The Bible describes the earth as round, a planet hung out in space, revolving on its axis.

And the only reason anyone does not believe the Bible is that, as Jesus said, he is a "fool and slow of heart to believe all that the prophets have spoken." Any honest heart who earnestly investigates the Bible will find that it proves itself the very Word of God, different from all the other books in the world.

V. The Bible Teaches the Earth Is One Among Many Planets

Was Paul a scientist with modern training? Had he looked through the giant telescopes with which modern scientists have discovered that the stars are not really simply pin points of light but are planets and suns, many of them far larger than this earth? Was Paul, I say, a modern scientist? No, but when Paul wrote certain books of the Bible he was inspired of God. The God who made the world inspired Paul so that not a word would be inaccurate. So in Hebrews 1:2 Paul speaks of "the worlds." He says that Christ has been appointed the heir of all things and that God made "the worlds" by Him.

Again, in Hebrews 11:3 we are told, "Through faith we understand that the worlds were framed by the word of God." God made all the planets or worlds, says the Scripture!

Is there more than one world? Yes. The scientists of Paul's day did not know that. It is only in recent centuries that scientists have learned the truth about our solar system and other worlds. Scientists in Paul's day supposed the sun was a light which was carried across the heavens daily, and that the moon was also such a light, and that the stars were lights fastened on a surface. They pictured the earth like a flat table, and the heavens like a bowl turned upside down over it. But the Bible, unlike other books, was written by divine inspiration; so Paul was led to speak with absolute scientific exactness of "THE WORLDS."

VI. The Inexorable Law That Blocks the Evolution Guess Is "After Their Kind"

Biologists have long tried to make their foolish theory, their hodgepodge of guesses and speculations called evolution, work. But one fact blocks them always. They are unable to make any plant or animal cross the line from its own kind to another kind. Horses may be developed into Shetland ponies or giant Percheron draft stock, or thoroughbred racers, but never become cows or giraffes, or hippopotamuses! Dogs may be developed into bulldogs, greyhounds, poodles, or collies; but they cannot be made into cats nor pigs nor sheep. And if animals are obviously of the same general family breed, as the horse and the donkey, then the resulting true hybrid will not reproduce itself. Millions and millions of mules have been raised from the time of Solomon until now, but every one of them had to be a separate cross between the horse and the donkey. Not a single mule ever had a mule for a father or a mule for a mother. If anyone tells you differently, first you should demand proof, scientific proof, not hearsay, and then laugh loudly! Mules do not reproduce. Publicity seekers have sometimes claimed to have a mule that could reproduce, but scientific investigation has always proven it a false claim. It is as if, in trying to develop new species or kinds, one were going up against some immutable law. And that is true.

In the plant world, the word *hybrid* is used very loosely. A new kind of rose may be called a hybrid rose, but actually it is not that. True hybrids are plants or animals which result from the crossing of different kinds, not two kinds of horses, and not two kinds of roses, but a horse and a donkey, and of a rose and some other flower. Actually, true hybrids do not reproduce as a new species. Like the mule, they usually are totally sterile. Extensive experiments have been carried on trying to produce "cattaloes" as a distinct species, by crossing domestic cattle with the "buffalo" or American bison. However, the hybrid would not reproduce when mated with a hybrid; and by the only mating possible, the resulting animals always reverted either to cattle or buffalo, indistinguishable from cattle or indistinguishable from buffalo, as the case might be. Other crossings of guinea pigs with South American cavies, of wheat with rye, of plums with apricots, etc., have had the same result. (See *After Its Kind* by Byron C. Nelson, Augsburg Press.)

It is utterly impossible to permanently cross the boundaries of species except by the Creator. Literally thousands and thousands of attempts have failed.

Instead of one "missing link," the evolutionist has yet to find a single link between two definitely distinct species.

These facts are now known by scientists after millions of separate observations and experiments. BUT THESE FACTS WERE CLEARLY STATED IN THE NATURAL LAW OF GOD GIVEN IN THE FIRST CHAPTER IN THE BIBLE, WRITTEN 3,500 YEARS AGO!

The Bible is absolutely scientifically accurate when it declares ten times in one chapter that both plants and animals reproduce "after their kind."

Scientists are learning a little of why this is so. Cell structure is different in different animals and even in plants. The hereditary characteristics are carried by little things called chromosomes. Different animals have a different number of chromosomes. And there is a fundamental difference in the blood of a man and the blood of a gorilla, for instance, which makes it impossible to cross them.

Here is a scientific fact which has balked all the dreams of people who for many decades now have been looking for "the missing link."

There is no missing link between man and animals. There never was and there never will be any missing link, because God has set a certain immutable law that both plants and animals are to bring forth only after their kind. There may be variations within the species, or within the immediate kind. Roses may be developed larger or of different color and habit of growth; they are still roses. Horses may vary in color or size, but they are still horses.

The guesses of the evolutionists have fallen through. They have never yet proven a single case of evolution from one species to another. They have never yet found a single case, a

known case, where an entirely new kind of animal or plant
has originated from another kind of animal or plant. The idea
that man came from animals or that higher animals came from
lower animals, or that animals and plants came from the
same single cell originally, is all foolish supposition without a
single scientific fact to back it! That doctrine has never gotten
beyond a hypothesis, a supposition, a guess. Honest scientists
do not claim that it is more than that. When anybody tells you
that "evolution is a proven fact," he shows himself to be an
ignoramus, parroting something he has read. He is not a
working scientist. He has not made wide-scale investigation.
He is not an open-minded scholar. The uncrossable boundary
lines between species is now becoming recognized widely as an
inescapable fact.

But the Bible, in the very first chapter of Genesis, has expressed that law as clearly as it could possibly be expressed
by any scientist. Genesis 1:11, 12 says:

*"And God said, Let the earth bring forth grass, the herb yielding
seed, and the fruit tree yielding FRUIT AFTER HIS KIND, whose
seed is in itself, upon the earth: and it was so. And the earth brought
forth grass, and herb, yielding SEED AFTER HIS KIND, and
the tree yielding fruit, whose seed was in itself, AFTER HIS KIND:
and God saw that it was good."*

And what the Lord said here about trees, herbs, and grass,
He says further over in the chapter about every kind of created
thing. In verse 21 we are told:

*"And God created great whales, and every living creature that
moveth, which the waters brought forth abundantly, AFTER THEIR
KIND, and every winged fowl AFTER HIS KIND: and God saw
that it was good."*

Again in verses 24 and 25 of that first chapter of Genesis, we
are told:

*"And God said, Let the earth bring forth the living creature AFTER
HIS KIND, cattle, and creeping thing, and beast of the earth AFTER
HIS KIND; and it was so. And God made the beast of the earth
AFTER HIS KIND, and cattle AFTER THEIR KIND, and every*

thing that creepeth upon the earth AFTER HIS KIND: and God saw that it was good."

Here we find that ten times in the first chapter in the Bible God says that trees, grass, herbs, fish, creeping things, cattle; that is, every living thing, is to reproduce only after one law. Each is to reproduce "AFTER HIS KIND." Not a single reliable scientist in the world can deny that inexorable law of God.

Living things do not bring forth according to exact identity, but after their own kind always.

Scientists are only beginning to catch up with the infallible Word of God in scientific matters. Up and down America for years, before great crowds, on many radio stations, in print again and again, I have challenged the infidels, reputable professors in great colleges and universities, to bring me one case where the Bible is proven scientifically incorrect. Not once has any such unbeliever appeared to face me before an American audience to attempt to prove a scientific inaccuracy in the Bible. It cannot be done! The Bible is the infallible Word of God, absolutely reliable in science as well as history or religion.

Modernist Fools Are "Slow of Heart to Believe"

Jesus said in Luke 24:25 that those who do not believe the Bible are really "slow of *heart* to believe all that the prophets have spoken." It is the heart which makes unbelievers. Wicked hearts that are not willing to *do* the will of God, do not want to accept His Word.

That is the same thing taught by our Saviour in John 3:19-21, where He said:

"And this is the condemnation, that light is come into the world, and men loved darkness rather than light, because their deeds were evil. For every one that doeth evil hateth the light, neither cometh to the light, lest his deeds should be reproved. But he that doeth truth cometh to the light, that his deeds may be made manifest, that they are wrought in God."

There is light for all who want the light. The Bible will prove itself to all who honestly explore its storehouse of wisdom. But people who love their sins and hate the light, will be turned over to a reprobate mind to believe a lie. It is not education that makes infidels and agnostics; but it is sin, the sin of self-will, the sin of pride, the sin of rejecting Christ as Saviour, the sin of deliberately seeking an explanation for the world that will discredit the Bible. Such sin, black-hearted, Christ-rejecting sin, is back of all the unbelief in the world.

If any honest unbeliever wants to learn further evidence of the accuracy of the Bible, actually wants to know the truth and will humbly seek to follow the truth and obey the light that he may find, please write your inquiry to the author at Wheaton, Illinois.

Let us reverently acknowledge that the Bible is the perfect Word of God, infallible in science or history as well as religion, and that "all scripture is given by inspiration of God, and is profitable" (II Tim. 3:16).

(This message, with other material added proving the historical accuracy of the Bible, is available from the publishers in a 28-page pamphlet at 15¢, seven for $1.00.)

III

The Universal Malady, Sin

"What then? are we better than they? No, in no wise: for we have before proved both Jews and Gentiles, that they are all under sin; as it is written, There is none righteous, no, not one: there is none that understandeth, there is none that seeketh after God. They are all gone out of the way, they are together become unprofitable; there is none that doeth good, no, not one. Their throat is an open sepulchre; with their tongues they have used deceit; the poison of asps is under their lips: whose mouth is full of cursing and bitterness: their feet are swift to shed blood: destruction and misery are in their ways: and the way of peace have they not known: there is no fear of God before their eyes. Now we know that what things soever the law saith, it saith to them who are under the law: that every mouth may be stopped, and all the world may become guilty before God. Therefore by the deeds of the law there shall no flesh be justified in his sight: for by the law is the knowledge of sin. But now the righteousness of God without the law is manifested, being witnessed by the law and the prophets; even the righteousness of God which is by faith of Jesus Christ unto all and upon all them that believe: for there is no difference: for all have sinned, and come short of the glory of God."—Romans 3:9–23.

GOD, I thank thee, that I am not as other men are, extortioners, unjust, adulterers, or even as this publican," said the Pharisee when he went up to the temple to pray (Luke 18:11). And so says the whole world! "I am not as other men are"! All of us want to think that we are better than others, different from others. But God's Word thunders back that we are no better than others, no different from others, "For there is no difference: for all have sinned, and come short of the glory of God."

No difference! No difference between the best moral man and the worst criminal in the fact of sin. No difference between the most chaste and refined woman and the street-walking harlot in the fact of sin! No difference in the bluebloods and the onion-eaters, in the down-and-outs and the up-and-outs, for all have sinned. There is no difference, God says, between the church member and the ranting atheist in the fact that both are alike sinners. There may be differences between men in other matters; there are rich and poor, ignorant and learned, pleasing and repulsive; but all are alike sinners. Saved and lost are simply saved sinners and lost sinners, forgiven sinners and condemned sinners. So God's Word here declares. Reader, there is no difference between you and Judas Iscariot in the fact of sin. He went to Hell, and you deserve to go, yea, will go unless you get cleansing and pardon and salvation. Doubtless millions are now in the fires and torment of Hell who were as good as you, as good outwardly, as good inwardly. They lived as well, they were as honest, they went to church as much, they prayed as much, they gave as much money and as much time and service. They loved their neighbors as well, were as kind to their families as you; and yet they are in Hell today, wicked sinners reaping what they sowed. They were sinners, and their sins found them out at last. "The wages of sin is death," God says, and "The soul that sinneth, it shall die." So they are in Hell. But you are as much a sinner as they. "There is no difference: for all have sinned."

Yes, those in Hell now and others who will go there later are no more sinners than you are. There is no difference. Some belong to the same church as you do. Millions were baptized like you and yet are in Hell. Millions took the same vows you took, and yet are in Hell! Others belonged to the same lodge as you but are in Hell. They had the same signs and passwords, the same grips and perhaps the same ridiculous and blasphemous oaths. Oh yes, there are millions of members of lodges and secret cults and even of churches now in Hell. They were sinners, and so are you. There is no difference, God says, for all have sinned and come short of the glory of God. And before I am through with this message I will prove beyond a doubt, God willing, that according to the Bible you are an awful sinner deserving of Hell, and worse yet, going to Hell unless you get salvation as a sinner with your sins covered by the blood of Christ.

Why We Must Preach About Sin

The Bible doctrine of sin is a foundation teaching absolutely necessary to the understanding of other great doctrines of the Bible. "Christian Science," falsely so-called, denies the reality of the fact of sin. But that denial is neither scientific nor Christian. Sin is a scientific fact, an omnipresent, awful, damning, hellish fact, and it is the part of a fool to deny it. No wonder the Bible says, "Fools make a mock at sin" (Prov. 14:9). The gospel of Christ is simply this: "Christ died for our SINS according to the scriptures" and rose again (1 Cor. 15:3); or that "Christ Jesus came into the world to save sinners" (1 Tim. 1:15). There can be no Christianity without admitting that all have sinned. So "Christian Science," so-called, is like the guinea pig which is neither pig nor guinea; or like grapenuts which contain neither grapes nor nuts; it is neither Christian nor scientific. Unwilling to accept the fact of sin, "Christian Science" sees no need of the atoning blood and denies it. Since it says there is no reality to sin, it thinks also there is no reality to Hell and judgment. Small wonder that it places a many-times-married woman on an equal with Jesus Christ and counts her silly book the key to the Bible and really a more authoritative, *later* divine revelation!

Why should Jesus die if men are not sinners? Why should anybody try to save sinners if men are not sinners? And if they are only small sinners, and if they can correct and atone for their own sins, why the horrible sufferings of Jesus on Calvary? The death of Christ was a stupid blunder, a terrible, senseless crime, unless men are sinners doomed to an awful Hell just like the Bible teaches.

The Bible teaching about sin is the only safeguard against false religions. Only the blood of Christ can solve the sin question. Self-righteousness, lodge membership, religious rites and ceremonies, human priest-craft and other fake remedies will never satisfy the heart that has learned the truth about the awful depravity of the human heart—the fact that "there is no difference: for all have sinned." This is why God's Holy Spirit inspired this passage in the third chapter of Romans, that "all the world may become guilty before God" (verse 19). "By the law is the knowledge of sin," says verse 20. So Paul preached the law to show men that they were sinners and to stop the mouth of every self-righteous boaster, to stop alibis and excuses until all should see themselves guilty, condemned sinners before God!

Some preachers preach always on the love of God and on trusting in Jesus Christ, and those are wonderful themes. But the Bible that says, "God is love," also says, "Our God is a consuming fire" (Heb. 12:29), and that "God is angry with the wicked every day" (Ps. 7:11). There is as much in the Bible about Hell as about Heaven; and if we do not preach Hell, sinners will see no reason to seek Heaven. If we do not preach about sin and bring conviction of mind and heart and conscience about sin, men will not repent of sin and cannot

trust in Christ as a Saviour from sin. Great revivals from
Heaven are always accompanied or preceded by deep conviction for sin. People who are not conscious of the guilt of sin
will not confess and forsake nor make restitution nor repent.

Analysis of Romans 3:9–23

Analyze the passage at the head of this sermon, Romans 3,
verses 9 to 23, and you will see how universally depraved and
wicked all men are by nature and life.

First is the plain statement that all the Jews and all the
Gentiles are sinners alike, that there is no difference. "What
then? are we better than they?" Are Jews better than others
who are not Jews? Is one race, one class, better than any other?
"No, in no wise," answers God through Paul's pen, "for we
have before proved both Jews and Gentiles, that they are all
under sin." Everybody who is not a Jew is a Gentile. There are
only those two classes, Jews and non-Jews; and you, reader,
are one or the other. And it makes no difference which you are,
for you are a sinner. There is no difference, all have sinned!

Verses 10 to 18 simply repeat and emphasize verse 9. After
stating the case that all alike are under sin, God brings fourteen indictments against the whole human race. Disregard the
verse numbers and copy God's list, and you will see that seven
times and then seven times again God brands man as naturally
wicked and godless and damned, with not one righteous
person, not one that doeth good in the whole natural race,
NO, NOT ONE! (Besides Jesus Christ, of course, who was
not born of natural birth, but supernaturally without a human
father, conceived by the Holy Ghost in the womb of the
virgin.)

1. "There is none righteous, no, not one" (vs. 10). There is
not a one righteous in the heart in the sight of God!

2. "There is none that understandeth" (vs. 11). There is
none that is even in tune with God by nature to understand
the things of God. The carnal mind is enmity against God.
"But the natural man receiveth not the things of the Spirit of

God: for they are foolishness unto him: neither can he know them, because they are spiritually discerned" (1 Cor. 2:14).

3. "There is none that seeketh after God" (vs. 11). Man is not righteous, does not understand God and His ways, and worse yet, does not even seek after God nor try to find the goodness of God. What is wrong with man is not only that he is a sinner by nature, but that he is a sinner by choice as well!

4. "They are all gone out of the way" (vs. 12). Here we find that the sinner not only does not seek God, he does deliberately go away from God. People are not *led* away from God, do not primarily *drift* away, but *go* away of their own choice. Satan tempts us, but we have a wicked nature that gladly listens and cooperates with Satan's efforts to get us to sin. Sin comes from the heart, not from outside.

5. "They are together become unprofitable" (vs. 12). Man is so far gone as to be unprofitable to God. God will never get back His investment in man, man can never pay his way since by nature men are such sinners. Therefore any kind dealing toward man must be on the basis of God's unmerited mercy. There is no ground of justice by which man could claim anything but condemnation and destruction. So when a Christian worker does all he can do, even to dying for the Saviour who loves him, he must say, 'I am an unprofitable servant' (Luke 17:10).

6. "There is none that doeth good, no, not one" (vs. 12). Men do not think this is so. They think that men do good in some respects, even unsaved men, heathen men. But God says, "No, not one!" All man's goodness is a fake goodness just as Satan's ministers appear as angels of light. Men often, like the Pharisees, "outwardly appear righteous unto men, but within ye are full of hypocrisy and iniquity," Jesus said (Matt. 23:28). In God's sight even "the plowing of the wicked, is sin" (Prov. 21:4). Even the prayer of the wicked is an abomination (Prov. 28:9). "The flesh profiteth nothing" (John 6:63).

7. "Their throat is an open sepulchre" (vs. 13). Like an open grave breathing out stench and foulness from decaying

bodies, so is the wickedness of the human heart which pours forth from the throat.

8. "With their tongues they have used deceit" (vs. 13). Lying comes naturally to the tongue of mankind. Children lie as soon as they can talk, and deceit is in the heart even of babies.

9. "The poison of asps is under their lips" (vs. 13). It is as natural for the human tongue to burn and hurt as it is for a poisonous snake (the adder) to bite. The poison in both is natural and inbred. "The tongue can no man tame; it is an unruly evil, full of deadly poison," says James 3:8, and again, "And the tongue is a fire, a world of iniquity: so is the tongue among our members, that it defileth the whole body, and setteth on fire the course of nature; and it is set on fire of hell"! (James 3:6).

10. "Whose mouth is full of cursing and bitterness" (vs. 14). "Out of the abundance of the heart the mouth speaketh." "Those things which proceed out of the mouth come forth from the heart," Jesus said in Matthew 15:18. Four times out of these fourteen indictments God refers to organs of speech, "throat," "tongues," "lips," "mouth." What a revelation of the wickedness of man! Cursing, blasphemy, bitterness and strife come naturally from corrupt human hearts!

11. "Their feet are swift to shed blood" (vs. 15). Mankind is a race of murderers. Cain was simply a natural man when he killed his brother. If you hold even a few weeks' old baby's head still, he will scream in anger at the restraint! Anger, hate, murder—that is the natural order when wicked human hearts bring forth their fruit. Every person living or who ever did live, save Jesus Christ alone, had feet that were inherently "swift to shed blood." This is the first explanation of war and crime.

12. "Destruction and misery are in their ways" (vs. 16). This is not *evolution*, it is *devolution*. It is not man climbing upward; it is man degenerating. Human government, human culture, human morals, have an inescapable tendency toward destruction and ruin. The whole world is getting farther from

God, with governments less stable, life and property less secure, homes less happy, and ruin inevitable for the race as a whole.

13. "And the way of peace have they not known" (vs. 17). Man in himself does not know the secret of peace. "There is no peace, saith my God, to the wicked" (Isa. 57:21). Sin in the heart is responsible for all the unrest in homes and nations. War is the natural result of the human nature. Man can have no peace except he gets it from above, from outside himself. Men strive for peace, but world peace is a delusion as long as men are sinners.

14. "There is no fear of God before their eyes" (vs. 18). The crowning climax of man's wickedness is that he does not fear God. Man does not do God's will, does not understand God, does not seek God, but goes headlong into sin and destruction. And in the midst of sin and ruin, man still does not fear God, mocks at the thought of judgment, scorns the idea of Hell and retribution! How wicked is man!

HERE IS GOD'S INDICTMENT, SEVEN TIMES, AND SEVEN TIMES AGAIN, OF THE WHOLE HUMAN RACE. It proves what God said that "There is no difference: For all have sinned, and come short of the glory of God." In this startling and terrible passage of Scripture, Romans 3, verses 9 to 23, several things stand out with shocking plainness.

1. There are no exceptions; God counts everybody the same. He says again and again, "All," "*all*," "*ALL*." *All* are under sin, *all* are gone out of the way, *all* have sinned and come short of the glory of God. Likewise, He says, "None," "*None*," "*NONE!*" There is *none* righteous, *none* that understands, *none* that seeks after God, *none* that does good; and then God cries out to us, "NO, NOT ONE!"

2. Another thing that stands out in the passage is that the present tense is used again and again. God is talking about today and about our hearts, talking to those of us who read this, this moment. All are under sin *now*. None is righteous.

The present tense is used throughout the passage. Then God says, "There is (present tense) no difference!"

3. God's conclusion is that "Therefore by the deeds of the law there shall no flesh be justified in his sight" (vs. 20). It is utterly impossible for anybody to be saved, or *partly* saved, or *kept* saved by good deeds, by keeping God's law or commandments. Man simply cannot save himself, cannot be justified by his deeds. Every man, woman, and child is so incurably wicked by nature that he or she cannot be saved except by the mercy of God and through the merit of the atoning blood of Jesus Christ, the righteous One.

Other Scriptures Prove Also That All Are Sinners

Do not think for a moment, dear reader, that this is an isolated passage and that it may be misinterpreted. No, the entire Bible is of the same tenor; and again and again God brings this charge that all alike are sinners and that there is no difference for all have sinned.

David, confessing the wickedness of his sin with Bath-sheba, cries out in Psalms 51:5, "Behold, I was shapen in inquity; and in sin did my mother conceive me."

In that inspired prayer of King Solomon when he dedicated the temple in Jerusalem, he said, "For there is no man that sinneth not" (I Kings 8:46; II Chron. 6:36).

Isaiah 53:6 says, "All we like sheep have gone astray; we have turned every one to his own way." There it is again, "All!" "Every one!"

Let us hear the words of Jesus Himself on this question. One came running to Jesus and said, "Good Master, what shall I do that I may inherit eternal life? And Jesus said unto him, Why callest thou me good? there is none good but one, that is, God!" (Mark 10:17, 18). "There is none good but one, that is, God!" Jesus meant that He should not be called Master or Rabbi, but God, or the Son of God, what He claimed to be— God, in human form. Unless Jesus was the very Son of God, then He was not good, for there is none good but God.

Do All Christians Sin?

There are some who say that they were once sinners; but now that they are saved, they are saved from sin and never sin any more. Some claim to be "sanctified" and to have "holiness." There is a true sanctification or holiness, being set apart for God; but it does not involve sinlessness. Some claim that the old sinful nature is altogether eradicated by a "second work of grace." But all such people are deceived. They may not want to sin, and they may think they do not sin, but they do sin. The Scriptures we have read say, "All," "*All*," "*ALL*." Not only all *have* sinned, but all *do* sin. All are now under sin. There is even yet no difference in the fact of sin. So the Bible says and so we must believe.

In fact, the saints of the Bible confessed, with great grief, their sin. Paul said (and it was the Holy Spirit who told him to say it and inspired it),

"*For we know that the law is spiritual: but I am carnal, sold under sin.*"—Rom. 7:14.

"*For that which I do I allow not: for what I would, that do I not; but what I hate, that do I.*"—Rom. 7:15.

And again he says by divine inspiration:

"*For the good that I would I do not: but the evil which I would not, that I do. Now if I do that I would not, it is no more I that do it, but sin that dwelleth in me.*"—Rom. 7:19, 20.

Paul cried out as many other earnest saints of God have, "O wretched man that I am! Who shall deliver me from the body of this death? I thank God through Jesus Christ our Lord. So then with the mind I myself serve the law of God; but with the flesh the law of sin" (Rom. 7:24, 25).

Paul thanked God that through Jesus Christ at the second coming He would be delivered entirely from the power of sin; but repeats that at present "With the mind I myself serve the law of God; but with the flesh the law of sin." Paul was saved, was an apostle, had been filled with the Holy Spirit, had laid down his life for the gospel, had been caught up to paradise and had had revealed to him things never before revealed to a human being; and yet Paul grieved that he still served with the flesh the law of sin! Do you, poor, ignorant, immature child of God, think you are better than Paul? To set Romans 8 against Romans 7, to make Scripture contradict Scripture, is wicked. No, Paul, a saint, was also, he grieved, a sinner.

John, the beloved disciple, wrote his first letter (First John) when he was nearly a hundred years old. John who once had rested his head on the breast of Jesus, John who loved to call himself the "disciple whom Jesus loved," John to whom the Saviour in His dying agony committed His mother Mary, John who was filled with the Holy Ghost at Pentecost, who wrote five books of the New Testament, and who was the last apostle alive on the earth, WAS STILL A SINNER! Writing by the inspiration of the Holy Spirit who told him what to say, John says in I John 1:8: "IF WE SAY THAT WE HAVE NO SIN, WE DECEIVE OURSELVES, AND THE TRUTH IS NOT IN US."

John says in effect something like this: "If I should say that in this old heart of mine even this second there is no sin, I would be fooling myself. Sin is there whether I know it or not. Although I am saved and forgiven, I am still a sinner." The only hope that John had for Heaven was that Christ died for him and paid for all his sins. And that is the only hope that anyone else has. If you say you have no sin, you are simply deceiving yourself and the truth is not in you. Let us beware lest we play the hypocrite and claim to be what we are not. Reader, there is no difference between you and the worst sinner on earth in the fact of sin. So teaches the Word of God from one end to the other.

If you think there are other Scriptures which contradict this teaching, you have misunderstood them. All Scripture is inspired, and the Bible never contradicts itself if honestly accepted and correctly interpreted. In every child of God there is part of the divine nature which does not sin. And God can put in the heart of His child a hatred for sin and a longing to please God when he creates the new nature within us. But as long as we are in the flesh, that is until Jesus comes to change our vile bodies like unto his glorious body, or until death, we will be sinners. There is no difference, so God says, in the fact of sin. All are sinners!

Weak, Sick, Aging Bodies, Coming Death, Prove We Are Sinners

And here is further proof of it, too. As long as Christians grow old, wear glasses, have bald heads or gray hair or failing memories or tottering steps or imperfect health, that is positive proof that sin is still in the body and will, if Jesus tarries, bring forth its natural fruit which is death. All sickness and disease and infirmity is the mark and product of sin, and all are under sin as certainly as all are in imperfect or failing human bodies.

If one reads this who insists that you are not a sinner, then that simply goes to prove that you are so sinful you are blind to spiritual truth. Jeremiah 17:9 says, "The heart is deceitful above all things, and desperately wicked: who can know it?" You do not know your own heart but are deceived. None of us can know the wickedness that resides inherently in our carnal natures. Millions of people have committed some ghastly sin and then have marveled and shuddered in surprise that they could ever do such wickedness. Whether you admit it or not, whether you can see it or not, you, too, dear reader, are a sinner. You are a sinner whether forgiven or condemned. You are a sinner whether a Pharisee with hidden, unconfessed sin, or a publican with tearfully confessed sin.

You Do Not Keep the Ten Commandments Nor Golden Rule: Men Are Sinners by Every Standard

Some man says, "Well, Brother Rice, I know I am not perfect, but I really try to live up to the Ten Commandments, and I believe I will get by." In the first place, why did you say, "I try?" Because you know very well you do not succeed!

You do not keep the commandments and neither did any other person that ever lived except Jesus Christ.

The rich young ruler claimed to have kept all the commandments from his youth up. But when Jesus told him to go and sell his goods and give to the poor and come and follow Him, he turned away sorrowfully. He had great riches and his riches were his god. He had not even kept the first commandment: "Thou shalt have no other gods before me." He did not love God with all his heart, mind, and soul and strength, and he did not love his neighbor as himself. And neither do you!

You say that you never killed? But God answers back, "Whosoever hateth his brother is a murderer" (I John 3:15). And you have had hate and grudges and unforgiveness in your heart and are a murderer in God's sight. Do you think you have not committed adultery? Then remember that Jesus said, "Whosoever looketh on a woman to lust after her hath committed adultery with her already in his heart" (Matt. 5:28). You see you are guilty in the sight of God who knows the heart. And you have stolen, too, for who is there who has not? Whether you have robbed God by withholding tithes and offerings, whether you have taken wages that you did not earn, or whether you have coveted in your heart that which was not yours, you have broken the commandment. You have broken all the law of God.

And if you foolishly suppose that you have not broken every commandment, you are still the same guilty sinner, the same lawbreaker in God's sight. If you break one commandment, you are guilty of breaking the whole law according to the plain statement of God's Word. James 2:10 says, "For whosoever shall keep the whole law, and yet offend in one point, he is guilty of all." And that proves that you, in God's sight, are guilty of murder, adultery, idolatry; in fact that you are no different from any other wicked, abandoned, evil sinner! If you sinned once, you are guilty of breaking the whole law of God!

Nor do you love your neighbor as yourself. You do not keep

the golden rule to do unto others as you would that they should do unto you. Every day there are others who do not have as much to eat as you have, do not sleep in as nice a home as you have, do not ride in as nice a car as you use. You may love your neighbor but not as God commands, not as much as yourself; and any lack here is sin.

Perhaps you say, as many have said to me, "Well, I do the best I can." But even that is not true. You do not do what you know to do. When you were angry the other day, did you really not know better? When you neglected to read your Bible or pray, did you really do the best you could? Have you done the best you could about giving, about loving? If you are honest, you will have to say that you have not even done the best you could and the best you knew.

By every standard in the world, then, we can see that God's Word is true and that "There is no difference: for all have sinned, and come short of the glory of God."

Other Witnesses of Man's Sin: War, Crime, Poverty, Conscience, Disease, and Death

The all-pervasive blight of sin is compellingly taught by the Bible. But that is not all, it is taught by many witnesses on every hand. If man will not believe what God says, then let him but look about him and see the overwhelming proof that all mankind has sinned.

What mean the wars and rumors of war on every hand that mark the history of mankind? All man's enlightenment, all man's training, all the treaties, all the trade pacts, all the exchange of scholars, all the amenities of international law cannot prevent war. Heathen nations war, yes, Japan attacked China and America; but what is the difference between that and the conscienceless siezure of Ethiopia and Greece by Italy, or of the most of Europe by Germany? And Italy and Germany are full of churches, and contain some of the highest and most ancient culture. There is war, bloodshed, and hate among the nomadic tribes of Asia and between the naked, gleaming blackbodied pygmies of Africa. But the highest culture cannot cover the wicked bent in the hearts of men that makes for war. Poison gas, the whining drone of great bombing planes aiming their missiles of death at hospitals, department stores, and masses of women and children, and the bombardment of great cities filled with non-combatants are in the plans of all the nations and will now have a place in all wars. War is incurable because it springs from the wicked hearts of human beings. War proves that all men are sinners. Those who hate war yet have the same selfishness, the same hates and prejudices and array class against class. The pacificists have law suits, quarrels and disagreements the same as other men. "And the way of peace have they not known" (Rom. 3:17).

Crime increases on every hand. There are more criminals than policemen. Crime is a bigger business than railroads, agriculture, or automobiles. Laws multiply, taxes increase, yet all our education, our reforms, and our laws cannot end crime because it springs from wicked human hearts. Man is a sinner. The race is a race of sinners.

The world is full of poverty. But there is only one reason why poverty abounds, and that reason is sin. If the race were good and thrifty and virtuous and hardworking and kind, every person in the world could live in happiness with clothes and food enough, with work and real prosperity and culture. The only thing that prevents this universal prosperity and brings stark poverty in every city and countryside is sin. The cause of all depressions is selfishness, godlessness, rebellion, and self-seeking. There is land enough, clothes enough, but sin everywhere brings poverty.

Divorce increases on every hand. It even increases faster among college people than ignorant people, faster in so-called Christian nations than heathen nations! And there is no remedy for the thousands of human lives blighted by unhappiness, the decay of morals and the awful hurt to little children caused by divorce. There can be no remedy except a remedy that would fix human hearts. Increasing divorce proves that we are a race of sinners.

On every hand are hospitals and undertaking parlors and graveyards. Disease and suffering and death are everywhere witnesses to man's sins. There was no disease in the Garden of Eden. No headstones or withering flowers marked graves of the dead in Eden. There they did not die because man had not sinned. The misery, the crying, the sorrow, the death on every hand are the ever-present witnesses that all mankind has sinned! Why should you need the Bible to tell you that you are a sinner?

Last of all I summon the witness of conscience. Is there nothing within your own soul that comes to whisper to you that you are a sinner? Do no memories live within you of the things you wish had never been? Is there never any fear in your heart that the hidden past may be uncovered or your secret thoughts revealed? Do you never feel warning in your soul that you, too, must die as others die and have an accounting with God whether prepared or unprepared? And if you never hear that still, small, reproving voice necessary because of sin, then you are alone in all the human race. Surely you do have "that little spark of celestial fire called conscience." Your conscience proves you are a sinner. By whatever standards you live you are a sinner. Deny the Bible if you will and yet your conscience confirms that the Bible is true and that "There is no difference: for all have sinned, and come short of the glory of God." Drown it in pleasure, ignore it, deny it, but still your conscience, enlightened by the law of God in your heart, reminds you stubbornly that you are a sinner!

How many times I have quoted this Scripture to lost men, or reminded them that all alike are sinners! Scores of them have answered me like this, "I do not know about everybody, but I do know that I am a sinner."

Yes, reader, the witnesses of the universe of God: war, crime, disease, death, and conscience join with the Bible to prove that all are sinners. And you are a part of this world, one guilty sinner in a world of sinners. You say you are different but God says, "There is no difference: for all have sinned, and come short of the glory of God."

The Final Proof of Sinful Hearts: Rejection of Christ

To men other men may appear righteous. But there is one way to reveal the wickedness of every human heart. That is to bring a man face to face with Jesus Christ. When one faces the Lord Jesus Christ—Christ the pure One, Christ the sinless One, Christ with such wisdom, such power, such holiness as no other man ever had or ever claimed—then facing Christ his sin is revealed.

One would have thought that those self-righteous Pharisees in the days of our Saviour's ministry were good men. They prayed, they tithed, they lived moral lives, they were active in religious services. But when they came face to face with the holy Jesus, they hated Him, they lied about Him, they rejected Him, they murdered Him! And now who is there in all the world who would count them guiltless and innocent and pure?

And so today a man claims to be moral and good. He is kind to his family, he says, true to his word, a good citizen, an honest business man, perhaps an active lodge man. But when he comes face to face with Jesus Christ, instead of loving Him, trusting Him, receiving Him as Saviour and Lord and following him every day, this so-called moral man turns his back upon Christ, does not love, does not trust, does not follow Him! Nothing in the world could so reveal the wickedness of his heart!

At Olton, Texas, several years ago in a revival service some 200 or 300 people gathered one morning to confess their sins. For two hours men and women confessed their drinking, their cursing, their dancing, their grudges, their neglect of duty. In the midst of these confessions, a man arose trembling to his feet to say, "I have been guilty of all the sins other people have mentioned. I drank, I cursed, I lived in revelry and sin. But

the meanest thing I ever did was that all my life until three
o'clock this morning I rejected Jesus Christ, I did not surrender
to Him nor love Him nor serve Him. That is my greatest
sin."

He was right, exactly right. Only a rotten heart full of sin
and love for sin can keep anybody away from Jesus Christ! If
you today are not a Christian, if you did not run to Jesus the
first time you ever heard about His love and mercy, then you
are a black-hearted sinner. You love sin; you choose sin; and
you purposely, deliberately turn your wicked heart away from
the light of God, away from truth, and away from righteousness and walk into the darkness and wickedness of sin! Nothing
in the world shows a wicked heart like staying away from
Christ.

And this is not a man's opinion, either, but the plain teaching of Jesus Himself. John 3:19–21 says:

*"And this is the condemnation, that light is come into the world, and
men loved darkness rather than light, because their deeds were evil. For
every one that doeth evil hateth the light, neither cometh to the light, lest
his deeds should be reproved. But he that doeth truth cometh to the
light, that his deeds may be made manifest, that they are wrought in
God."*

All who trust in Christ are forgiven and have everlasting
life, but all who have not believed in Him are condemned
already. And the reason they are condemned, Jesus said, is
that they hate the light and will not come to the light because
their deeds are evil. They love the darkness of sin and deliberately stay out in the darkness because they are not willing to
surrender their sins! Anybody who really tries to do right and
loves the right will run to Christ the first time he ever hears
that Jesus died to save sinners.

There is only one way that anybody in the world is a lost
sinner. That is, that his wicked heart is against Christ, hates
Christ, turns away from Christ to continue in sin.

Again, I will show from the Bible that that is true. Jesus
Himself said,

"No man can serve two masters: for either he will hate the one, and love the other; or else he will hold to the one, and despise the other. Ye cannot serve God and mammon."—Matt. 6:24.

There is no halfway ground. If you do not love Jesus Christ and trust Him and serve Him, then you hate Him and despise Him. That is the plain statement of the Word of God. Nothing in the world proves you are a sinner as clearly and forcibly as the simple fact that you do not love and have not trusted and surrendered your whole heart to Jesus Christ as Saviour and Lord to follow Him and obey Him all your life. If Christ is pure and good and holy, then only a black-hearted sinner, a deliberate sinner, one who loves sin and holds on to sin would despise Jesus or reject Him or hate Him.

Again we say in the words of Holy Scripture that, "There is no difference: for all have sinned, and come short of the glory of God." All the world is alike in the fact of sin. Everyone who ever heard the gospel and did not the first instant accept it gladly and turn to Christ, simply proved the awful depravity of his heart by nature.

And if you, dear reader, deny that you are a sinner, that itself proves only the blackness and stubbornness of your heart that will not believe the Word of God, will not admit the truth about your own wicked heart, will not repent and come to Christ. And in that inborn taint, that hellish bent to sinning, that awful turning of the heart away from God, there is not a particle of difference between the lowest and the highest, the best and the worst. All alike are sinners! Only the infinite grace of God could ever save any human being on earth.

But If You Are a Sinner, You Deserve the Wrath of God, Eternal Torment

By this time, I trust, every honest reader has come to the place God intended these Scriptures to bring us. They were given, He said, "That every mouth may be stopped, and all the world may become guilty before God" (Rom. 3:19). If you are honest, by this time you have admitted that you are a sinner, the same kind of sinner as the street-walking harlot, or the criminal behind the bars. If you are honest, you have listened to the voice of conscience joined in with the Word of God to condemn you as a sinner. There is no difference. We are all in the same boat and are all passed under condemnation alike. We are in the boat of sin and the boat is sinking!

There are some terrible Scriptures in the Bible, but they are true. The Scripture says, "The soul that sinneth, it shall die" (Ezek. 18:4). The solemn warning of God is, "Be sure your sin will find you out"! (Num. 32:23). The alarming law of the Bible is that "The wages of sin is death" (Rom. 6:23). When a sinner dies, he has earned the death of his body. When he goes to a Hell of torment he need not complain for he has only gotten what is his just wages. People do not go to Hell because God hates them. No, they go to Hell because they deserve to go, because they ought to go, because they are sinners. They stay in Hell because they are still sinners, still unregenerate enemies of God. The stern Word of God to every sinner is, "Be not deceived; God is not mocked: for whatsoever a man soweth, that shall he also reap" (Gal. 6:7). That is the reason the Bible says that "so death passed upon all men, for that all have sinned" (Rom. 5:12). The wrath of God burns always against sinners. "God is angry with the wicked every day" (Ps. 7:11), and "It is a fearful thing to fall into the hands of the living God" (Heb. 10:31). Therefore, unless you, dear sinner, find some way to escape what you deserve, and some one else who loves you enough to save you and pay for your sin, you are eternally doomed!

All Bible Doctrine Depends On the Fact of Sin

Here are some conclusions from the fact of sin. If you believe the Bible and accept this proven fact that all are sinners, then several great conclusions, which you must acknowledge, come quickly to mind.

1. Man is a fallen creature. Then the foolish theory of evolution is not so. Man is not climbing upward toward God. Lost man, made in the image of God, is now a fallen creature. The

fact of sin, proved to us on every hand, is conclusive proof that the first chapters of Genesis are true. Adam sinned and so bent the mind and heart of the whole race away from God.

2. Next, the fact of sin fully understood explains and makes necessary the certainty of judgment and eternal punishment for unrepentent sinners which is so clearly taught in the Bible. Men who do not believe in Hell evidently do not believe in sin as the Bible teaches it. The Bible doctrine of sin is the foundation of every important doctrine in Christianity.

3. The fact that all men everywhere are sinners, sinners justly deserving death and eternal condemnation, makes necessary and logical the crucifixion of Christ. Christ died to save men from an awful Hell. He, the Sinless One, died for our sins. His blood made an atonement for us. Christ is the sinner's Substitute, Christ died, not as an example, not as a martyr, and not as a good man, a victim of circumstances. No, He, the Son of God, the Son of man, purchased salvation for sinners by His death on the cross. You can never understand the atonement of God's plan of salvation if you do not believe what God says about sin.

4. Jesus said, "Ye must be born again." The need for the new birth is denied only by men who do not accept God's teaching about sin. Men are by nature wicked sinners with hearts that must be changed. Men are dead in trespasses and sin and must be made alive by the Holy Spirit if they are ever to see God. One who does not believe he must be born again simply needs to learn what God has said about him, that he is no wise different, but a poor wicked-hearted sinner like all others.

5. The fact of sin, as so clearly taught in God's Word and witnessed on every hand by history and observation and the human conscience, explains why many men turn away from the Bible and away from Christ. Men hate the Bible because it brands them as guilty sinners! Men will not come to Christ and receive Him, because He will only receive them as confessed and Hell-deserving sinners! And this is the explanation of modernism. Foolish, wicked, self-righteous men wish to be

known as Christians but they do not accept the Bible as infallibly inspired, nor Christ as very God, nor the death of Christ as an atonement for sin because this would mean they would have to confess to be fallen, guilty and black-hearted sinners, fully under the condemnation of an angry God! Christ-rejectors love their sin but hide it and deny it.

Some of you may shrink from the plain words of this message, but I warn you that man shuts his heart to every great doctrine in the Bible if he does not accept God's plain teaching that "There is no difference: for all have sinned and come short of glory of God." And all who deny that they are sinners shut the door of hope and mercy and grace and salvation, for God offers these only to confessed sinners!

All Have Sinned, But Thank God, All Can Be Saved!

We have been repeating that "all have sinned," and if that were all there was to say on the question, everyone of us would be doomed forever. Thank God, that is not all; God has another word on the subject. It is still true that "There is no difference: for all have sinned and come short of the glory of God." But in the book of Romans there is another place that says too, "There is no difference." Turn to Romans 10:12, 13.

"For there is no difference between the Jew and the Greek: for the same Lord over all is rich unto all that call upon him. For whosoever shall call upon the name of the Lord shall be saved."

No difference, all have sinned! So says Romans 3:22, 23. And now, thank God, we read that there is no difference, all may be saved! All of us are sinners; we are all in the same boat. But, thank God, Jesus Christ will save the whole boatload if we will let Him! If sin is universal, then salvation is offered just as freely and universally. "But where sin abounded, grace did much more abound" (Rom. 5:20).

If you go back and read Romans 3:23, "For all have sinned, and come short of the glory of God," you will find it is followed by the blessed promise, "Being justified freely by his grace through the redemption that is in Christ Jesus."

Isaiah 53:6 told us that "All we like sheep have gone astray; we have turned every one to his own way." Then the verse continues, "And the Lord hath laid on Him the iniquity of us all." Jesus Christ bore our sins!

This is the gospel, that "Christ died for our sins according to the Scriptures" (I Cor. 15:3). It is a blessed, blessed thought, worthy of all acceptation, God had Paul to say, "that Christ Jesus came into the world to save sinners." And Paul said that he himself was the chief of sinners (I Tim. 1:15).

Jesus died to save sinners and nobody else! He said, "I came not to call the righteous, but sinners to repentance" (Luke 5:32). If you are a sinner, then there is hope for you, love for you, mercy for you, salvation for you! Do you know why the poor publican in the temple, so ashamed that he could not lift up his eyes toward Heaven, got wonderfully saved and went down to his house justified and saved? He prayed, "God be merciful to me a *sinner!*" (Luke 18:13). Any one who comes to Jesus Christ for mercy, confessing he is a poor, undone sinner, will be saved. God cannot give a sinner *justice* in saving him as if he were righteous. But He can offer, and delights to offer, *mercy* to those who admit they are sinners.

It is only the blood of Christ, then, which is a hope for the sinner. The blood has paid for sin! Your sins are laid on Jesus Christ. That perfect and holy Jesus was tempted in all points like as we are, yet did no sin. He suffered as a sinner, but it was my sins He suffered for, and yours. "For he hath made him to be sin for us, who knew no sin; that we might be made the righteousness of God in him" (II Cor. 5:21). God the Father is well satisfied with the price His Son has paid. He has accepted Christ as a substitute and is willing, yea, anxious, to have us reconciled to Him.

"All Is Forgiven: Come Home!"

In the "personals" column of a daily newspaper long ago I saw an ad that touched my heart. It ran about like this—

"Emma, come home. All is forgiven. Mother is sick and wants to see you." I do not know what wayward girl had broken her mother's and father's hearts with her sin. I just know that the anxious, loving hearts of her parents reached out through the great city begging her to return and to accept the forgiveness which was already offered before she even asked it!

So God the Father sends this message today saying, "Dear sinner, all is forgiven if you will trust in my dear Son who has paid for your sins. We love you and want you to come home to Heaven instead of being lost in Hell."

"There is no difference!" All have sinned, but all may be forgiven, too. All must come alike, simply trusting in the blood of Jesus Christ.

In a Texas revival years ago, I talked to a lost woman who seemed so troubled, so burdened with her sins that she longed to be saved. But she could not believe God would save her. I wondered what was in her way but could not find the secret that troubled her and kept her from Jesus. At last she wrote me a letter and brought it to me saying with downcast face, "When you have read this, please tell me if you think I can be saved." She went away and I read the letter. It was the pitiful outpouring of a shamed, broken heart. She told me how she had been a common woman, had gone far in sin. Her husband, she said, had led her to it, only God knows why! Now in despair and shame she wondered if God could ever save her.

That night after the meeting I saw her and opened my Bible to show her Isaiah 1:18. I pointed my finger to it and read it over and over.

"*Come now, and let us reason together, saith the Lord: though your sins be as scarlet, they shall be as white as snow; though they be red like crimson, they shall be as wool.*"

Doubting, fearing, hoping, she listened and prayed and yet went away not sure. But the next night she came back to the meeting with glowing face and rejoicing heart and told me this:

"Last night I had a dream or vision—I do not know which.

Someone held a Bible before me and pointed to the same verse of Scripture that you showed me which promises, 'Though your sins be as scarlet, they shall be as white as snow; though they be red like crimson, they shall be as wool.' In my dream I wept and wondered if it was for me. Then I looked up to see who it was whose finger pointed to the verse, and Brother Rice, it was Jesus! I saw Him and knew Him and then I knew the promise was for me. He paid for my sins and so I know that now everything is forgiven!" I baptized that woman and she became a happy soul winner, a true Christian.

Dear, troubled, dying sinner, won't you come too and be saved today? Confess to Christ that you are a sinner, but receive Him as your Substitute and be washed today as white as snow!

There is no difference, for all have sinned; but—

"There is no difference between the Jew and the Greek: for the same Lord over all is rich unto all that call upon him. For whosoever shall call upon the name of the Lord shall be saved!"—Rom. 10:12–13.

If you have never been converted, but today will take Christ as your own Saviour and Redeemer, will you write me and tell me that you have trusted Christ? You may copy the form below, or write me in your own words. I will be so glad and will pray for you and write you a personal letter.

Date......................

Dr. John R. Rice,
Wheaton, Illinois

Dear Dr. Rice:

I confess I am a sinner. I do not deserve salvation. But I am glad that Jesus died for my sins. Here and now I receive Him into my heart. With all my heart I turn away from my sin and turn to Christ. I trust Him to forgive my sins, and take Him as my personal Saviour. I will claim Him openly and try to live for Him the rest of my life by His help.

Signed...

Address...

....

(This message, under the title of *All Have Sinned*, is available from the publishers in a 32-page pamphlet at 15¢ each, seven for $1.00.)

IV

Double Theme of All the Prophets

I. All Bear Witness to Christ
II. All Teach Salvation by Simple Faith

"To him give all the prophets witness, that through his name whosoever believeth in him shall receive remission of sins."—Acts 10:43.

WHEN PETER WENT to preach to Cornelius, the Roman centurion, God let him sum up all the Old Testament in one verse as given in Acts 10:43: "To him give all the prophets witness, that through his name whosoever believeth in him shall receive remission of sins." Cornelius and his entire household, who had been prayerfully seeking God, saw the way of salvation at once and were instantly saved and gloriously filled with the Holy Spirit.

What a marvelous unity there is the Bible! The theme of the whole Bible is Christ. And this verse says that the Old Testament prophets, every one, gave witness to Christ, and that every one of them taught that whoever put his trust in Christ received remission of his sins, forgiveness, salvation!

This is wonderful proof of the divine authenticity of the Scriptures. Only God could have about forty men, writing over a period of 1600 years, all unite in one theme and never a one contradict the others. All pointed to Christ! And all showed that salvation was by simple faith in Him alone.

I. Christ Is the Theme of All Old Testament Prophets

1. *Christ is everywhere in the book of Genesis.* When the serpent, under Satan's leadership and which is a constant symbol of Satan, deceived Adam and Eve and led them into sin and death, God comforted them by His statement to the serpent, "And I will put enmity between thee and the woman, and between thy seed and her seed; it shall bruise thy head, and thou shalt bruise his heel" (Gen. 3:15). That seed of the woman who will finally crush Satan is Christ.

When God promised Abraham that "In thee shall all families of the earth be blessed" (Gen. 12:3), He referred to Christ. When He promised that Abraham's seed should inherit the land of Canaan forever, that with Abraham's seed He would make an everlasting covenant, He referred to Christ, the great descendant of Abraham. So Galatians 3:16 says, "Now to Abraham and his seed were the promises made. He saith not, And to seeds, as of many; but as of one, And to thy seed, which is Christ."

When Abraham offered Isaac, he did it in faith, knowing that Isaac was a type of Jesus Christ. Like the Lord Jesus, Isaac was a long-expected and promised son. He was counted the only-begotten son. He was offered as a sacrifice and, symbolically, raised from the dead! In all this Abraham saw the coming Saviour. When on the way up Mount Moriah with Isaac he said, "My son, God will provide himself a lamb for a burnt-offering" (Gen. 22:8), he referred to Christ; for the Saviour said in John 8:56, "Your father Abraham rejoiced to see my day: and he saw it, and was glad." And Hebrews 11:17–19 tells us that, "By faith Abraham, when he was tried, offered up Isaac: and he that had received the promises offered up his only begotten son. Of whom it was said, That in Isaac shall thy seed be called: Accounting that God was able to raise him up, even from the dead; from whence also he received him in a figure."

2. *Christ is pictured repeatedly throughout the ceremonial law.*

Christ was pictured by the passover lamb, a male lamb of the first year (in its full prime) without a blemish, as Christ was without sin or fault. The lamb roasted whole with fire and without water represented Christ who suffered all the torments of the damned for us without alleviation. The lamb was eaten with bitter herbs, representing the sufferings of Christ.

All the sacrifices picture Christ. The lamb pictured Him as the innocent one suffering for the guilty. The young bullock pictured Him as our burden-bearing Saviour. The scapegoat pictured Him as taking our blame, carrying away our sins from the presence of God. The mourning turtledove pictured Him as the man of sorrows and acquainted with grief, who bare our sickness and our sorrows. The pure white pigeon pictured Him as the sinless one. The offering of fine flour pictured Christ, our bruised Saviour. It was anointed with oil, picturing Christ filled with the Holy Spirit. It was offered with frankincense, picturing how He intercedes for us with the Father and how pleased God is with the offering of His own Son, how satisfied with the payment of our debt.

Christ is pictured in the priesthood. He alone can enter into the Holy of Holies to make intercession for us according to the will of God. He alone can be our mediator, our priest, our Saviour.

The tabernacle pictured Christ. Its boards of acacia wood pictured the humanity of Christ. They were covered with gold which pictured His deity. The inner veil pictured His flesh, torn on the cross (Matt. 27:51; Heb. 10:20). The white linen covering of the tabernacle pictured His righteousness. The blue covering pictured His heavenly nature, His deity. The ramskins dyed red pictured His atoning blood. The badger skins which were the outer covering pictured how He is unlovely to those of the outside world, who do not perceive His beauties. In the tabernacle the table of shewbread continually pictured Christ as the bread of life. The seven golden lamps pictured Christ as the light of the world, not an incomplete or imperfect light but the perfect light, perfection being pictured by seven. These lamps were fed by olive oil which pictured the Holy Spirit. Christ in His human ministry was completely filled and empowered with the Holy Spirit. The altar of incense before the veil which separated it from the Holy of Holies pictured Christ in His perfect mediatorial work, His prayer, His intercession for us before the Father and how pleased God is with His offering.

The high priest pictured Christ, our own High Priest, who has now entered into the Holy of Holies in Heaven for us and has made atonement with His own blood (Heb. chapters 9 and 10).

3. *Incidents on the wilderness journey of Israel pictured Christ.* The manna which fell every day from Heaven pictured Him as the true bread from Heaven (John 6:31–35). Christ was the Rock smitten in the wilderness out of which came an abundance of water that all the people might drink (Exod. 17:5, 6; I Cor. 10:4). And being once smitten, the Rock needs never to be smitten again, but only spoken to for the continued fullness of His blessing (Num. 20:7–12).

The brazen serpent, lifted upon a pole in the wilderness, so that snake-bitten Israelites might look and be healed by God's mercy (Num. 21:5–9) pictured Jesus. For Jesus told Nicodemus, "As Moses lifted up the serpent in the wilderness, even so must the Son of man be lifted up: that whosoever believeth in him should not perish, but have eternal life" (John 3:14, 15).

In Deuteronomy 18:15 Moses prophesied, "The Lord thy God will raise up unto thee a Prophet from the midst of thee, of thy brethren, like unto me; unto him ye shall hearken."

In fact, Christ is so clearly portrayed in Genesis, Exodus, Leviticus, Numbers and Deuteronomy, that Jesus Himself said, "For had ye believed Moses, ye would have believed me: for he wrote of me. But if ye believe not his writings, how shall ye believe my words?" (John 5:46, 47).

4. *Jesus was a favorite theme of the prophets who wrote the Psalms.* Psalm 2 tells how the kings and rulers would set themselves together to take counsel against God's Anointed. (The word

Anointed is translated *Christ* in Acts 4:26.) In Psalm 2:7 God says, "Thou art my Son; this day have I begotten thee." And in verse 12 the sinners are exhorted, "Kiss the Son, lest he be angry, and ye perish from the way, when his wrath is kindled but a little. Blessed are all they that put their trust in him." Psalm 22 plainly tells of the Saviour's death on the cross, even the words of His prayer. Psalm 16:10 tells of His resurrection.

5. *Christ was the Coming Seed of David who was promised to reign on David's throne forever beginning at some future time* (II Sam. 7:10–16; I Chron. 17:4–15). The same promise is continued in the eighty-ninth Psalm. It was repeated to Mary by the Angel Gabriel (Luke 1:32, 33).

6. *Christ is often foretold in Isaiah.* He is the "Branch" out of the stem of Jesse, David's father, in Isaiah 11, and His glorious reign on the earth is foretold. He is the man of sorrows and acquainted with grief, the suffering servant of Isaiah 53. Even the beating and marring of His face and form were foretold in Isaiah 52:13, 14. Isaiah 61:1 tells how Christ was to be anointed with the Holy Spirit to preach the good tidings to the meek, to bind up the brokenhearted, to proclaim liberty to the captives and the opening of the prison to them that are bound. Jesus Himself read this Scripture in the synagogue in Galilee, and said, "This day is this scripture fulfilled in your ears" (Luke 4:14–21).

7. *Other prophets throughout the Old Testament pictured Jesus clearly.* Jeremiah 23:5 pictured His return and reign when it said, "Behold, the days come, saith the Lord, that I will raise unto David a righteous Branch, and a King shall reign and prosper, and shall execute judgment and justice in the earth." Ezekiel spoke of Him when he promised the restoration of Israel and said, "And I will set up one shepherd over them, and he shall feed them, even my servant David; he shall feed them, and he shall be their shepherd. And I the Lord will be their God, and my servant David a prince among them" (Ezek. 34:23, 24). That "David" is the greater David, Jesus

Christ, descended from David according to the flesh, and promised to sit on his throne.

Daniel 9:25, 26 tells of "the Messiah the Prince," and tells exactly when He should come, sixty-nine weeks of years, 483 years, from the decree to rebuild Jerusalem in the days of Ezra and Nehemiah. And Micah 5:2 promised clearly that in Bethlehem of Judea Jesus would be born, a ruler in Israel. Jonah, by being three days and nights in the belly of the whale, pictured that Christ would be three days and three nights in the heart of the earth, that is, buried three days and nights before His resurrection (Matt. 12:40).

Zechariah 12:10 foretells the piercing of the Saviour's side with a spear and how one day, at His second coming, Jews will see this and repent; while Zechariah 13:6 tells how they will discover the wounds made by the nails in His hands when He was crucified! Zechariah 14 tells plainly of the Saviour's second coming, and verse 9 tells us, "And the Lord shall be king over all the earth." And that Lord is Christ!

The Old Testament Scriptures close with Malachi, and there in chapter 3, verse 1, we are told, "Behold, I will send my messenger (John the Baptist), and he shall prepare the way before me; and the Lord, whom ye seek, shall suddenly come to his temple, even the messenger of the covenant, whom ye delight in; behold, he shall come, saith the Lord of hosts."

Christ is the theme of the Old Testament as well as the New. Peter truly said to Cornelius that, "To him give all the prophets witness"!

If you read the Old Testament with a spiritual mind and a prayerful heart, you will find hundreds of references to Christ not here mentioned, but clearly intended by the Holy Spirit, as you will see.

II. All the Prophets Teach Exactly the Same Plan of Salvation, by Faith in Christ

Some foolish people have supposed that God had various plans of salvation down through the ages. It has been taught that some were saved by keeping the Ten Commandments. Others have believed that Jews were saved through the blood of the sacrifices of animals. But Hebrews 10:4 says, "For it is not possible that the blood of bulls and of goats should take away sins." No, no, all those sacrifices only pointed toward the salvation which is offered freely, purchased for us by the blood of Christ, and received by those who trust in Him. Others have supposed that in the days of John the Baptist people were saved in the act of baptism. But John the Baptist himself plainly said in John 3:36, "He that believeth on the Son hath everlasting life: and he that believeth not the Son shall not see life; but the wrath of God abideth on him." That is exactly the same plan of salvation as that in John 3:16; Habakkuk 2:4; Acts 16:31; and Romans 3:28. No, there are no different plans of salvation. The testimony of all the prophets is this, that "through his name whosoever believeth in him should have remission of sins."

Throughout the Bible then we will find the foretelling of Christ's death, we will find reminders of the blood that would be shed. And throughout the whole Old Testament it is made clear that all who trust in Him are saved. "To him give all the prophets witness, that through his name whosoever believeth in him shall receive remission of sins," as our text in Acts 10:43 declares.

1. *In Genesis people were saved by faith in the coming Saviour.* Before Adam and Eve had been cast out of the garden, but after they had sinned, they made aprons of fig leaves sewed together (Gen. 3:7). That pictures the way frail human beings try to cover their nakedness and sin, by their own works. But how frail and unsatisfactory is such a covering! As a child I tried the same thing with my playmates. We pinned grape leaves and oak leaves together with straws. But they were soon dried and brittle and fell apart, just as all of man's self-righteousness fails him! But God had a better way to cover man's nakedness and sin than that; He made coats of skins and clothed them (Gen. 3:21). Thus the first animal was

slain, picturing Christ, and so we are covered with a robe of Christ's own righteousness and our nakedness and sin is hidden from God's face when we trust in Christ.

Cain brought an offering to God of the fruits of the ground which he had raised with his toil and sweat, but God would not receive such an offering. That pictured the truth that God is never pleased when men come in their own name and righteousness, depending on their own works. But at the same time Abel brought of the firstlings of his flock and the fat thereof (Gen. 4:1–5). And Hebrews 11:4 says, "By faith Abel offered unto God a more excellent sacrifice than Cain, by which he obtained witness that he was righteous, God testifying of his gifts; and by it he being dead yet speaketh." It was not that God was pleased with *Abel* in himself, but that God was pleased with his *gift* which he offered by faith. For that gift pictured the coming Saviour, the innocent Lamb of God that should take away the sin of the world.

Noah was commanded of God to build an ark. The heavenly specifications were given. Noah and his family, eight souls, were saved from the mighty flood in that ark. But the ark pictured Christ. The seams of the ark were pitched with pitch. The same word for "pitch" in Genesis 6:14 is the Hebrew word translated "atonement" in Leviticus 17:12, etc. Noah was saved not by his goodness but by simply stepping into the ark. Hebrews 11:7 tells us, "By faith Noah, being warned of God of things not seen as yet, moved with fear, prepared an ark to the saving of his house; by the which he condemned the world, and became heir of the righteousness which is by faith."

Note again that Noah was saved exactly as we are. He "became heir of the righteousness which is by faith." Noah understood that that ark pictured Christ. He understood that he would be counted righteous by putting his trust in this coming Saviour. So he stepped into the ark, took his family in with him and was carried safely through the flood. But

inwardly a greater blessing came. Noah was saved by faith in
the coming "ark" of God, Jesus Christ.

How was Abraham saved? Abraham "believed in the Lord;
and he counted it to him for righteousness" (Gen. 15:6).
Romans, chapter 4, holds Abraham up as the example for all
ages, both for Jews and Gentiles, teaching that he was saved
wholly by grace when he trusted in the coming Saviour, and
so sin was not imputed to him. Just so we are saved when we
put our trust in Christ.

2. *God's dealing with the children of Israel in Egypt and the
wilderness pictures salvation by simple faith in the shed blood of Christ.*
No gospel text in the New Testament is stronger than the
lesson given on salvation in Exodus, chapter 12, where the
children of Israel were commanded to take the blood of the
passover lamb and smite some of it on the two doorposts and
on the lintel above the door with a bunch of hyssop. Thereafter the firstborn son of such a home was safe. At midnight
the death angel passed over the land of Egypt, and in every
home on whose door there was not that mark of blood the
firstborn of man and the firstborn of all cattle suddenly died!
And God said plainly, "When I see the blood, I will pass
over you" (Exod. 12:13).

That rescue of the firstborn sons from physical death pictured God's way in which every soul may be saved from
eternal death. The Israelites trusted in the blood on the door.
They deliberately applied the blood as directed. Then they
sat down safely within the home. They did not work for their
safety. They did not earn it. They did not deserve it. They
simply believed God's blessed promise that when He saw the
blood, He would pass over them, and the death angel would
not come within that blood-protected home to strike. What an
accurate and beautiful picture of saving faith that is!

The firstborn sons were not saved by being better than the
Egyptians. They were not saved by keeping laws and commandments. They were saved simply because they put their

trust in the blood that was on the door. Spiritually-minded Jews may have seen what we can see, that the blood dripping from the lintel of the door was like the trickle that ran down the face of the Saviour from the thorns on His brow, and like the blood from the spikes through His feet, or like the river of blood that ran down from His side where the spear entered. The blood on each doorpost may have pictured to them, as it does to me, the outstretched hands of Jesus pierced by the nails for us and dripping blood. Let no one think that anybody in the Old Testament was ever saved in any way but exactly as we are saved. They believed that God would furnish a Passover Lamb, and that this Lamb of God should take away the sins of the world. Those who were saved simply depended upon and trusted in the blood that should be poured out, believing God's word.

Another picture of salvation was when the children of Israel thirsted for water in the wilderness and complained and murmured. Then God told Moses to take the rod in his hand and smite upon the rock in Horeb. And when he did, there came out a river of water that the people and their cattle drank abundantly (Exod. 17:1–6).

What a picture of salvation! They did not work for it, they did not buy it, they did not get it by circumcision nor ceremonies. Moses, with the rod of God in his hand, smote the rock. Just so Christ was smitten by the rod of God and chastised for our sins, and from Christ, the smitten Rock, there flows a fountain of everlasting life, and whosoever will may come and drink. Thus salvation is free. All who come to the smitten Christ may drink of the water of life and never thirst again.

The blessed fact that salvation is eternal, that God does not cast away His children, is taught very plainly in Numbers 20:2–13. The people thirsted again, long afterward. God said to Moses, "Take the rod, and gather thou the assembly together, thou, and Aaron thy brother, and speak ye unto the rock before their eyes; and it shall give forth his water and thou shalt bring forth to them water out of the rock: so thou shalt give the congregation and their beasts drink" (Num. 20:8). Note that in this second time Moses was commanded to *speak* to the rock and not to smite it. But in anger and vexation Moses smote the rock before the children of Israel. Thus God's lesson was missed by Israel (but not by the prophet who wrote). For Christ being once crucified need not be crucified again. Our sins are settled forever when He is crucified once and when we have taken of Him once. Salvation is settled once for all with one smiting of Christ and one believing by a sinner. Thereafter we may come again and drink and drink and never thirst again.

The same blessed lesson was taught in Exodus 12 in the story of the passover lamb. Israelites were to eat of the passover lamb that one night, and all of it was to be eaten. If any remained until the morning it was to be burned. By this God meant to teach that salvation is not a gradual process but a transaction once for all whereby a believer partakes of Christ and so is saved. There are not varying steps in salvation. Rather, "He that believeth on the Son hath everlasting life" (John 3:36; John 5:24; John 6:47). Why it is evident that the Old Testament has exactly the same gospel as the New and that "To him [Jesus] give all the prophets witness, that through his name whosoever believeth in him shall receive remission of sins."

When the snake-bitten Israelites were commanded simply to look at the brass snake lifted up on a pole to be healed, as told in Numbers 21:5-9, that was a clear picture of how people are saved today. In fact, Jesus used exactly that illustration to show Nicodemus that "As Moses lifted up the serpent in the wilderness, even so must the Son of man be lifted up: that whosoever believeth in him should not perish, but have eternal life" (John 3:14, 15). Looking to the brass snake on the pole symbolized a poor sinner, dying with the snakebite of sin, looking to the crucified Saviour for salvation. And as the snake-bitten, dying man was healed when he believed the

word of God and looked, so a poor lost sinner, when he believes
what God has said and depends upon the crucified Saviour,
looking to Calvary in his heart, is forgiven and saved!

For forty years the children of Israel were fed by manna
from Heaven. Every day it fell, except on the Sabbath.
Enough fell on Friday to do for both Friday and Saturday.
It was called angels' food and it pictured Christ who said
He was the bread from Heaven. But notice how the people
took it. They did not buy it. They could not hoard it even
when they tried. Even those who did not gather as much as
others, had just as much when it was all measured out. There
was no element of merit in that manna whatever. They did
not grow it in the field. They did not buy it with money.
They did not deserve it by righteousness. They simply believed God and took it and ate it. And that is the way sinners
are saved. They simply take of Jesus Christ and eat the Bread
from Heaven. John 1:12 says, "As many as received him,
to them gave he power to become the sons of God, even to
them that believe on his name." So those that received the
manna took it and ate and were saved from death in the
wilderness. What a beautiful picture of receiving Christ by
faith, simply taking the salvation He offers!

3. *The way people offered the bloody sacrifices of the Old Testament
pictures salvation by faith in Christ.* We have reminded you that
all the sacrifices pictured Christ. Now let me remind you that
they also taught that salvation is by simple faith. When a Jew
brought his sin-offering, he admitted his own sin; but the
beast was killed instead of the sinner! When he brought a
peace offering, it pictured that his peace was gained by the
death of another. Again and again we are told in varying
words that, "It is the blood that maketh an atonement for the
soul" (Lev. 17:11). We know that they were never saved by
the blood of animals, and they knew it too. The blood of bulls
and of goats never did take away sin (Heb. 10:4). When they
brought a sacrifice, that sacrifice never purged their conscience
nor made them perfect before God. But it did picture to them

that God would have a sacrifice provided, "the Lamb of God which taketh away the sin of the world." And those who were saved did not depend upon the animal sacrifice but depended upon God's Lamb who was yet to come.

Likewise the priesthood was a constant reminder to the people that they were not fit to appear before God. They must have some intercessor, someone who would make an offering in their behalf. So all who truly understood the significance of the priesthood knew they must look forward to God's High Priest who would come.

Some people very foolishly make a distinction between the Judaism of the Old Testament and the Christianity of the New Testament. But true Judaism points as clearly to Christ and His atoning blood on Calvary as Christianity. The God of the Old Testament and of the New is the same God. The Christ of the Old Testament and the New is the same Christ. The plan of salvation of the Old Testament and the New is the same plan of salvation.

4. *Many promises of the Old Testament point to salvation by simple faith in Christ, the coming Saviour.* In studying the meaning of Acts 10:43 and searching for illustrations of it, I have just been impressed anew with a remarkable truth. Some of the greatest texts on salvation by faith in Christ are first in the Old Testament and then quoted in the New Testament! For instance, Martin Luther's great text of the reformation, "The just shall live by faith," is found in Romans 1:17, Galatians 3:11 and in Hebrews 10:38. *But every one of these Scriptures is quoting from the Old Testament to prove salvation by faith.* For the statement is originally found in Habakkuk 2:4.

Likewise that sweet promise of Romans 10:13, "For whosoever shall call upon the name of the Lord shall be saved" is found first in the Old Testament in Joel 2:32, "And it shall come to pass, that whosoever shall call on the name of the Lord shall be delivered." Peter quoted that Scripture on the day of Pentecost, as recorded in Acts 2:21, "And it shall come to pass, that whosoever shall call on the name of the Lord shall be saved"; saying plainly that "This is that which was spoken by the prophet Joel."

You see all the New Testament apostles used Old Testament texts to preach that people are saved when they simply put their trust in Christ.

In Romans 9:31–33 we find the argument of Paul, divinely inspired, that Israel as a whole was not saved, "because they sought it not by faith." Then he quoted from Isaiah 28:16, as follows: "As it is written, Behold, I lay in zion a stumbling-stone and rock of offense: and whosoever believeth on him shall not be ashamed." Then in the tenth chapter, Paul shows the terrible error of the Jews who seek to establish their own righteousness and have not submitted themselves unto the righteousness of God, and says in Romans 10:9–11, "That if thou shalt confess with thy mouth the Lord Jesus, and shalt believe in thine heart that God hath raised him from the dead, thou shalt be saved. For with the heart man believeth unto righteousness; and with the mouth confession is made unto salvation. For the scripture saith, *Whosoever believeth on him shall not be ashamed.*" Here again Isaiah 28:16 is quoted, proving that salvation is by faith in Christ alone and that all who put their trust in Christ will never be left to be embarrassed and lost and ashamed over their sins, but are forgiven and saved.

Therefore true Judaism, as taught in the Old Testament, is Christianity. It is as proper to preach revival sermons from the Old Testament as from the New Testament. The passover supper pictured the death of Christ for sinners, salvation by faith, in *exactly* the same way as the Lord's Supper does now.

I have just carefully looked over, in Young's Analytical Concordance, every time the word *trust* is used in the Old Testament. I find that in the Psalms alone people are commanded to trust in the Lord and are given sweet and precious promises of their safety if they put their trust in the Lord, or are rebuked for not trusting Him, about seventy times! The word *trust* is used in Jeremiah and Isaiah more times than in the entire New Testament! It is used more often of trusting *in the Lord* by far than the same word is used with that meaning in the New Testament! In the book of John the word *believe* is often used as *trust* is used in the Old Testament. But in the book of Psalms alone, the word *trust* is used more often of the Lord than the word *believe* is used of God and of Christ in the book of John!

Now let us review. Trusting Christ for salvation is as often taught in the Old Testament as in the New. Consider that Abraham believed God and it was counted unto him for righteousness, and that in Romans chapter 4, Abraham is held up as a great example of salvation by faith. Consider that Jesus in teaching Nicodemus how to be saved used the example of the brazen serpent on a pole to picture the Son of man, and the Israelites' looking to the brass snake on the pole to illustrate a sinner believing in the crucified Saviour. Consider the galaxy of Old Testament heroes mentioned in Hebrews chapter 11 and that every one of them did what he did *by faith*, not by merit or works of righteousness. Consider that nearly the entire book of Hebrews is used to show how the Old Testament tabernacle worship, offerings, and priesthood, pointed to salvation by faith in a crucified Saviour. Consider that Peter's sermon at Pentecost and Paul's great message on salvation in Romans 10:1–13 are based on Old Testament quotations, "Whosoever believeth on him shall not be ashamed" and, "Whosoever shall call upon the name of the Lord shall be saved." Consider that "The just shall live by faith," great texts in Romans 1:17, Galatians 3:11 and Hebrews 10:38, are all quoted from Habakkuk 2:4. Now is that not overwhelming proof that every prophet in the Old Testament taught exactly the same plan of salvation as the prophets in the New Testament?

What Peter said by divine inspiration in Acts 10:43, "To him give all the prophets witness, that through his name whosoever believeth in him shall receive remission of sins" is true!

Dear reader, I hope you will study further this blessed, blessed truth. Begin now to try to find all through the Bible pictures of Christ and of His atoning blood and of the doctrine that one who puts his trust in Christ is saved. You may find help from the notes in the Scofield Bible as you study the Old Testament. You will find help from *Christ in the Pentateuch* by Dr. J. B. Tidwell, a large book of 364 pages published by Zondervan. You will find help from the five-volume set on the Pentateuch by C. H. McIntosh. You will find help in the book *Simple Talks on the Tabernacle* by Dr. D. H. Dolman. You will find help in the great book on *The Tabernacle, Priesthood and Offerings* by the late Dr. I. M. Haldeman. But most of all you need a believing, humble mind and heart, led by the Holy Spirit as you really search the Scriptures. And soon you will be finding Christ on every page, and salvation offered in every type and promise! This article has only barely scratched the surface.

And dear sinner friend, if you read this, will you, like Cornelius and his household, take the testimony of all the prophets that "Whosoever believeth in him, [in Jesus Christ as your personal Saviour] shall receive remission of sins"? Oh, trust Him today!

V

"Paul's Gospel" or "Kingdom Gospel"

1. Carnal Christians Cause Divisions Over Dispensation. 2. Only One Gospel. 3. Is Repentance for Today? 4. The Gospel of the Kingdom. 5. Was John's Baptism for Jews Only? 6. "One Baptism" but Which Baptism? 7. Were Miracles for Jews Only?

DON'T MAJOR on minors! That was the trouble with the Pharisees who tithed mint, anise and cummin, and yet neglected the weightier matters of the law: judgment, mercy and faith, and rejected Christ! (Matt. 23:23). So many people become such ardent students of dispensations or the smaller incidentals of prophecy that they neglect the weightier matters of the Bible. For example, a woman wrote me very earnestly asking if she might not be taking the mark of the Beast if she bought defense bonds. Another letter asks what the mark of the Beast will be like and if we these days might take it without knowing it. Now the Bible mentions the mark of the Beast, but certainly for us today it is an incidental matter about which very little information is given. Speculation about it is not helpful, since the Beast himself (the one several times mentioned in Revelation, chapters 13 to 20) has not appeared, and no one can know yet what is his mark, and no one could possibly take it.

I. Carnal Christians Cause Divisions Over Dispensations

Likewise some Christians are so allured by the dispensational teachings of the Bible that they carry the matter to extremes. They imagine new dispensations here and new dispensations there. Sometimes they imagine that Jews were saved one way and Gentiles another. They imagine that John the Baptist had one kind of gospel and Paul another kind of gospel. Some of them talk about "a transition period." Some of them say that material blessings were all for the Jews and spiritual blessings all for the Gentiles. Some of them say that circumcision was essential to salvation in the Old Testament, that baptism was essential to salvation to Jews in the time of Christ, and that now baptism, like circumcision, is forbidden for Christians! All this confusion is very much like that of the carnal Christians at Corinth. Read carefully the following Scriptures and see the Holy Spirit's application.

"And I, brethren, could not speak unto you as unto spiritual, but as unto carnal, even as unto babes in Christ. I have fed you with milk, and not with meat: for hitherto ye were not able to bear it, neither yet now are ye able. For ye are yet carnal: for whereas there is among you envying, and strife, and divisions, are ye not carnal, and walk as men? For while one saith, I am of Paul; and another, I am of Apollos; are ye not carnal? Who then is Paul, and who is Apollos, but ministers by whom ye believed, even as the Lord gave to every man? I have planted, Apollos watered; but God gave the increase. So then neither is he that planteth any thing, neither he that watereth; but God that giveth the increase. Now he that planteth and he that watereth are one: and every man shall receive his own reward according to his own labour.

"Therefore let no man glory in men. For all things are your's; Whether Paul, or Apollos, or Cephas, or the world, or life, or death, or things present, or things to come; all are your's; And ye are Christ's; and Christ is God's."—I Cor. 3:1–8; 21–23.

"And these things, brethren, I have in a figure transferred to myself

and to Apollos for your sakes; that ye might learn in us not to think of men above that which is written, that no one of you be puffed up for one against another."—I Cor. 4:6.

Now consider the mistakes of these carnal Christians at Corinth. They had divisions and strife because one of them would say, "I am of Paul," thinking that Paul's gospel was different from that of Apollos or of Peter. But those very divisions proved that they were babes in the gospel, not able to bear strong meat, as Paul had said in verses 1 and 2 above. In verse 5 Paul simply disclaims any difference in his gospel and that of Apollos or of any other minister by whom people might believe in Christ. In verse 8 he expressly says that "he that planteth [Paul] and he that watereth [Apollos] are one" —that is, that they exactly agreed.

Then in verse 22 Paul says that whether Paul or Apollos, or Cephas—one who had the one, had the other. There was no difference in their doctrine. Neither one could give them anything that the other could not give them. One who believed under Paul's preaching was no better nor no better informed than those converted under the preaching of Apollos.

Then in I Corinthians 4:6 we are simply warned not to think of men (especially of Paul or Apollos or Peter) more highly than we ought to, and that no one should set himself up as a follower of Paul instead of Peter or instead of any other Bible preacher or writer of the Bible.

An earnest good Christian brother wrote me asking, "Are we under Paul's preaching of grace, as of Galatians 1:6–10 and Ephesians 2:8, 9 . . . or under the kingdom gospel of the twelve . . . ?" That honest question of a useful, good man encourages me to answer the questions of others on this subject.

II. Only One Gospel!

Did Paul have one gospel different from the gospel preached by others? Was the kingdom gospel and Paul's gospel different? I answer quickly and say, "Absolutely not!" There is only one gospel, only one plan of salvation. That gospel never did change and never will.

In Galatians 1:6–8 Paul says, "I marvel that ye are so soon removed from him that called you into the grace of Christ unto another gospel: which is not another; but there be some that trouble you, and would pervert the gospel of Christ. But though we, or an angel from Heaven, preach any other gospel unto you than that which we have preached unto you, let him be accursed."

Paul says that that which the Judaizers brought to Galatia was claimed to be another gospel; but it was not really a gospel. Then he gives them the solemn warning that the original gospel which he preached to them early in his second missionary journey (Acts 16:6) was the only gospel, and none other was to be tolerated. If he, Paul, or even an angel from Heaven, should later come to them with any different gospel, he was to be accursed!

Thus we know that Paul never did change his gospel. Any new revelation Paul received from Heaven did not affect the old, old gospel. It was just the same, never to be changed.

Mark 1:1, 2 says, "The beginning of the gospel of Jesus Christ, the Son of God; as it is written in the prophets, Behold, I send my messenger before thy face, which shall prepare thy way before thee." Then there follows a discussion of the ministry of John the Baptist, fulfilling that prophecy quoted from Malachi 3:1 as it applied to the ministry of John the Baptist. So John the Baptist began preaching the true gospel. To put John the Baptist in the Old Testament order and to have him preaching law and not grace is here made utterly impossible. John the Baptist preached the gospel, exactly the same gospel as Jesus preached. Those who heeded the gospel preached by John the Baptist believed in Christ, and depending on Him were saved. For John the Baptist preached, "Behold the Lamb of God, which taketh away the sin of the world" (John 1:29). Neither Paul nor any other preacher ever made the gospel of salvation by simple faith alone any clearer than did John the Baptist in John 3:27-36, ending with this matchless statement of it: "He that believeth on the Son hath everlasting life: and he that believeth not the Son shall not see life; but the wrath of God abideth on him."

That plan of salvation, that gospel invitation, as expressed in John 3:36 is exactly the same as Jesus Himself told Nicodemus in John 3:16, the same that Paul and Silas told the Philippian jailer in Acts 16:31, is the same Paul wrote to the Ephesian Christians in Ephesians 2:8, 9. The preaching of John the Baptist was gospel preaching. All who heeded John the Baptist turned to Christ in personal faith, depending on Him alone to save.

III. Is Repentance for Today?

John the Baptist said, "Repent ye: for the kingdom of heaven is at hand" (Matt. 3:2). Some have foolishly supposed that repentance was for Jews only. But that is not true. Jesus preached the same, exactly, when He came, saying, "Repent: for the kingdom of heaven is at hand" (Matt. 4:17). The same word *repent* is emphasized just as strongly in the gospel of Luke as in the gospel of Matthew. Jesus said there twice, "Except ye repent, ye shall all likewise perish" (Luke 13:3, 5). To the disciples waiting before Pentecost, Jesus commanded, "that repentance and remission of sins should be preached in his name among all nations, beginning at Jerusalem" (Luke 24:47). So the teaching of repentance is a part of the gospel for *all nations*, and not merely for Jews. Paul, preaching to the Gentiles on Mars' hill at Athens, said that God "now commandeth all men every where to repent" (Acts 17:30). Repentance is commanded of "all men every where." In II Peter 3:9 we are told that God is "not willing that any should perish, but that all should come to repentance." Paul's preaching in the great Gentile city of Ephesus was "repentance toward God, and faith toward our Lord Jesus Christ" (Acts 20:21).

Dr. H. A. Ironside has done us a great service in his book,

Except Ye Repent, in which he urges that everywhere gospel preachers should stress the fact today, as gospel preachers did in Bible times, that turning to God means a heart-turning away from sin, repentance. Faith in Christ is impossible without a revulsion against sin and a turning of the heart to God, that is, a change of mind, or repentance. All the great preachers who have won thousands of souls have preached that men need to repent of their sins, that there ought to be a godly sorrow which leads to a genuine turning of heart to hate sin and love God. And at the same time the heart puts its trust in Jesus Christ, depending on Christ to forgive the sins that the poor sinner now hates and turns from. Repentance is a part of God's plan of salvation, or rather, is one facet of the single plan of salvation. It is the gospel in one of its simple statements. The gospel that Christ died for our sins and rose again according to the Scriptures is not apprehended nor received honestly by any heart that does not turn away from sin, that does not repent.

So the preaching of John the Baptist was gospel preaching. It was not any different in its dispensation from that of Paul.

IV. "The Gospel of the Kingdom"

But John the Baptist preached, "The kingdom of heaven is at hand" (Matt. 3:2). So did Jesus (Matt. 4:17). Matthew 4:23 tells us that Jesus preached "the gospel of the kingdom." Does that mean that Jesus preached in Galilee a different gospel from that which He preached to Nicodemus in Jerusalem as recorded in the third chapter of John? Certainly not! By "the gospel of the kingdom" it is simply meant that Jesus was offering the kingdom, the literal kingdom on earth when He the "Seed of David" should reign at Jerusalem. This offer of the kingdom as being at hand, or nigh, or available, was simply used as an urgent reason why they should repent and be saved. For no Jew or Gentile will enter that kingdom who is not truly born again!

Suppose I go to a tuberculosis sanitarium and in a ward

of hopeless cases of those who are certain to die soon, I am allowed to preach. And suppose that there I preach to them a "gospel for the dying." Does that mean that I would give them a different gospel? Certainly not! By the "gospel for the dying" I would only mean that I had the same gospel, but I would present it with a particular urgency in view of the fact that those who heard me had such a short time to receive it. There are many motives and reasons for urging people to accept the gospel. The opportunity of Jews to receive their kingdom was one. So the gospel that men should repent and be born again so they would be fit to enter the kingdom of Christ on earth was called simply "the gospel of the kingdom."

Now, the imminency of the kingdom does not press upon us. We know that the earthly kingdom has been postponed because the King was rejected of the Jews. We know that now the next thing we are taught to look for is the coming of Christ to receive His saints into the air, not to reign, yet, on earth. And so we may preach the gospel in view of the coming of the Saviour, instead of preaching the same gospel in view of the coming of the kingdom. It is perfectly legitimate now to connect the imminent coming of Christ with our urging of men to accept Him and depend upon Him as Saviour. It was fitting then that the prospect of the kingdom should be urged upon the people as a reason why they should repent, trust in Christ and be saved. But in both cases it would be the same gospel. People would be saved by simple faith in Christ, turning their hearts from the love of sin to love God, whether they did it in view of the kingdom under the preaching of John the Baptist or Jesus, or whether they do it now in view of the coming of the Saviour from Heaven, which coming we expect at any time.

But in the great tribulation time after the rapture is over and when it is time for Christ to return again to reign on earth, then the same gospel will be preached; but it will again be connected with a prophecy and an urgent warning that the kingdom is coming. In view of the coming kingdom, people will be urged to repent and trust in Christ for salvation. And this same gospel then will be called, "this gospel of the kingdom"; and it "shall be preached in all the world for a witness unto all nations"; and the end of the great tribulation will come (Matt. 24:14). But it will not differ a particle from the old gospel, and people will be saved exactly the same way as through all the ages.

It is an interesting fact that the kingdom is mentioned in the book of Matthew fifty times, according to Young's Analytical Concordance, and forty-four times in the book of Luke. Possibly some will be surprised to learn that Luke mentions the kingdom almost as frequently as does Matthew, despite the fact that the book of Luke presents Jesus as the Son of man and is obviously addressed to all mankind, while Matthew has more particular meaning for Israel than does Luke. And Paul in his epistles talks about the kingdom of God fourteen times, while Peter, whom some people suppose to be writing principally for Jews, mentions it in his epistles only once! It is certainly unscriptural, and a mark of careless study, to talk about John the Baptist and Jesus preaching "a kingdom gospel" and of Paul as bringing "a gospel of grace," as if it differed from the kingdom gospel. The kingdom teaching was for all, and the gospel of grace was for all.

V. Was John's Baptism for Jews Only?

John the Baptist baptized converts. Some carnal Christians, these babes who are not yet able to digest strong meat, but need the sincere milk of the Word; these who, like the Corinthians, say, "I am of Paul" and cause divisions and strife, setting Paul against Peter or Paul against James or Paul against John the Baptist and against Christ—some of these, I say, teach that John baptized but that that was only for Jews and that baptism was a part of "the kingdom message." They would have us to think that baptism is connected with the law and not with grace, that it was for Jews and not for Gentiles. But here again it is because they do not know well the Bible and have never understood the great fundamental meaning connected with the plan of salvation and with baptism as a picture and symbol of salvation by grace. But baptism means today exactly what it meant with John the Baptist. And Paul describes it in Romans 6:4–6 as follows: "Therefore we are buried with him by baptism into death: that like as Christ was raised up from the dead by the glory of the Father, even so we also should walk in newness of life. For if we have been planted together in the likeness of his death, we shall be also in the likeness of his resurrection: knowing this, that our old man is crucified with him, that the body of sin might be destroyed, that henceforth we should not serve sin."

When a Christian is baptized, he means to picture that Christ died for our sins and rose again; that by faith in Him we too have been counted dead to sin. Now the old life is buried and we are counted dead, so we raise up to live a new life in Christ. Baptism should mean that to every new convert.

Do not scorn the baptism of John the Baptist. Jesus walked perhaps ninety miles to be baptized of John the Baptist in the Jordan River. He said, "Thus it becometh us to fulfil all righteousness." It is a righteous act, that is, an act of faith showing that Christ in dying on the cross for us and being buried for us and being risen again for our justification, has fulfilled all the law, all righteousness. Baptism clearly pictures grace, not law. Remember that Jesus was not only baptized Himself, but He taught others to be baptized. All of the twelve apostles were baptized with the baptism of John, and no one could be one of the twelve to bear witness to Jesus, without this (Acts 1:21, 22). Paul himself was baptized, and he baptized others wherever he went.

It is true that Paul did not make baptism the end to which he strove. He said, "For Christ sent me not to baptize, but to preach the gospel" (I Cor. 1:17). No, that was not the end Paul aimed at. But do you think that he sinned every time he baptized people? Does Paul mean to say that he had misunderstood God's call and that he had violated God's command, and that every time he had baptized a new convert, he had preached a false gospel? No, no! Rather, Paul meant that though he had converts baptized everywhere he went, and sometimes baptized them even with his own hands, yet baptism was not the first matter. What he was sent to do was to preach the gospel. Sometimes he preached it with his voice, and sometimes with his pen, and sometimes in the blessed picture presented by baptism. But the *gospel* was the end, and baptism was only an incidental picture which God had commanded to keep the gospel clear in the minds of the congregations who saw it. Baptism was a means, not the end. It still is.

No Bible preacher *ever* was sent primarily to baptize. I have baptized hundreds of new converts, and yet I never preached a sermon aiming primarily to get people baptized. Certainly John the Baptist did not come primarily to baptize. He baptized, as a duty, just as Paul did; but always his preaching was primarily *to get men to repent!* Baptism only pictured their repentance and was a symbol of the heart turning from sin to trust in Christ. It pictured the burial and resurrection of the Saviour and pictured the new convert's death to sin and the newness of life which he expected to live by God's grace.

VI. "One Baptism"—But Which Baptism?

In Ephesians 4:5 the Scripture says that there is "one Lord, one faith, one baptism." So, many babes in Christ who have not been well taught in the Scriptures and who hasten after dispensational teaching before they know the greater fundamentals, say that this phrase of two words, "one baptism," proves that baptism in water is now out of date, is entirely done away with, and that henceforth for the Christian there is no duty to be baptized; that we should ignore both the example and the teaching of Jesus on the question. They say that Paul received new light that other Bible preachers did not have. They say that the Great Commission in which Jesus commanded us to "teach all nations, baptizing them in the name of the Father, and of the Son, and of the Holy Ghost: teaching them to observe all things whatsoever I have commanded you" is really not binding on us, though Jesus expressly said it was for all nations and even to the end of the world.

But that is a very shortsighted and unscriptural opinion. I can show that to a prayerful heart, I believe, in a few moments.

Several baptisms are mentioned in the Bible. I mention the following:

1. *The baptism of a new convert in water.* John said, "I indeed baptize you with water," literally *in* water (Matt. 3:11). "And Jesus, when he was baptized, went up straightway out of the water" (Matt. 3:16). The baptism, of course, was a burial of the new convert in water, and his resurrection from the water, as described in Romans 6:4, 5.

2. *The baptism in the Holy Ghost.* Jesus did the baptizing in the Holy Spirit as we are plainly told (Matt. 3:11), covering, surrounding, immersing His disciples in the Holy Ghost. This was the enduement of power from on high promised in Luke 24:49, the power to witness for Jesus promised in Acts 1:8.

3. At conversion one is *baptized or buried into the body of Christ* as a stone is put into a stone wall, buried there in mortar and stone (I Cor. 12:13; Eph. 2:19–22; I Peter 2:5). Notice that the Holy Spirit is the One who does this, that one is baptized by the Holy Spirit into the mystical body of Christ. This is surely not the same as being baptized (or covered, or immersed) by Christ in the Holy Spirit. Baptism number two above is a baptism in the Holy Spirit for soul-winning power, and some Christians never have this power. But baptism number three every one gets as soon as he is saved, being put into the body of Christ and buried there, that is, immersed, baptized there by the Holy Spirit, made a part of the body.

4. *Christ's baptism in suffering.* He was overwhelmed, or sur-

rounded, with grief and trouble. "But I have a baptism to be baptized with, and how am I straitened till it be accomplished" (Luke 12:50).

Now above are four different baptisms mentioned in the Bible. Then when Ephesians 4:5 says, "One baptism," which of these baptisms does it mean?

That is easy when you ask the simple question, which of these is a literal, physical baptizing or burial? Which others of these are only figures of speech; have a clear meaning but are not literal burials or immersions?

It is quite clear that when Christ "poured out" the Holy Spirit at Pentecost and the disciples were "baptized in the Holy Ghost," these are figures of speech. Christ did not put the Holy Spirit in a pitcher and pour Him out like water. Neither were the Christians literally dipped, immersed, plunged, or buried in the Holy Spirit. But in a figurative and spiritual sense they were surrounded, covered, overwhelmed with the power of God. So the Bible uses this beautiful figure of speech and calls it, in a few cases, "baptized with the Holy Ghost." But actually other terms are usually used. The Bible in Acts 2:4 says, "And they were all *filled* with the Holy Ghost." In Luke 24:49 Jesus used the phrase "endued with power from on high." Joel's prophecy, quoted in Acts 2:18 says, "I will pour out in those days of my Spirit." In Acts 2:38 the promise is, "Ye shall receive the gift of the Holy Ghost." It is obvious that all these Scriptures are talking about what happened at Pentecost. The term "baptism" is only one of the terms used, and that a very figurative term. *Other terms are usually used in the Bible about what happened then.* "Baptized in the Holy Ghost" is a figure of speech, not a literal use of the word. That baptism is not a literal baptism.

Likewise, when a new convert is buried into the body of Christ at his regeneration, there is no literal, physical immersion. Only in a figurative, mystical sense the new convert becomes a part of the body of Christ which will be called out at the rapture.

And only in a figurative sense, likewise, was Christ baptized or buried in suffering. These are figurative uses of the term.

But baptism in water is a literal baptism, a literal immersion, a literal, physical burial. And remember that many, many thousands of people were baptized by John the Baptist, and many other thousands baptized by the disciples of Jesus, and at the Saviour's own command, long before Pentecost. Matthew 3 tells of the preaching of John the Baptist, and verses 5 and 6 say, "Then went out to him Jerusalem, and all Judaea, and all the region round about Jordan, and were baptized of him in Jordan, confessing their sins." For perhaps three and a half years or more the people had been accustomed to new converts being baptized in water. So literal baptism, in the Bible sense, was understood to be immersion of a new convert in water. The word was used first in that way and had a very definite, literal, physical meaning. The other uses of the term were only figurative and derived meanings. By nation-wide use the word *baptism* meant the immersion of a convert physically, literally in water.

Therefore, when Ephesians 4:5 says, "One Lord, one faith, one baptism," of course it refers to baptism in water, the only literal baptism, the only physical immersion in the Bible. Remember that baptism in water has no other name in the Bible. Remember that though we say, "*water* baptism," because we have confused the terms, the Bible simply says, "baptism," and always means baptism in water, unless the context clearly shows otherwise.

And Ephesians 4:5 does not mean that the term baptism could not now be used in a figurative sense for sufferings, or for power, or for the body of Christ. But in the literal sense there is only one baptism.

But actually Ephesians 4:5 is not saying, "There once were two baptisms, but one of them is done away with, and now we only have one." No, no! What that verse is really saying is, "We all have the same Lord, we all have the same faith, we all have the same baptism. We all have the same God, we all are members of the same body, we all have the same Holy Spirit, we all are called in the same hope." That is the literal meaning of the Scripture in Ephesians 4:4, 5. Paul, inspired by the Holy Spirit, is stressing the unity of Christians. How strange it is that carnal-minded Christians, "smart alecks" not well informed on Bible doctrine, should use this very Scripture to bring *disunity* instead of unity, and should divide Christians instead of uniting them!

What the Lord says here is that we all have the same baptism and should give the same testimony. And in the preceding verse, He has already mentioned that we have the same Holy Spirit; so this baptism does not refer to the baptism of the Spirit, but to baptism in water.

It is foolish and unscriptural to make a new dispensation here and try to do away with baptism.

VII. Were Miracles for Jews Only?

Those who cause divisions and say, "I am of Paul," Christians who need to be given milk because they cannot yet bear strong meat, Christians who start out to try to teach dispensations before they know other great fundamentals of the Bible, sometimes carelessly say that miracles and signs and wonders followed the gospel among the Jews but not among the Gentiles; that the gospel of the kingdom involved miracles but the gospel of grace, Paul's gospel, did not.

They have in mind such Scriptures as Mark 16:17, 18 which says, "And these signs shall follow them that believe; in my name shall they cast out devils; they shall speak with new tongues; they shall take up serpents; and if they drink any deadly thing, it shall not hurt them; they shall lay hands on the sick, and they shall recover."

They also have in mind the miracles which are recorded in the ministry of Jesus and in the book of Acts. They say that such miracles do not occur today, and therefore that the gospel has been changed. But their mistake is twofold: first, they misunderstand the place of miracles in the time of Christ;

and second, out of their ignorance they suppose that no miracles are occurring today.

Mark 16:17, 18 did not promise that miracles would follow in the case of everybody who trusted Christ for salvation. Nothing can be plainer than that miracles were the exception, even in Bible times. Aside from Paul and Barnabas, who ever cast out devils in the book of Acts? Aside from Paul on the island of Melita (Acts 28:3–5), who ever took up serpents in the New Testament? Of course that was involuntary with Paul, and God protected him. It was not an everyday business and was not done for a show by anybody. It is true that the apostles sometimes laid hands on the sick and they recovered. But that was unusual. And I Corinthians 12:29, 30 plainly says, "Are all workers of miracles? have all the gifts of healing? do all speak with tongues? do all interpret?" These are searching questions showing that such miracles and gifts were widely scattered. The Bible never anywhere intimates that all New Testament Christians did miracles. No, Stephen was stoned and left dead, and nobody of all the Christians of Jerusalem had the power to raise him. The Apostle James was imprisoned and finally killed by Herod, and all the apostles did not have power to release him from jail nor raise his dead body (Acts 12:1, 2). Peter raised only one person from the dead (Acts 9:36–43), and Paul only one, as I recall (Acts 20:9–12). Miracles were unusual and striking, even in New Testament times, and even at Jerusalem and immediately following Pentecost. They are unusual today and even more widely scattered, because of our unbelief, no doubt.

No, God never did promise that everyone who trusted Christ for salvation would be able to work miracles, raise the dead, cast out devils, and talk with new tongues. These things are promised only to "follow them that believe," that is, *those who have faith for these particular miracles!* Where God gives the faith, God gives the miracles.

But it is an equally sad mistake to say that God works no miracles these days. The history of the church fathers tells again and again of miracles in answer to prayer. The literature of the China Inland Mission and of other orthodox and fundamental and reliable foreign missions these days tells marvelous stories of the casting out of devils, of instant healing of the sick in answer to prayer. You should read *Pastor Hsi* by Mrs. Howard Taylor, the true, well-authenticated story of a Chinese Christian who many times cast out devils. The book is perfectly reliable. Or you should read the book, *The Ministry of Healing* by Dr. A. J. Gordon, which gives reports down through the ages, reliably authenticated, telling of many, many miracles. Dr. W. B. Riley; Dr. R. A. Torrey; D. L. Moody; Dr. Charles Blanchard, former president of Wheaton College; and many others have published accounts of miraculous answers to prayer. They are rare, but they do happen where God gives faith. And those who have never seen such wonders of God should very modestly keep quiet in the presence of others who know they have seen God work in supernatural, even miraculous, power in modern times.

God has never changed His gospel. Even in Old Testament times people were saved exactly the same as they are today. In Acts 10:43 Peter said by divine inspiration, "To him [Christ] give all the prophets witness, that through his name whosoever believeth in him shall receive remission of sins." Every prophet in the Old Testament taught that one who trusted in Christ would be saved. Jesus said, "Abraham rejoiced to see my day: and he saw it, and was glad" (John 8:56). He said, "Moses . . . wrote of me" (John 5:46). And in Romans, chapter 4, Abraham is held up as an Old Testament example of one who was saved by faith without works. Circumcision, sacrifices, ceremonies—these never saved anybody in Old Testament times. They were given to picture the coming of the Saviour. And since John the Baptist in New Testament times, baptism, church membership, the Lord's Supper, godly living—these have not saved men. But they are proper outward symbols and illustrations and manifestations of the wonderful gospel. They picture the death of Christ and

His resurrection and proclaim to the world what God will do for a sinner who trusts Him.

So we say to you in the words of Paul, "But though we, or an angel from heaven, preach any other gospel unto you than that which we have preached unto you, let him be accursed" (Gal. 1:8). Paul never changed his gospel. And Paul never abandoned those outward rites, baptism and the Lord's Supper, which so beautifully picture the death and burial of Christ and His resurrection and our participation in His death and in His resurrected life. The Great Commission is still ours to go and teach all nations, to preach the gospel to every creature, and to baptize them in the name of the Father and the Son and the Holy Spirit, and then to teach them to observe all things that God commanded the apostles to observe.

It is time for us to go back to the fundamentals and essentials. There are clear dispensational teachings in the Bible. But when people insist on making intricate divisions in the Scriptures, setting one part against another, magnifying one divinely inspired writer more than another, finding new interpretations to discredit certain plain commands of Christ, certain duties of Christians commanded in the Bible and followed by the best Christians for centuries; they are not true to the dispensational teachings of the Bible. And when they spend more time chopping the Scriptures up into artificial dispensations, dividing between John the Baptist and Christ, between Peter and Paul, than they do in studying and teaching the great themes of the Bible as clearly traced in the Scriptures themselves, then all kinds of divisions and carnal strifes will appear among the people of God.

"A little learning is a dangerous thing." It is certain to result badly when men get "smart" with God, when they consider themselves wiser than others about the Word of God. God "hath hid these things from the wise and prudent and hath revealed them unto babes" (Matt. 11:25).

If new converts were taught more about the plan of salvation, the duties of a Christian life, the power of the Holy

Spirit, how to win souls, and such other fundamentals; then they would later be better able to learn incidentals, such as the mark of the Beast, or to understand such terms as "the gospel of the kingdom" without setting Paul against Peter or against Christ, in his teaching, and without starting new-fangled cults or departing from the Great Commission or leaving off Bible baptism or the Lord's Supper.

Again let us impress upon our minds the solemn warning of the Apostle Paul, inspired by the Holy Spirit, "But though we, or an angel from heaven, preach any other gospel unto you than that which we have preached unto you, let him be accursed. As we said before, so say I now again, if any man preach any other gospel unto you than that ye have received, let him be accursed" (Gal. 1:8, 9).

There is only one gospel; there has never been another, and there will never be another. It is the blessed gospel of grace, that Christ died for our sins according to the Scriptures and rose again the third day according to the Scriptures, that "whosoever believeth in him should not perish, but have everlasting life."

VI

"The Love of the Spirit"

—Rom. 15:30

**The Christian's Best Friend, the Holy Spirit; How
He Loves Us, What He Will Do for Us, and How
We Should Treat Him**

YOUR BEST FRIEND is the one who loves you the
most and does the most for you and stays the closest by you.
And that Friend is the Holy Spirit of God.

In Romans 15:30 Paul says,

*"Now I beseech you, brethren, for the Lord Jesus Christ's sake, and
for the love of the Spirit, that ye strive together with me in your prayers
to God for me."*

Paul wanted, and was led by the Holy Spirit to ask it, that
the Christians at Rome pray for him. They were to pray for
him for Jesus' sake, that is, because the work Paul was doing
honored the Lord Jesus, and it would please our Lord for them
earnestly to be partakers in his ministry by prayer. And they
were to do it also because of the love of the Spirit. The Holy
Spirit loved Paul and loved the Christians at Rome. With
unspeakable concern He longed to bless Paul in the ministry
and to bless these Christians who would have a part in Paul's
ministry by prayer. And so Paul is led to ask them to pray for
him because of the love of the Holy Spirit for him and them.
It is as if Paul said, "The Holy Spirit loves me so much that
He wants you to pray for me; and if you listen to Him, He will
lead you to pray for me."

"The love of the Spirit"! The Holy Spirit loves us! This dear, unseen Person who loves us so is our best Friend.

The Holy Spirit is the personal representative of God and of Christ on earth. He is called many times "the Spirit of God" (Matt. 3:16; Gen. 1:2), and God many times speaks of "my Spirit" (Gen. 6:3; Isa. 44:3; Joel 2:28; Acts 2:17, 18). He is also called, "the Spirit of Christ" (Rom. 8:9).

In John 14:16–26 the Saviour told His sorrowing disciples that through the Holy Spirit both He and the Father would manifest Themselves to the disciples and would come and make Their abode with Christians.

The Holy Spirit is God's executive officer in dealing with mankind.

The Holy Spirit dictated the Bible. "Holy men of God spake as they were moved by the Holy Ghost" (II Pet. 1:21). We are told that the things God has prepared for us are not known by eye, nor ear, nor heart of man; "But God hath revealed them unto us by his Spirit" (I Cor. 2:10). And even the very words of divine revelation are given by the Holy Spirit. "Which things also we speak, not in the words which man's wisdom teacheth, but which the Holy Ghost teacheth; comparing spiritual things with spiritual" (I Cor. 2:13). The Holy Spirit is the author of the Bible. So the Word of God is fittingly called, "the sword of the Spirit" (Eph. 6:17).

But as wonderful as is the fact that the Holy Spirit is the author of the Bible, here is a fact even more wonderful—the entire ministry of Jesus Christ on earth was wrought in the power and wisdom of the Holy Spirit!

It was by the Holy Spirit that Christ was conceived in the womb of a virgin girl (Matt. 1:20; Luke 1:35). Joseph was told, "That which is conceived in her is of the Holy Ghost"; and the angel Gabriel explained to Mary, "The Holy Ghost shall come upon thee, and the power of the highest shall overshadow thee: therefore also that holy thing which shall be born of thee shall be called the Son of God."

And all the ministry of the Lord Jesus was NOT in His

power as the Son of God, by which He created the worlds, but rather in the power of the Holy Spirit. He never worked a miracle nor healed the sick nor cleansed a leper nor preached a sermon nor won a soul until His baptism when, praying, He received the Holy Spirit coming upon Him. After that He did His first miracle at Cana of Galilee and then went to Nazareth and in the synagogue read and explained Isaiah 61:1: "The Spirit of the Lord is upon me, because he hath anointed me to preach the gospel to the poor; he hath sent me to heal the brokenhearted, to preach deliverance to the captives, and recovering of sight to the blind, to set at liberty them that are bruised, to preach the acceptable year of the Lord." Then Jesus said, "This day is this scripture fulfilled in your ears" (Luke 4:16–21). Thereafter Jesus was always full of the Holy Spirit and did His work under the Holy Spirit's complete anointing. See Acts 10:38. Even after His resurrection Jesus gave his apostles instructions through the power and wisdom of the Holy Spirit (Acts 1:1, 2). When Jesus returns to the earth to reign, His reign will be as the Spirit-filled Son of man. "And the spirit of the Lord shall rest upon him, the spirit of wisdom and understanding, the spirit of counsel and might, the spirit of knowledge and of the fear of the Lord" (Isa. 11:2). That is why we may do the same work that Jesus did; we may have the same power and wisdom that was given to Him through the same Holy Spirit.

It is the Holy Spirit who convicts sinners, for "When he is come, he will reprove the world of sin, and of righteousness, and of judgment," Jesus said (John 16:8).

Every soul that is regenerated is literally "born of the Spirit." Just as God breathed His Spirit or breath into the nostrils of the man, Adam, the first man whom He had made out of dust, and he became a living soul; so the Holy Spirit of God comes into the body and life of a poor lost child of wrath and makes him into a child of God. He is "born of the Spirit" (John 3:5). We say, "Let Jesus come into your heart," and that is perfectly proper. But in truth the Lord Jesus has a human body. He has scars in His hands and His feet. He ate and drank before the disciples, and their hands handled Him. When Jesus comes again, it will be the same Jesus; and every eye shall see Him, this Christ with a human body, with hands and feet and flesh and bones. So in a sense, Christ could not come into your heart. What we mean is that when we were converted we let the Spirit of Christ come into our hearts, Christ's own representative, doing His work; and He took us over, regenerated us, and made us children of God.

And now this blessed Holy Spirit dwells literally in our bodies. "What? know ye not that your body is the temple of the Holy Ghost which is in you, which ye have of God, and ye are not your own? For ye are bought with a price: therefore glorify God in your body, and in your spirit, which are God's" (I Cor. 6:19, 20). Ever since the day Jesus rose from the dead and breathed on the disciples and said, "Receive ye the Holy Ghost," the Holy Spirit of God has lived literally in the body of every Christian, every child of God (John 7:37–39; John 20:22). When you were converted, the Holy Spirit who made you a member of the body of Christ buried you into this body as a stone is buried in the mortar and other stones of a wall so as to become a part of the building (I Cor. 12:13; I Pet. 2:5; Eph. 2:19–22). All this work is done by the Holy Spirit as the representative of God and of Christ on the earth.

What the Loving Holy Spirit Does for a Christian

One can see thus how intimate is the relationship of the Holy Spirit of God to the Christian. If God loved the whole world enough to give His Son, and if Christ loved poor sinners with such infinite compassion that He gladly went to the cross, then how must the Spirit of God love His own! Those He has sought and convicted of sin, those He has won to trust in Christ, those whose hearts He has changed, those into whose bodies He has come to dwell forever, those He has made a part of that mystical body of Christ which will be called together at the rapture and assembled in Heaven, the

church of the firstborn—how He must love them! So Romans
15:30 urges us to pray one for another "for the love of the
Spirit." The Holy Spirit loves us with tender compassion that
can never leave us. The Holy Spirit is our best Friend.

And now, keeping always in mind how the Holy Spirit loves
us and yearns over us, let us see some of the things that the
Holy Spirit does for a Christian.

First, the Holy Spirit comforts the Christian. He is called by our
Saviour "the Comforter," that is, one called alongside to
help. Acts 9:31 tells us how the churches "were edified; and
walking in the fear of the Lord, and IN THE COMFORT
OF THE HOLY GHOST, were multiplied." New Testament
Christians had the comfort of the Holy Ghost! How many
thousands of others have been comforted by this Holy Spirit
who loves us, who lives within us, and who does the work of
God within us. Romans 14:17 tells us, "For the kingdom of
God is not meat and drink, but righteousness, and peace, and
joy in the Holy Ghost." It is the Holy Spirit who sets the
songs singing in the heart of a Christian as you see when you
read together Ephesians 5:18, 19, which say: ". . . be filled
with the Spirit; speaking to yourselves in psalms and hymns
and spiritual songs, singing and making melody in your heart
to the Lord." So it is the Holy Spirit who is the author of
spiritual songs; the Holy Spirit makes melody in the heart of a
Christian. He is the Comforter, the joy of the redeemed!

God promises to Israel, despised and hated of men, that one
time He will comfort them. "As one whom his mother comforteth, so will I comfort you" (Isa. 66:13). That is, when
Jews cease to reject the Saviour but are born again and the
Spirit of God comes into their hearts and abides in their
bodies, then they, too, will know the Comforter that the
saints of God all know when they let the Holy Spirit have His
way. God comforts His people through the Holy Spirit.

This verse indicates that the mother-work of God is done
by the Holy Spirit. God is a masculine God, and the pronouns
He and *Him* are used of God the Father. But there is some-

thing so intimate, so personal, so affectionate, and so detailed about the way the Holy Spirit of God, the indwelling Comforter, warms and consoles the heart of God's child, that God says, "As one whom his mother comforteth, so will I comfort you."

Now for forty years I have missed my mother. How strangely my mind goes back to certain little details of a mother's love and affection. Mother cooked the loveliest birthday cakes and could write my name on them with little cinnamon drops! Mother made the straight little trousers out of a pair of my father's worn ones and made the little red waist with the big collar. And she brushed my hair so nicely and said how fine I looked when she took me to church, and had me sing out of her book (though I could not read), and called me her preacher boy! Then long, orphaned years I spent after my mother died before I got another birthday cake, made just for me!

Mother knew just what to do when I exploringly pushed a pea up my nose. After she took me out and had me look at the sun and I had sneezed violently and the pea shot out, how we laughed together! And when I tried a circular washer on my hand and it fit so tight I couldn't get it off, it was mother who assured me I would not have to wear it all my life as I feared; and she knew the marvel that soapy water would work in just such cases! Even now, man that I am, there are many times when I long for my mother. What a comfort it would be if I could only kneel down at her knees or lay my head in her lap or have her hands on my face and have her praise me or strengthen me or comfort me!

But, bless God, I have One who can comfort me "as one whom his mother comforteth." The blessed Holy Spirit does this blessed mother's work for the Lord in my heart! And does not this picture how sweetly the Spirit loves us?

Second. The Holy Spirit is "the spirit of wisdom" (Eph. 1:17; Isa. 11:2). Do not be misled by the fact that sometimes the Bible does not spell the word Spirit with a capital letter. The

translators could not always decide, and in the original lan
guages capitalization of words did not mean always the same
as it does in English. The Lord Jesus called Him "the Spirit
of truth" (John 14:17). And again He promised, "When he,
the Spirit of truth, is come, he will guide you into all truth:
for he shall not speak of himself; but whatsoever he shall hear,
that shall he speak: and he will shew you things to come. He
shall glorify me: for he shall receive of mine, and shall shew
it unto you" (John 16:13, 14). Thus spiritual wisdom is given
by the blessed Holy Spirit who is dwelling in the Christian's
body. He reveals the things of Christ to the Christian. He
will guide the Christian into all truth. Not only that, but He
will help us to remember spiritual truths and the Scriptures,
for Jesus said, "But the Comforter, which is the Holy Ghost,
whom the Father will send in my name, he shall teach you all
things, and bring all things to your remembrance, whatsoever
I have said unto you" (John 14:26).

Always teaching, always reminding, always guiding—that
is the work of the blessed Spirit of God who loves us and is
tenderly anxious to guide us into the truth.

When we come to read or study the Bible then, we should
be conscious of the Spirit's presence. We should always ask
Him to teach us the Word of God. Many times when I write
an article or preach a sermon, I earnestly pray for the Spirit
to bring to my remembrance the Scriptures on the subject
and to help me to understand them. And strangely, often
when I am in the pulpit, in the midst of a sermon, Scriptures
come to mind that I did not think about when I prepared the
sermon. And oftentimes after I have read the Scriptures in
the pulpit, there comes to me such light on the Word of God
as I did not have in the study and preparation. But that only
happens, of course, as I am led by the Spirit of God and when
I am surrendered to Him and have an open receptive heart.
He is the Comforter, the Guide, and the Teacher of the Christian.

In this dark world every Christian needs a guide. How can

I know what will come tomorrow? How can I know which way to turn, what to do? A thousand details must be settled day after day. The preacher must know what text to preach on, what illustrations to use, he must know whether to accept this invitation and reject another, or vice versa. What is the will of God about this matter, or that, or that? And the only way that a Christian can day by day *know* that he is following the will of God for his life is by the clear leading of the Holy Spirit of God.

And thank God, every Christian can have that leading. Isaiah 30:21 says, "And thine ears shall hear a word behind thee, saying, This is the way, walk ye in it, when ye turn to the right hand, and when ye turn to the left." And that word of direction every Christian can hear from the Holy Spirit. The way may be dark, but a Christian can say, "Though I walk through the valley of the shadow of death, I will fear no evil: for thou art with me."

How clearly the Holy Spirit led Christians in the Bible! Note how "The angel of the Lord spake unto Philip, saying, Arise, and go toward the south unto the way that goeth down from Jerusalem unto Gaza, which is desert" (Acts 8:26). The word *angel* means messenger or agent. It seems likely that this is simply another way of saying that the Spirit of God told Philip what to do. He may have spoken even with an audible voice, or it may not have been with an audible voice; but Philip knew exactly what to do. Then we read in verse 29, "Then the Spirit said unto Philip, Go near, and join thyself to this chariot." The Spirit then taught Philip how to win the eunuch to Christ, and then "The Spirit of the Lord caught away Philip, that the eunuch saw him no more."

Now read in the tenth chapter of Acts how the Holy Spirit dealt with Peter, preparing him to go to speak to Cornelius and win him and his family to Christ. How definite was the leading of the Holy Spirit and how wonderful the results when Peter obeyed! Read how the Holy Spirit directed the praying group of workers at Antioch to "Separate me Barnabas and Saul for the work whereunto I have called them." How clearly and definitely the Holy Spirit led Paul in his work is indicated by Acts 16:6-10 which says:

"Now when they had gone throughout Phrygia and the region of Galatia, and were forbidden of the Holy Ghost to preach the word in Asia, after they were come to Mysia, they assayed to go into Bithynia: but the Spirit suffered them not. And they passing by Mysia came down to Troas. And a vision appeared to Paul in the night; There stood a man of Macedonia, and prayed him, saying, Come over into Macedonia, and help us. And after he had seen the vision, immediately we endeavored to go into Macedonia, assuredly gathering that the Lord had called us for to preach the gospel unto them."

Oh, Christian, the dear Holy Spirit who loves you wants to lead you in the will of God. You can walk day by day with sweet assurance that you are where God wants you, that you are busy about the things that please Him, that you are acting in His wisdom. The wisdom of God is ours when we are led day by day and guided by the Spirit.

Next, the Holy Spirit is our help in prayer. When God promises to pour upon the house of David and the inhabitants of Jerusalem "the spirit of grace and of supplication," so that they will see the Saviour and know He is their Messiah, and will seek Him with mourning and confession, He simply means that the Holy Spirit will be poured upon them. In fact, again and again God does promise to pour out the Holy Spirit upon Israel, as in Joel 2:28, quoted in Acts 2:17. So that "the spirit of supplication" is simply the Holy Spirit doing His blessed work in helping people pray!

And if the Holy Spirit would create a hunger in the heart of a lost man and lead him to be convicted and seek God, how much more will the Spirit help a Christian to pray! We are told, "Likewise the Spirit also helpeth our infirmities: for we know not what we should pray for as we ought: but the Spirit itself maketh intercession for us with groanings which cannot be uttered. And he that searcheth the hearts knoweth what is the mind of the Spirit, because he maketh intercession for the saints according to the will of God" (Rom. 8:26, 27).

You know how our mothers pray for us. My mother prayed for me to be a preacher, giving me to God when I was born. The Syrophenician woman came to Jesus and said, "Have mercy on me, O Lord, thou son of David; my daughter is grievously vexed with a devil" (Matt. 15:22). Many a mother has written to a judge asking leniency for her wayward boy who was charged with a crime. The mother of James and John came to Jesus interceding for them that they should sit on His right hand and on His left in the coming kingdom. How many times has my good wife come to me when there was a question of punishing one of our daughters and said, "But, Daddy, she is such a little girl." So the Holy Spirit pleads to God for us. He is "the spirit of supplication," and the Spirit "maketh intercession for us with groanings which cannot be uttered."

And so the Holy Spirit helps us to pray. He puts in our minds what we should pray for, gives us a heart to pray if we wait on Him and listen to His tender wooing and follow His loving leading. When a Christian really prays, and prays aright, then you may be sure that the Holy Spirit is helping him pray.

The blessed Spirit always prays in the will of God. "He that searcheth the hearts knoweth what is the mind of the Spirit, because he maketh intercession for the saints *according to the will of God*."

People are often timid about praying; and they feel, they tell me, that they dare not be very bold in prayer since they may be asking something contrary to the will of God. But usually a Christian can pray in the will of God. Usually one can know ahead of time, first by the Scriptures, and second by the sweet whispering of the Holy Spirit in his heart, whether the prayer he wants to bring is according to the will of God. Every prayer, when the Holy Spirit helps, is a prayer born in Heaven, a request that is patterned after the answer God wants to give; and such a prayer is always heard! Oh, the blessedness that we are not orphans, that we need not be untaught, unguided in our ignorance and frailty when we come to pray. The blessed Spirit of God prays with us, and prays for us!

Recently I spent two weeks in a pastor's home as his guest during a revival campaign. Each morning we joined hands around the breakfast table and each one prayed. The father, holding his five-year-old son's hand, put the words in his mouth each morning as he prayed. Each evening as we kneeled in the home, the father took the little one down on the floor beside him with his arms about him and whispered into his ear the words he should pray, a line at a time. And that baby boy prayed sensible, wise prayers, such prayers as if he knew well the Bible and as if he had a mature, well-disciplined heart; all because he was taught to pray, and helped to pray by such a Christian, his father.

Just so the blessed Holy Spirit kneels with every Christian who prays, and as if loving arms were about us, and as if a loving voice whispered in our ears, so we may know what we should pray for and how to pray, and so we may hear Another praying with us—the blessed Holy Spirit—joining with us in prayer for the things that please God and that He has revealed as His sweet will for us. Thank God for the love of the Spirit as shown in His help in prayer.

So a Christian can know how to pray, can pray for the right things, and can have a sweet assurance that God hears him when he prays! A Christian needs only to submit himself to the blessed Spirit of God and to the will of God as written down in the Word of God by the same Holy Spirit, and he can pray in the will of God and pray with faith and joy and victory and get the answer from God to a prayer that has already been made in Heaven!

Likewise the only power a Christian can have is the power of the Holy Spirit. In Acts 1:8 Jesus promised the disciples, "But ye

shall receive power, after that the Holy Ghost is come upon
you: and ye shall be witnesses unto me both in Jerusalem,
and in all Judaea, and in Samaria, and unto the uttermost
part of the earth." And Jesus commanded the disciples, "And,
behold, I send the promise of my Father upon you; but tarry
ye in the city of Jerusalem, until ye be endued with power
from on high" (Luke 24:49). Pentecost was simply an example
of Christians under the mighty power of the Holy Spirit carrying out the Great Commission. As D. L. Moody said, Pentecost
is simply a specimen case of what God can do when people are
filled with His Spirit. The Holy Spirit, when He controls and
fills and masters Christians, brings revivals and gives wonder-
working power to the people of God. That is what the prophet
means when he says, "Not by might, nor by power, but by
my spirit, saith the Lord of hosts" (Zech. 4:6). Again D. L.
Moody said that it is foolish to try to do the work of God
without the power of God.

None of us know the secrets of unsaved people's hearts.
None of us by nature or training have the keys to unlock the
sealed vaults of the will. Only the Spirit of God knows just
how to convict the sinner and bring him to repentance and
faith in Christ. Our fruitfulness in soul winning must depend
altogether on having the power of the Holy Spirit, being filled
with Him, controlled and mastered and used by Him. His
loving heart yearns to use our hands, our feet, our voices, our
heart's love in winning souls. He loves us so that He longs for
us to have that highest honor, that sweetest joy, that greatest
reward that can ever come to a child of God—the honor and
joy and reward of soul winning.

The Holy Spirit and the Christian's Body

The body is not the soul; and a Christian's body, of course,
is not as important as his spirit. The Scripture says, "Keep
thy *heart* with all diligence; for out of it are the issues of life"
(Prov. 4:23). Yet the bodies of those we love are dear to us.
To a baby, a mother is not just a spirit, but a loving spirit

and a maternal body all in one. Mother's lap, mother's soft breast, mother's tender hands, mother's gentle smile, and mother's goodnight kiss— all these go to make up Mother. Our personalities are woven up, in part, of the fleshly body, and we want the bodies of our loved ones. Every marriage should be a marriage of heart, but it is obviously and properly a marriage of human bodies, which God prepared, husband for wife and wife for husband. And every mother and father watch the little bodies grow with delight, have matched little hands and little feet by father's and mother's, have kissed every dimple, have loved the bare, clear, baby skin, the soft baby hair, and wet little smile, the fat little creases, the first little teeth. And so, since the Holy Spirit loves us, He has much to do with our bodies. In fact He lives in the body of every Christian. Again notice I Corinthians 6:19, 20 which says, "What? know ye not that your BODY is the temple of the Holy Ghost which is in you, which ye have of God, and ye are not your own? For ye are bought with a price: therefore glorify God in your BODY, and in your spirit, which are God's." It is only partly true to say we have Christ in our hearts or the Holy Spirit in our hearts. Actually, the Holy Spirit is in our bodies. When we go to serve God and glorify God, we are to glorify Him first in our bodies, says this Scripture above, and then in our spirits.

So when a Christian is baptized, and his body is buried in the watery grave, picturing the burial and resurrection of the Saviour, it also means that the Christian counts his old body dead and the fleshly nature dead; and he is commanded to reckon himself alive from the dead. That means that his body is no longer his own but is counted as belonging to God alone. In Romans 12:1 we are commanded, "I beseech you therefore, brethren, by the mercies of God, that ye present your BODIES a living sacrifice, holy, acceptable unto God, which is your reasonable service." We deceive ourselves when we talk about giving our hearts to God and making Him first in our hearts, if we do not really give Him our *bodies*. Every

Christian should offer his body freely to God. It belongs to God. Of course that means he is to put his body under the control of the Holy Spirit who lives within him. Your body is dear to the Holy Spirit. He wants it to be a holy body, a living sacrifice, acceptable unto God, so that every member of it will be used to God's glory and for your own good.

When the body is defiled, it grieves the Spirit. We are told that "If any man defile the temple of God, him shall God destroy; for the temple of God is holy, which temple ye are" (I Cor. 3:17). This indicates that Christians who defile their bodies will die prematurely, and we know that some died in the church at Corinth because of their sins (I Cor. 11:29–32).

It is the Holy Spirit who heals the body. James 5:14, 15 tells us that the elders of the churches, when called upon to do so, shall anoint the sick with oil, and that the prayer of faith shall save the sick. The oil here is certainly a symbol of the Holy Spirit of God, the loving, brooding, indwelling Presence in every Christian's body. The meaning of the anointing with oil must be that it is the Holy Spirit which heals the body when God gives the faith for healing.

Thus sins which grieve the Holy Spirit, defiling the body and misusing it, whether the mouth, the stomach, hands or eyes or feet, or things said sadden the blessed Holy Spirit, who loves us so. Ill health and sickness is often the result of such sins, and the blessed Holy Spirit longs to cleanse us of the sins and to heal our bodies of the diseases that sin brings.

The blessed Holy Spirit never leaves a Christian. As the angels of God, sent forth to be ministers to those who shall be the heirs of salvation (Heb. 1:14) constantly watch over us and go with us and surround us, as the angels in chariots of fire surrounded Elisha at Dothan, so the Holy Spirit goes always within the Christian's body, wherever he goes. Jesus said in Matthew 28:20, "Lo, I am with you alway, even unto the end of the world." The way He is with the Christian is in the always abiding presence of the Holy Spirit; consciously felt and with obvious power and joy when the Holy Spirit is in control, unobtrusively and rather passively when the Christian is worldly-minded and not walking in the Spirit nor filled with the Spirit. But always the abiding Holy Spirit goes with the Christian, stays where he stays, abides within his body. Sometimes He manifests Himself happily, revealing the truth of God, giving us light on the way, giving power for our tasks, comforting our hearts. Other times He seems to speak only reluctantly and sadly because He is so grieved by our sins. But whether happily or sadly, the Spirit stays always within the body of a child of God. That is His home, His temple; and He never leaves it.

I have heard Christians say, "If you go to the tavern, the Holy Spirit will not go with you." Or, "If you go to the theater, or the dance hall, the Holy Spirit will not go with you there." But they are mistaken; wherever a child of God goes, the Holy Spirit goes. That body belongs to Him. It is in His charge; it is His temple, His home. Since He always goes with us everywhere, sleeping or waking, working or playing, laughing or sober, living holily or carnally, then how earnestly we ought to seek to please Him and always be conscious of His presence.

When the Christian dies, he is still not done with the blessed Holy Spirit for it is the Holy Spirit who will raise up our mortal bodies and make them glorified bodies. Romans 8:11 says, "But if the Spirit of him that raised up Jesus from the dead dwell in you, he that raised up Christ from the dead shall also quicken your mortal bodies by his Spirit that dwelleth in you." It was the Holy Spirit who raised Christ from the dead. The same Holy Spirit of God who over-shadowed Mary and conceived the Holy Son of God and formed the child in her womb was the Holy Spirit that came upon Jesus with wisdom and power for all His ministry. Then the same Holy Spirit raised His body from the grave! And now the same Holy Spirit dwells in us who are saved, and He that raised Christ from the dead shall also quicken our mortal bodies by the same Holy Spirit!

Dr. J. Wilbur Chapman, preaching at Dayton, Ohio, at a Bible conference of ministers and workers, said, "I was sitting in my home in the country, reading the account of an address delivered by Dr. Moorehead at a Bible conference, and he said he believed it was true that when one became a Son of God the Spirit of God came into him to dwell, and he continued to dwell always. 'I don't know but that in some way unknown to me He will continue to abide, even though in the tomb, until the resurrection morning. But,' said he, 'if any of my brethren deny me the privilege of this belief, I will say, when I became a son of God, the Spirit of God came into my life, and He continues to abide through life, and then if I am placed in the tomb He will still hover over me. He hovers over that tomb keeping watch until the day breaks in glorious resurrection.' I could not read the closing sentences, for the tears had filled my eyes, and I told my man to hitch the horse to the carriage, and my wife and I rode out to the little grave where we had buried our firstborn boy, and as we stood there that morning we said, 'Thank God, he is keeping watch,' and peace filled our souls. And I shall never forget going across the country to stand beside the grave of my mother, and I said, 'Thank God, thank God, for thirty years He has been keeping watch, and when the morning breaks He will lift them up, to be united by the Spirit again—the body in the grave and the spirit in His presence.' That is the work of the Holy Ghost."

The loving Holy Spirit of God will then complete the sanctification which He has been working in our natures when we let Him, and then will completely perfect these bodies which He has inhabited and loved and cared for so long. Blessed, loving Holy Spirit!

How Christians Should Treat This Best Friend

There are four plain commands for Christians about the Holy Spirit.

The first of these that we will mention is in Ephesians 4:30

which says, "And grieve not the Holy Spirit of God, whereby ye are sealed unto the day of redemption."

(1.) If we have an important and greatly respected guest in the home, how careful we are to see that nothing should offend. There are clean towels in the room; the housewife is so careful to see that just such food is served as will please the guest. The guest is given the best bed, a place of honor at the table; the best silverware is brought out, the loveliest cut glass and china. Dad tries to be more than usually entertaining; mother makes the best desserts, and the children try to be on their best behavior. But how a sensitive and cultured guest might be grieved if there were filth in the home, if there were wrangling, quarreling, profane language and drunkenness!

And how do you suppose the blessed Holy Spirit feels, He who dwells always lovingly within the body of the Christian, when the life is given over to things unclean and worldly? Many people are made physically ill by tobacco smoke. When I ride in a railway coach where people smoke, I have a headache. When I visit in a home where tobacco is used, I can usually smell it. When I sit at restaurant tables, if the ash trays have been used I ask that they be removed. I have not developed a tolerance for tobacco. But how do you suppose the Holy Spirit feels about the same foul-smelling stuff? And how do you think He feels about tobacco stains on fingers that ought to be holy and tobacco smell on a breath that ought to speak only of the praise of God? And how does He feel about the use of beer in a Christian's body, and about Christian eyes that look on the foul scenes of the movies, and Christians who enjoy the lust of the dance and of promiscuous petting?

But in this passage where we are urged, "And grieve not the Holy Spirit" several sins of the tongue are mentioned: "corrupt communications," "bitterness, and wrath, and anger, and clamour, and evil speaking." God also mentions here malice and fornication and all uncleanness, covetousness, and filthiness as sins that grieve the dear Holy Spirit.

2. Again the Scripture says, "Quench not the Spirit" (I Thess. 5:19). I take it that as water quenches fire and as discouragement quenches enthusiasm, so rebellion of heart on the part of a Christian quenches the Holy Spirit's leadership in his life.

Perhaps someone reads this who does not any longer feel the leading of the Spirit, does not hear His voice, is not conscious of His presence. Do not feel that the Holy Spirit has left you. He has not, nor will He ever leave His temple. But rebellion may have so broken His heart that He cannot make His way clear to you nor give in your heart the witness of your salvation nor help you pray until you have renounced your rebellion and confessed and forsaken this grievous sin.

We should well remember that the tender Holy Spirit is the most sensitive of all beings. The purest and most fastidious woman would not be offended by anything ugly or unclean as soon as would the dear Holy Spirit. The gentlest and most trusting and loving child would not be hurt as soon by neglect and harshness as He. I remind you that it is only against the Holy Spirit that a lost man can commit the unpardonable sin. So sin can grieve the Spirit, and so rebellion can quench His leadership in the life. If you have been quenching the Spirit, offering alibis, excuses, rebellion, instead of listening to every command, instead of following where He leads, then I beg you today confess to Him your sin, surrender your will and resolve to follow anywhere He leads.

3. Another command of the Holy Spirit is, "Walk in the Spirit" (Gal. 5:16, 25). I think this means that a Christian may walk in the *conscious* fellowship of the Spirit, may know day by day that he is in the sweet will of God. The presence of the Spirit is one thing, and consciously walking together, led by Him, listening to the slightest call, would be walking in the Spirit.

4. The next command I will mention is, "And be not drunk with wine, wherein is excess; but be filled with the Spirit" (Eph. 5:18). Oh, to be filled with the loving Holy Spirit! To

have His power, to have His wisdom, to bear His fruits! That will mean a surrender of the will; that will mean a conscious and deliberate confessing and forsaking of sin, and it will mean waiting on God until He prepares your heart and life for the perfect fullness of the Spirit. He who lives in your body wants to take charge of you, soul and body, and have His way. How foolish to live in our barrenness when we may have His fullness and His fruitfulness!

Then, Christians, let us seek and long and pray and wait and surrender to be filled with Him. Thus in our lives we may have shown all the fullness of God, and the marvelous results that followed New Testament Christians will follow us, too.

Your best friend is the Holy Spirit. I hope you will rejoice in "the love of the Spirit," and for His sake, as well as for Christ's sake, do God's will.

VII

Can a Saved Person Ever Be Lost?

T HE MOST important question that ever faced any man is that of the salvation of his own soul. If any man has not settled that question, then let him do so today at any cost, no matter what else must be neglected. To the man who has already trusted in Christ for salvation and thus has been born again, the most important question is the one expressed in the title, "Can a saved person ever be lost?"

Everywhere I go I find people troubled because they do not know but that at any time, because of their sins, their negligence, the sudden besetting of temptation which they might not withstand, they may lose the salvation which they have and so become, not the children of God, but the children of the Devil. Such Christians know that their own hearts are deceitful, they know that they do not deserve the mercies of God; and the fear haunts them that they may lose their salvation and so, perchance, die to be forever lost. For such as these, I bring this message today.

There are many Scriptures which doubtful Christians think teach that a saved person can be lost. I want to review those Scriptures and show you that not one of them either teaches or implies that a saved person can be lost.

John 15:6

For instance there is John 15:6 which says:

"If a man abide not in me, he is cast forth as a branch, and is withered; and men gather them, and cast them into the fire, and they are burned."

You see here that a man may be cast forth as a branch and may wither. And there is the startling statement about being cast into the fire! Does this mean that God will cast away one of His children and that that soul will be cast into Hell? No, read it again and see that a man may be out of touch with Christ after he has been saved and so cannot bear fruit; he may be withered and lose all the joy which he had, as Christians many times do. But notice that those that are gathered, in this verse, and cast into the fire are the branches cut from the grapevines, and not men at all. Notice too, that it is *men* that gather them, while we are plainly told in Matthew 13:41, 42 that it is angels, not men, who will put the lost in Hell. The Saviour in John 15 is talking to His disciples on the subject of fruit bearing. Again and again He refers to it in the chapter, teaching that we cannot bear fruit except by abiding in fellowship with Christ and through His power. A withered branch, so worthless to men because it will not bear grapes and is therefore burned up, is used to show how useless is a Christian in God's service who does not abide in Christ. Of course, the difference between men and God is this, that men value grapevines for the grapes, and Christ loves us for ourselves. This Scripture does not teach that a saved person can be lost and does not say so.

Take the Bible at face value. It means exactly what it says and says exactly what it means. Do not add to the meaning of God's Word. In this case *fire* means fire, and does not mean Hell. I think the branches of the vine mean just that, and men cast them into the fire and they are burned, but it does not mean that a Christian man is cast into Hell and burned.

Ezekiel 3:20, 21

Perhaps you have had Ezekiel 3:20, 21 pointed out as a Scripture which teaches that a saved person may be lost. It says:

"Again, when a righteous man doth turn from his righteousness, and commit iniquity, and I lay a stumblingblock before him, he shall die: because thou hast not given him warning, he shall die in his sin, and his righteousness which he hath done shall not be remembered; but his blood will I require at thine hand. Nevertheless, if thou warn the righteous man, that the righteous sin not, and he doth not sin, he shall surely live, because he is warned; also thou hast delivered thy soul."

But careful reading of these verses and of the chapter will show that it has no reference to the salvation of a soul nor to the loss of a soul. The message is to Israel (see vs. 17). The righteousness of the righteous man mentioned here does not refer to salvation but to a citizen of Israel keeping the Mosaic Law. The penalty mentioned is not eternal damnation nor the loss of a soul, but simply physical death. The only salvation mentioned for the wicked in this case is "to save his life" (verse 18). We preachers have spiritualized this passage and made it mean what it does not say. The righteousness mentioned is not the righteousness of Christ but the self-righteousness of a Jew under the law. The Jew who had never committed a murder, adultery, nor any other major crime, would yet, if he turned from his righteous way and committed such a crime, be taken out and stoned; that is, he should die in his sin. This passage clearly has no reference to a saved person becoming lost. Ezekiel 18:24 and 33:12, 13 are two other passages nearly identical in meaning. Read these and see.

Do you see the danger of spiritualizing away the plain meaning of the Bible, and making it mean something it does not say?

II Peter 2:20-22, Dogs and Sows

"For if after they have escaped the pollutions of the world through the knowledge of the Lord and Saviour Jesus Christ, they are again

entangled therein, and overcome, the latter end is worse with them than the beginning. For it had been better for them not to have known the way of righteousness, than, after they have known it, to turn from the holy commandment delivered unto them. But it is happened unto them according to the true proverb, the dog is turned to his own vomit again; and the sow that was washed to her wallowing in the mire."

Whoever the people indicated in these Scriptures were, we can see the latter end is worse with them than the beginning. Many people believe that this Scripture tells the story of a man once saved but who is entangled in the pollutions of the world and finally lost.

But notice these things about this passage: the escape was through the knowledge of the Lord and Saviour Jesus Christ. The Scripture does not say that these trusted Jesus. Many lost people know about the gospel and about Christ. We see from verse 21 that they knew the way of righteousness. But the Scripture does not indicate that they ever walked in it. In verse 22 the dog is still a dog and the sow is still a sow. The dog returning again to his vomit is a picture of a sinner returning again to the sin that made him sick. The sow that was washed returns to wallowing in the mud because she is still a sow with a sow's nature. God never calls His people either dogs or hogs anywhere in the Bible. Both are used as symbols of the unsaved. If God had made this sow into a sheep and changed her nature as He does the nature of one who is born again, the sheep would not have delighted in the mud like a sow, even if through carelessness she became soiled. There are too many people who are still sows and the only washing they ever had was on the outside with no change of their sinful natures. In this chapter from verses 1 and 2 it is easily seen that the Lord is not talking to saved people at all but to enlightened lost people who return to their sins and do not accept Christ.

Hebrew 10:26–29, Jew Rejecting Christ

"For if we sin wilfully after that we have received the knowledge of the truth, there remaineth no more sacrifice for sins, But a certain fearful

looking for of judgment and fiery indignation, which shall devour the adversaries. He that despised Moses' law died without mercy under two or three witnesses: Of how much sorer punishment, suppose ye, shall he be thought worthy, who hath trodden under foot the Son of God, and hath counted the blood of the covenant, wherewith he was sanctified, an unholy thing, and hath done despite unto the Spirit of grace?"

Does this Scripture teach that a saved person can be lost? It speaks of one who has been sanctified in verse 29.

But this does not refer to a Christian. It is in the book of Hebrews addressed to Israel. The covenant mentioned in verse 29 is God's covenant with Israel, whereby Israel was sanctified, that is, set apart, as a chosen people to God. The Hebrew sacrifices of the Old Testament, all of them, were reminders of this covenant; and the blood was a picture of that which Jesus would shed as the complete sacrifice for Israel's sin. This Scripture then applies to those of Israel who looked forward to the coming Saviour; but when He came, or when they received knowledge of Him, they would not accept Him. Those who wilfully reject the Christ cannot find any other sacrifice to take away their sins. Verse 39 in the same chapter referring to Christian Jews says: "But we are not of them who draw back unto perdition; but of them that believe to the saving of the soul." This Scripture, then, does not teach that a saved person can be lost. It does teach that if a Jew, after coming to the knowledge of the truth that Christ is our sacrifice for sin, then continues wilfully in the sin of unbelief, rejecting Christ, no other sacrifice can take away his sins and there is no other way for him to be saved.

Matthew 14:43–45, The Unclean Spirit

This is sometimes held to teach that saved souls may be lost. It says:

"When the unclean spirit is gone out of a man, he walketh through dry places, seeking rest, and findeth none. Then he saith, I will return into my house from whence I came out; and when he is come, he findeth it empty, swept, and garnished. Then goeth he, and taketh with himself

*seven other spirits more wicked than himself, and they enter in and
dwell there: and the last state of that man is worse than the first. Even
so shall it be also unto this wicked generation."*

But notice that the unclean spirit is not driven out of the
man but goes out himself. He says, "I will return into *my*
house." The house still belongs to him; the man is unsaved.
Notice too, that he found the house empty, that is, Christ was
not in it. This is a picture of a man who reforms without
salvation. Notice in the last sentence of this Scripture that
Jesus applies it to the ungodly Pharisees about whom He is
talking (vs. 38).

Galatians 5:4, Falling From Grace

But does not the Scripture say in Galatians 5:4, *"Ye are
fallen from grace"*? Yes, but read the whole verse and see that
this refers to one who would be justified by the law, that is,
one who is counting on his own righteousness to save him.

*"Christ is become of no effect unto you, whosoever of you are justified
by the law; ye are fallen from grace."*

Grace is a higher plan than the law, and these Galatians
had begun to teach salvation by circumcision and the laws of
Moses instead of staying with God's high gospel of mercy
that people could be saved by faith. You can see it has no
reference to a saved person becoming lost. "Ye are fallen
from grace" here means "you have departed from God's plan
of salvation by grace; you have fallen into false doctrine."

Does God Blot Christians Out of His Book?

In Exodus 32:31–33, we are told of Moses' prayer to God
for Israel after they had sinned so terribly in worshipping the
golden calf which Aaron made. That Scripture says:

*"And Moses returned unto the Lord, and said, Oh, this people have
sinned a great sin, and have made them gods of gold. Yet now, if thou
wilt forgive their sin—; and if not, blot me, I pray thee, out of thy
book which thou hast written. And the Lord said unto Moses, Whosoever hath sinned against me, him will I blot out of my book."*

Christians sometimes believe that Moses here referred to the book of life, and that the Lord threatened to blot out of the book of life the names of people who have sinned after they were converted. But that is not the meaning of the Scripture, as a careful reading will show you. In the first place, there is no reason to believe that God had then written all of the book of life. That book had never been mentioned in the Bible up to this time. But God had given definite and clear promises to Abraham, Isaac, and Jacob and then to the whole nation through Moses about the land of Canaan and that Israel should go into the land and possess it. Moses meant that he would be willing to be left out of Canaan, left out of God's promises for Israel as a nation, in order for the sins of the people to be forgiven. Yet God said, "Whosoever hath sinned against me, him will I blot out of my book." God meant evidently that those who rebelled against God and worshipped idols would be left out of His plan and would miss the privilege of going into the land of Canaan. A little later we find that not a single one of the grown men who were present at that time was allowed to go into the land of Canaan, but were blotted out of God's promises for the nation because of their sin, and their little children later went into the land and inherited it. God is not talking about salvation here but is dealing with Israel under covenant and law. It is not here primarily a question of Heaven and Hell but of physical life and death, of being carried into Canaan under God's covenant or of being rejected and leaving their dead bodies in the wilderness.

Revelation 3:5 is another Scripture that mentions the blotting out of names. That verse says:

"He that overcometh, the same shall be clothed in white raiment; and I will not blot out his name out of the book of life, but I will confess his name before my Father, and before his angels."

I remember that a woman once brought me this Scripture as proof that a saved person could be lost. When we examined it together, I said, "But notice this verse promises that God will NOT blot out one's name. When you find a verse that says He will blot out one's name from the book of life, that will be different."

This time it is the book of life God discusses. But to comfort those striving to overcome, God promises He will not blot out their names. Do not read into the Book more than it says. Do not add to the Bible. God said what He meant. Had He meant more He would have said more. God does not say and does not mean that He will blot out the name of any child of His from the book of life.

"God Shall Take Away His Part out of the Book of Life" —Revelation 22:19

Another Scripture which sometimes troubles Christians who fear that they may become lost is Revelation 22:19, which says:

"And if any man shall take away from the words of the book of this prophecy, God shall take away his part out of the book of life, and out of the holy city, and from the things which are written in this book."

This time the Scripture clearly says concerning certain people that God shall take away his part out of the book of life. But it does not say that God will blot out any one's name which is written in the book of life. What then does the Lord mean here? This Scripture evidently means that salvation is bought and paid for for every man and woman in the world. In I John 2:2 we are told, "He is the propitiation for our sins: and not for our's only, but also for the sins of the whole world." Every sinner has a part purchased for him in the book of life and in "the holy city," bought by the blood of Christ, which he may occupy if he will accept the Saviour as his own and the eternal life which is freely offered. That PART is prepared for every man, and it is his opportunity. But one who rejects the Bible and turns his back on God's revelation will thereby, of course, miss the way of salvation pictured in the Bible and will not accept the Saviour and therefore will miss Heaven. This Scripture evidently means that those who reject the Bible will miss the plan of salvation and all the good things which Christ has bought for them. It certainly does not mean that one of God's children will be lost, that one whose name is written in the book of life already will have his name blotted out.

"Lest I Should Be a Castaway"—I Corinthians 9:27

In I Corinthians 9:27 Paul tells how carefully he controlled and buffeted his fleshly nature, lest he should be a castaway. Did Paul mean that he was afraid he would lose his soul? Read that verse and see.

"But I keep under my body, and bring it into subjection: lest that by any means, when I have preached to others, I myself should be a castaway."

The word "castaway" here is translated from a Greek word meaning literally "not approved." Paul really means that after God has greatly used him to preach the gospel and has shown his approval on Paul's ministry by Holy Spirit power, that even Paul could lose that Holy Spirit power and find himself not approved of God for the ministry if he lets the fleshly nature control his life. How many preachers there are who once held great revivals, once had a great ministry and won many souls and blessed many hearts, but now they have no power, have few if any conversions, and their ministry is marked "not approved" by the Lord! As far as the ministry is concerned, some men who were once used are now castaways, unprofitable servants, instruments not fit for God's use in the ministry.

In John 6:37 Jesus plainly promises that the individual soul that comes to Him for salvation will in no wise be cast out. The Christian is in no danger of losing his soul. He may lose the approval of God on his service and be laid on the shelf. It was this disapproval of God, the possibility of losing his power and being set aside as a preacher, which Paul feared. Paul was not afraid of losing his salvation.

Do Good Works Keep a Christian Saved?

There are several passages in the Bible which emphasize Christians' works, and people many times believe that these passages imply one will not remain saved unless he works.

Philippians 2:12, Working out Your Salvation

For instance, Philippians 2:12 says, "*Work out your own salvation with fear and trembling.*" But when you read the following verse, "*For it is God which worketh in you both to will and to do of his good pleasure,*" you will see that Paul here speaks of working out that which you already have. A man cannot work out his cotton crop until he has a cotton crop; a man cannot let his light shine out until he has a light in his heart; a man cannot work out his salvation to a lost world until he has the salvation. The Saviour promised that we could have a well of water within us for a thirsty world and that we should be the light of the world and the salt of the earth. This does not mean work for your salvation, but it does mean work your salvation out to others.

Matthew 24:13, Enduring to the End

"*But he that shall endure unto the end, the same shall be saved.*"
This Scripture seems, to the careless reader, to teach that salvation depends upon holding out faithfully or enduring unto the end. But if you read carefully the chapter, you will see that Jesus is talking about the great tribulation period at the end of this age, that the salvation mentioned is salvation of the flesh, not salvation of the soul. Verse 21 says, "*For then shall be great tribulation, such as was not since the beginning of the world to this time, no nor ever shall be.*" The time mentioned here is the great tribulation time. And verse 22 says, "*And except those days should be shortened, there should no flesh be saved.*" The salvation mentioned here is the salvation of the flesh, that is, the rescue of literal Jews from physical death during the great tribulation period. Take the Bible at face value. You see that

this Scripture does not teach salvation by works or by holding out faithfully.

To those Jews who will be so terribly persecuted in the tribulation period Jesus says in effect, "If you are able to endure these persecutions to the end of the tribulation period, I will come and rescue you out of the hands of the Antichrist."

Hebrews 6:4–6, The Unpardonable Sin

"For it is impossible for those who were once enlightened, and have tasted of the heavenly gift, and were made partakers of the Holy Ghost, and have tasted the good word of God, and the powers of the world to come, if they shall fall away, to renew them again unto repentance; seeing they crucify to themselves the Son of God afresh, and put him to an open shame."

Notice this Scripture says, "If they shall fall away." Is the one mentioned in this Scripture a saved man? He has been enlightened, has tasted the heavenly gift and the good Word of God and the powers of the world to come. He has even had something to do with the Holy Ghost. The words here, "partakers of the Holy Ghost," in the marginal reading are, "going along with the Holy Ghost." But there are several things that show this is not a saved person who has become lost. A lost man can be enlightened, that is, may learn about Christ. He can have tasted the heavenly gift of the Word of God, etc.; and you notice here this one did not eat, but simply tasted. The Holy Ghost goes along with a lost man convicting him as He did Saul of Tarsus, pricking his conscience day by day. This is a lost man. Some Christians may say, "These verses fit my case exactly, I was a Christian and right with God, and I fell away like this Scripture says." If this be true, whoever has done according to this Scripture is lost without hope forever, *"For it is impossible . . . to renew them again unto repentance; seeing they crucify to themselves the Son of God afresh, and put him to an open shame."* No, dear friend, this is not about a Christian who has fallen into sin, but this is that one unpardonable sin of a lost man who, after great enlightenment, deliberately, maliciously, and finally rejects Christ and blasphemes the Holy Ghost (Matt. 12:31).

In Matthew 12:31, 32, Jesus said that every kind of sin and blasphemy in the world would be forgiven except the blasphemy against the Holy Ghost. That means there can only be one unpardonable sin and all other sins can be forgiven. But the sin mentioned here in Hebrews 6:4–6 cannot be forgiven, because the Scripture says, "*It is impossible . . . to renew them again unto repentance.*" This, then, is the unpardonable sin of a lost man who has never been saved and does not refer at all to a child of God becoming lost.

Bible Characters Who Fell Into Sin

Judas

Many prominent men of the Bible fell into grievous sin· Were these men saved? If so, did they become lost? Judas Iscariot is most often mentioned in this connection. He betrayed the Saviour, and, according to Acts 1:25, I believe that Judas went to Hell as a lost soul. Acts 1:25 says:

"*That he may take part of this ministry and apostleship, from which Judas by transgression fell, that he might go to his own place.*"

In John 6:64–71 the Saviour plainly tells us that Judas never believed and was never saved. He knew from the beginning that Judas would betray Him, and He knew that Judas was a devil. Read some of these verses and see what Jesus said about Judas Iscariot:

"*But there are some of you that believe not. For Jesus knew from the beginning who they were that believed not, and who should betray him.*"—vs. 64.

"*Then said Jesus unto the twelve, Will ye also go away? Then Simon Peter answered him, Lord, to whom shall we go? thou hast the words of eternal life. And we believe and are sure that thou art that Christ, the Son of the living God. Jesus answered them, Have not I chosen you twelve, and one of you is a devil? He spake of Judas Iscariot the son of Simon: for he it was that should betray him, being one of the twelve.*"—vss. 67–71.

Judas was never saved, and so never lost his salvation. He never did believe in Christ, but was a devil; so when he died he went to his own place. Certainly Judas is not an example of a Christian losing salvation.

Lot—A Backslidden Christian

Lot was guilty of terrible sins. He ran in bad company; he let his town go to Hell without winning a soul; he drank, and so was indirectly responsible for the ruin of his own daughters. If any man could lose his salvation, it seems that Lot would have lost his. But we must not guess about this matter. Let us turn to II Peter 2:7, 8 and find what God's Word says about Lot:

"And delivered just Lot, vexed with the filthy conversation of the wicked. (For that righteous man dwelling among them, in seeing and hearing, vexed his righteous soul from day to day with their unlawful deeds;)"

Lot, even in the midst of Sodom, is called "just Lot," is called "that righteous man," and it is said that he had a "righteous soul"! Lot's righteousness was the same as the righteousness of present Christians, the imputed righteousness of Christ. He was justified by faith, without the deeds of the law (Rom. 3:28), not of his works but of God's grace. Lot certainly sinned, but certainly was not lost when God said these things about him. We know that Lot lost his family, lost his money, lost his joy, because of his sins; but he did not lose his soul, for God said he was a just man with a righteous soul.

David's Sins

David committed sins of murder and adultery. We must condemn his sins. They were bad. But David's sins were under the blood of Christ, and in the fifty-first Psalm, the prayer of David shows that he had not lost his salvation, but lost the joy of salvation. Psalm 51:11, 12 says:

"Cast me not away from thy presence; and take not thy holy spirit from me. Restore unto me the joy of thy salvation; and uphold me with thy free spirit."

David does not ask for the restoration of salvation, but he does ask that God will restore the *joy* of salvation. He prays that God will not break the fellowship, will not cast him away from God's presence, will not take away the communion of the Holy Spirit. A backslider like David ought to pray for the joy of salvation to be restored, but he should not believe that God has cast away His child. David sinned, but he did not become a lost sinner again. So David praised God, under divine inspiration, saying:

"Blessed is he whose trangression is forgiven, whose sin is covered. Blessed is the man unto whom the Lord imputeth not iniquity.—Ps. 32:1, 2.

The Scripture shows why David did not lose his salvation and why a saved man cannot be lost.

"Implied" Doctrines

Perhaps, my troubled friends, there are other Scriptures which come to your mind. I have given those upon which the doctrine of losing salvation is generally based. But you say some other Scriptures "seem to imply" that a saved person can be lost. That is one of the sad things that has filled the world with false doctrine today: people teach some doctrine which the Bible does not anywhere plainly teach but which they think is "implied" somewhere. A question so important as this ought to be settled by the Word of God; and I promise you if you will prayerfully take the Scripture which I give you, word-for-word, this matter will be settled forever in your own heart that a saved person can never be lost.

A Positive Bible Teaching That a Saved Person Cannot Be Lost

I have shown that there is no teaching in the Bible that a saved person may become lost. Now let us turn to some of the many passages wherein the Bible very clearly and unmistakably teaches the eternal security and safety of the man who has trusted in Christ. Every teaching about salvation is a teaching of everlasting salvation.

A Christian Has Been Born Again

Salvation is likened to a birth in John 1:13 and John 3:3, 5–7. Saved people are now the children of God (I John 3:2). A child cannot become unborn, and the relationship of a father and child cannot be ended. Notice too, that the Bible mentions many times the second birth but never a third birth. To be born again once is enough. When I have become God's child, that is as settled as when I was born my father's child.

a child be could inherited disenherited couldn't He

Again I beg you to take the Bible at face value. When Jesus teaches that a Christian is born again, has become a child of God, has a right to call God "our Father," He means exactly that. There is a real change when a sinner is converted. He becomes a child of God and is born into the family of God as definitely as my children are born into my family. II Peter 1:4 says:

"*Whereby are given unto us exceeding great and precious promises: that by these ye might be PARTAKERS OF THE DIVINE NATURE, having escaped the corruption that is in the world through lust.*"

A Christian is literally a child of God and has become a partaker of the divine nature. Whatever that man does, God has become his Father and he has become a child of God. My children stay in my family, not by virtue of their goodness but by virtue of their birth. We are God's children on the same basis, born into His family. That is the meaning of Romans 8:14–17 which says:

"*For as many as are led by the Spirit of God, they are the sons of God. For ye have not received the spirit of bondage again to fear; but ye have received the Spirit of adoption, whereby we cry, Abba, Father. The Spirit itself beareth witness with our spirit, that we are the children of God: and if children, then heirs; heirs of God, and joint-heirs with Christ; if so be that we suffer with him, that we may be also glorified together.*"

If the mother's love fails for her baby, God's love is greater. Even though a child on account of sin may lose fellowship with his earthly father, yet the child partakes of the nature of the father. They may have the same eyes or hair or ways. So, though a Christian may lose sweet fellowship with the Father by his sins, yet he is still God's child, partaker of the divine nature. God punishes His children when they sin, but they are His children still.

The Bible could not honestly use this picture of a birth and a relation of father and child concerning God and His people if it were not so that when one is saved he enters into a permanent relationship with God which does not change. One's fellowship changes, but his relationship does not.

Everlasting Life

More than forty-five times the terms *eternal life* and *everlasting life* are used in the Bible. Besides, many other times such terms as *eternal redemption, eternal glory, eternal salvation, eternal inheritance,* etc., are used. These terms are used more often in the gospel of John than elsewhere, but everywhere they are used the promise of everlasting life is given to those who believe. John 3:16 is a glorious example of this. One hundred and one times in the gospel of John the words *believe, believing* or *believed* are used, and most of the times referring to the plan of salvation. And many times, with instance piled upon instance, it is stated that a man has everlasting life when he believes.

The Believer Has Everlasting Life Already

God promises everlasting life to the believer, and that everlasting life is a PRESENT POSSESSION of the believer. John 3:36 says: *"He that believeth on the Son HATH EVERLASTING LIFE."* Put that in modern English and it simply says: *"He that believes (or trusts) on the Son HAS EVERLASTING LIFE."* That is literally what the Bible says. I have trusted

Him, so I HAVE IT; THANK GOD, I HAVE EVER-LASTING LIFE! The Scripture does not say that the believer WILL HAVE everlasting life, but says that the believer HAS IT NOW!

The same thing is repeated again and again in the Bible. John 6:47 says: *"Verily, verily, I say unto you, He that believeth on me HATH EVERLASTING LIFE."* There again, God says the believer HAS EVERLASTING LIFE. John 5:24 says: *"Verily, verily, I say unto you, He that heareth my word, and believeth on Him that sent me, HATH EVERLASTING LIFE, and shall not come into condemnation; but is passed from death unto life."* *Brother, take God's Word for it and be happy.* If you have trusted in Christ, you now have life, everlasting life, life that will last forever; and you will not lose it! Praise the Lord!

When I believed in Jesus I had the life and I had the everlasting also. Suppose that ten years after I got everlasting life I should sin and lose it. Then that would not be everlasting because it only lasted ten years. But God has guaranteed everlasting life to the one who trusts Christ. You notice that in each case the word "believeth" is used in the present tense, but the everlasting life runs on into eternity. Anybody who has everlasting life can never lose it. Doubting soul, look not at your own unworthiness, but look to the eternal promises of God that when you believed in Christ you got everlasting life. There is no other honest way to interpret these promises of God than to take them at their face value and thank God.

But the Lord piles promise on top of promise. In John 6:37 he promises that a saved person will never be cast out.

"All that the Father giveth me shall come to me; and HIM THAT COMETH TO ME I WILL IN NO WISE CAST OUT."

Thank God for that "in no wise." Jesus says He will not cast out a saved person under any condition in the world. Your sins, even since you were saved, may have been mighty black, and in fact it is quite sure that they have been! But He will not cast you out. He said so Himself.

That great old hymn, "How Firm a Foundation," the

hymn my mother wanted sung to her a few minutes before
she went home to Heaven, says it so sweetly:

> The soul that on Jesus hath leaned for repose,
> I will not, I will not desert to its foes;
> That soul, though all Hell should endeavor to shake,
> I'll never, no, never, no, never forsake!

This safety is not earned. We do not deserve it. This safety
of a child of God depends on the goodness of God, His faith-
fulness to keep His promises. Thank God, it does not depend
on my efforts nor on my deserts. I can safely trust His promise,
who said that He would never cast me out!

No Condemnation to One Who Has Believed

The saved person will not come into condemnation, for
John 5:24 says:

*"Verily, verily, I say unto you, He that heareth my word, and be-
lieveth on him that sent me, hath everlasting life, and shall not come
into condemnation; but is passed from death unto life."*

A believer shall not come into condemnation! That reaches
on through to the end of eternity without any limit. The
reason is given here: because the sinner is passed from death
unto life. The Revised Version will make it clearer even yet,
for as translated there this verse says about the believer that
he "hath eternal life, and cometh not into judgment." The
reason a saved person will not ever be condemned is because
he will not even come before the court to be tried! Christ has
already been tried, counted guilty, and borne the punishment
for all the sins that a believer ever has done or ever will do;
and the sinner has passed out of the death of sin and will not
come into condemnation nor ever come to judgment. *"Who
is he that condemneth? It is Christ that died, yea, rather, that is risen
again, who is even at the right hand of God, who also maketh intercession for us."*—Rom. 8:34.

None Can Take Us out of the Hands of Christ

Another such blessed promise is in John 10:28. Speaking of His sheep Jesus said:

"And I give unto them eternal life; and they shall never perish, neither shall any man pluck them out of my hand."

Notice a triple promise here concerning the security of God's sheep. First, Christ gives them *eternal* life. Second, they shall *never* perish, and third, neither shall any pluck them out of Christ's hand. Brother, are you one of Christ's sheep? If so, you have eternal life, you will never perish and cannot be taken from His hand. The last promise is all the stronger when you notice in your Bible that the word *man* in this verse is in italics which shows it was not in the original at all. No one, either man or devil, can take one of Christ's sheep out of His hands. And the following verse adds for extra security that God the Father, who gave us to Jesus Christ, is greater than any one and no one can take us out of the hands of the Father. What blessed, blessed safety is ours who have trusted in Christ Jesus!

Nothing Can Separate the Believer From the Love of God

Paul was certainly confident about the safety of his soul. To the young preacher, Timothy, he wrote,

"For I know whom I have believed, and am persuaded that he is able to keep that which I have committed unto him against that day."
—II Tim. 1:12.

Paul was certainly "persuaded" about this matter, for he uses the same word in Romans 8:38, 39, under divine inspiration.

"For I am persuaded, that neither death, nor life, nor angels, nor principalities, nor powers, nor things present, nor things to come, nor height, nor depth, nor any other creature, shall be able to separate us from the love of God, which is in Christ Jesus our Lord."

Nothing in death, nothing in life, can separate us from the

[Handwritten marginal note: "Doesn't say we can't leave Christ though. This would make man loose his free moral Agency when he desired a Christian if he couldn't leave Christ."]

love of God. Angels cannot. Remember that the devil seems to be a fallen angel. Principalities and powers cannot. Certainly the devil is a power. Things present cannot separate us from the love of God, nor can anything that ever will come in the future, says Paul here. Nothing in the height all the way up to Heaven can come between us and God, and nothing in the depth all the way down to Hell can separate us from His love. Then the Lord, knowing our doubts, our unbelief, and our conscious unworthiness, after He has named everything that a poor forgiven sinner might be afraid of, yet adds the other words, "*nor any other creature.*" Nothing ever created can separate us from the love of God which is in Christ Jesus our Lord! That is the kind of salvation I have, the kind every believer has, and the kind every lost sinner can have if he will trust in Christ!

Are We Saved by Works or by Grace?

Many Christians think this blessed teaching is too good to be true and some call it a dangerous doctrine to say a saved man cannot be lost. But one is never on dangerous ground when he takes the promises of God. What then is the basis for this great salvation? It is all in the merits of Christ. Salvation is of grace, "*not of works, lest any man should boast*" (Eph. 2:9). Paul wrote to Titus that it was "*Not by works of righteousness which we have done, but according to his mercy he saved us*" (Titus 3:5). No man ever got saved by doing good, for "*Therefore by the deeds of the law there shall no flesh be justified in his sight*" (Rom. 3:20). And "*Therefore we conclude that a man is justified by faith without the deeds of the law*" (Rom. 3:28). Man cannot get saved by his work nor keep saved by his works. You did not deserve salvation when you got it, and you never have deserved it any single day you have ever lived since you got it. Salvation is of grace, that is, the loving mercy of God. If a man's safety after salvation depends on his works, then he is really saved by his works and must earn his salvation. That would take glory from Christ and put it on man. The fact is that if any person in the world got what he deserved, he would go to Hell for all have sinned and do sin, day by day. *"If we say that we have no sin, we deceive ourselves and the truth is not in us"* (I John 1:8). And the wages of sin is death. There can be no salvation either obtained or kept by man's goodness, lest in eternity *"any man should boast."* Salvation is *"the gift of God,"* we are *"freely justified."* No man deserves it or ever will, either before he gets it or after.

Sin Is Not Charged Up to the Christian

Read prayerfully that blessed fourth chapter of Romans and see how Abraham believed God and it was reckoned to him for righteousness. There we are told in verses 5 to 8 that the same thing is true of every believer:

"But to him that worketh not, but believeth on him that justifieth the ungodly, his faith is counted for righteousness. Even as David also describeth the blessedness of the man, unto whom God imputeth righteousness without works, saying, Blessed are they whose iniquities are forgiven, and whose sins are covered. Blessed is the man to whom the Lord will not impute sin."

The righteousness which I have as a Christian is really the righteousness of Christ which is charged to my account when I trust in Him. My sins likewise were charged up to Christ, and He has already paid for them. When Christ died on the cross, He died for all the sins that I ever have committed or ever will, though I had not yet been born. That one sacrifice had to be sufficient to pay for all sin, and there will never be another sacrifice for man's sins. So when I trusted Christ, I got forgiveness for all my sins; and from this time on my sins are charged back to Christ and are not charged against me at all. That is what God means when He says, *"Blessed are they whose iniquities are forgiven and whose SINS ARE COVERED. Blessed is the man to whom the Lord WILL NOT IMPUTE SIN."* That is the reason that a Christian will not come into condemnation and will not even come into judgment as far as his soul's salvation is concerned. The security of my soul depends then, not at all on my goodness, for I am not good; but it depends on the righteousness of Christ and His faithful promises.

Does It Matter How a Christian Lives?

Perhaps some one will say then that it does not matter how a Christian lives if there is no danger of his losing his soul. How foolish and shortsighted such a statement is! Would you say to my daughter that it does not matter how she lives since her position as my daughter is secure? It is true she is my daughter; she always will be; and I dare say that even my poor human father-love would not fail her no matter what she did. But she could easily lose the sweet communion with her father, crush all his pride in her, and lose all the happiness which she now has. So it is with God's children; sin breaks the communion with the father, takes away the joy of salvation and loses much of the reward a Christian might have. First Corinthians 3:12-15 is talking about this reward and shows that the evil works of a Christian will be burned up and only the good works remain. But the Scripture goes on to say,

"If any man's work abide which he hath built thereupon, he shall receive a reward. If any man's work shall be burned, he shall suffer loss: BUT HE HIMSELF SHALL BE SAVED; YET SO AS BY FIRE."

It certainly does matter how a Christian lives!

Sin Does Not Pay

Besides the matter of fellowship and rewards, God punishes His own children for their sins. My daughters are mine and therefore I feel responsible for them and must chasten them for their good. So God whips His children because of His love and chastises them for their sins (Heb. 12:5-8). Christians are punished in this life and may be judged and ashamed at the judgment seat of Christ, where all of us must stand (II Cor. 5:9-11), but do not ever go to Hell.

On account of David's sin, his baby died; and evidently

because of his example, his son, Amnon, ruined his own sister, Tamar. Amnon was murdered by another brother, Absalom, who was also David's son. Then Absalom tried to take the kingdom away from David and was killed. Sin did not pay with David and it never pays anybody else. God whips His children for their sins, but thank God, He never does forsake them nor allow their souls to be lost for whom Christ died and who trusted in Him.

In fact, dear friend, if you have thus settled that your soul is kept safe by the power of God through the merits of Jesus Christ, you are prepared to serve Him as never before. Love is a greater motive than fear. *"Behold, what manner of love the Father hath bestowed upon us, that we should be called the sons of God!"* (I John 3:1). Oh, the depth of the riches of God! His salvation is everlasting, and one He has saved shall not come into condemnation but is passed from death unto life!

Wonderful Saviour!

Wonderful salvation given free to "whosoever will" trust Christ who died for sinners!

Wonderful life, everlasting life, life that never ends, beginning the moment you trust Christ!

Thank God, a saved person can never be lost!

(This message available from the publishers in a 24-page pamphlet at 15¢, seven for $1.00.)

VIII

Sunday or Sabbath—

Which Should Christians Observe?

A Bible Answer to Honest Seventh Day Adventists

Many HONEST PEOPLE are greatly confused about the Sabbath question. The trouble here, as in the case of other doctrines, is because many follow human leadership and tradition instead of the Word of God. Seventh Day Adventists say that the Sabbath is the seventh day and that all Christian people ought to keep the seventh day as a day of rest and worship. Some even go so far as to say that salvation depends upon the Old Testament Sabbath and that "the mark of the beast" mentioned in Revelation is keeping Sunday instead of Saturday as a day of rest and worship! Another group of men answer back that since the resurrection of Christ, the Sabbath is changed from the seventh day to the first day and that now all Christians ought to observe Sunday as a day of rest and worship. These call Sunday "the Christian Sabbath," call Sunday School "the Sabbath School," and believe that all the commands in the Old Testament about the Sabbath, or Saturday, the seventh day of the week, ought to be applied to Sunday, the first day of the week.

BOTH ARE MISTAKEN as you will soon see from the Scripture. We may be sure that the Bible has a very clear teaching on this subject and that when we are willing to search the Word of God and take God at His word we can know without doubt God's will for us concerning this and other necessary matters of Bible doctrine and Christian life. The Bible does not say that Christians should observe the Sabbath today. The Bible says nothing about "the mark of the beast" being the observation of Sunday. On the other hand, the Bible certainly does not call Sunday "the Christian Sabbath" nor any other kind of Sabbath.

The Old Testament Sabbath Is the Seventh Day

Exodus 20:10 plainly says, "But the seventh day is the sabbath of the Lord thy God." Concerning this there can be no differences of opinion. In some languages the word for Sabbath means seventh. The Sabbath of rest followed six days of labor and was counted the last day of the week. Saturday is the Old Testament Sabbath.

The Sabbath Is an Old Testament and Not a New Testament Command

The average Bible student has strangely missed this fact: the Sabbath is a part of Mosaic Law and was never given to anybody but Jews under the law. Many preachers who would not think of urging Gentile congregations to observe the command about circumcision or to refrain from pork and catfish, yet sincerely preach to them, "Remember the sabbath day, to keep it holy."

Such preachers mean, "Remember Sunday to keep it holy" and call Sunday the Sabbath. However, there is no more command for Christians to keep the Sabbath than there is for Christians to avoid pork or catfish or to be circumcised. Read very carefully the scriptural proof which I will now give you and get the matter settled in your heart.

First, in the entire New Testament there is not a single command to observe the Sabbath! Every other one of the Ten Commandments is repeated in the New Testament (some many times), with the exception of the Sabbath. Of all the sins mentioned in the New Testament, Sabbath-breaking is never once mentioned as a sin! Jesus did not command His disciples to keep the Sabbath. He was repeatedly called into question on this matter of the Sabbath and never once asked the public to observe the Sabbath. In fact, we are told in John 5:18 that the Jews, rigorous Sabbath-keepers that they were, sought to kill Jesus—

"Because he not only HAD BROKEN THE SABBATH, but said also that God was His Father making himself equal with God."

Jews hated Jesus because He Himself did not keep the Jewish Sabbath. In rebuking them for their criticism when the disciples gathered grain to eat on the Sabbath (Matt. 12:1–8), Jesus referred them to the Scripture, "I desired mercy, and not sacrifice" (Hosea 6:6), and said that if they had understood that Scripture, they would not have condemned the guiltless. Jesus clearly meant that the Sabbath was a part of the ceremonial law, like the sacrifices, which was fulfilled in Jesus.

Jesus did not teach anybody to keep the Sabbath. This fact cannot be denied! The apostles did not teach the New Testament churches to observe the Sabbath. The council at Jerusalem, sending word to the Gentile converts as to what they should do, did not even mention the Sabbath (Acts 15:19–24). The books of Hebrews and James, written to dispersed Israel, do not even refer to the Sabbath as a day to be kept; and Paul in all his epistles to the churches never once intimated that Christians are to observe the Sabbath! The Sabbath is Old Testament, not New Testament. Make sure of this before you go any further.

The Sabbath Is Mosaic Law, Given to Israel Under the Law

As remarkable as is the absence of the Sabbath command in the New Testament, is its absence before Mount Sinai in the Old Testament. Genesis 2:1–3 teaches that when God had finished creation he rested on the seventh day and blessed that day and sanctified it. But no command is given to man concerning that day either in the Garden of Eden or afterward until Mount Sinai. There is no record that God ever spoke to Adam or Enoch or Noah or Abraham about the Sabbath, nor that any of them ever observed it or ever heard of it! Remember that this passage here in Genesis 2:1–3 was not written until Moses wrote these first five books of the Bible under divine inspiration in the wilderness, after Mount Sinai. The first time the word *Sabbath* is used in the Bible is in Exodus 16:23, and men never heard of it until that time.

This is all the more remarkable when you remember that the people already had the week as a period of time (Gen. 29:27; Gen. 8:10–12). When you read about the incident in Exodus 16:23–36, it is quite clear that it was a strange new teaching to the people of Israel and that they had never observed it before.

Now we turn to Nehemiah 9:13–14 which says:

"*Thou camest down also upon mount Sinai, and spakest with them from heaven, and gavest them right judgments and true laws, good statutes and commandments: and madest known unto them thy holy sabbath, and commandest them precepts, statutes, and laws, by the hand of Moses thy servant.*"

After recounting the oppression in Egypt and the crossing of the Red Sea, the Scriptures tell us that God came down upon Mount Sinai and "*made known*" to the people His holy Sabbath. The Sabbath, then, was a part of the Mosaic Law. It was not a previous command incorporated in the Mosaic Law, like marriage, the tithe, or even circumcision. No, the Sabbath was given to Israel as a part of the ceremonial law. It was "made known" on Mount Sinai! No man on earth ever heard of it before then.

This same teaching, that the Sabbath was first given or made known at Mount Sinai, is taught again in Ezekiel 20:10–12.

"*Wherefore I caused them to go forth out of the land of Egypt, and brought them into the wilderness. And I gave them my statutes, and shewed them my judgments, which if a man do, he shall even live in them. Moreover also I gave them my sabbaths, to be a sign between me and them, that they might know that I am the Lord that sanctify them."*

Notice carefully that the Lord Himself says concerning Israel at Mount Sinai: "I gave them my sabbaths to be a sign between me and them." No man ever heard of the Sabbath before it was given to Israel as recorded in Exodus 16:23-36.

The Sabbath Given As a Special Sign to Israel

That matter was quite clear to Israel. On Mount Sinai the Lord revealed to Moses that this command was given to Israel as a special covenant between God and that nation. In Exodus 31:12, 13, 16, 17 the Lord says:

"And the Lord spoke unto Moses, saying, Speak thou also unto the children of Israel, saying, Verily my sabbaths ye shall keep; for it is a sign between me and you throughout your generations; that ye may know that I am the Lord that doth sanctify you. Wherefore the children of Israel shall keep the sabbath, to observe the sabbath throughout their generations, for a perpetual covenant. IT IS A SIGN BETWEEN ME AND THE CHILDREN OF ISRAEL FOREVER: for in six days the Lord made heaven and earth, and on the seventh day he rested and was refreshed."

Ezekiel 20:12 repeats that explanation of the meaning of the Sabbath. It was a sign between God and Israel.

It becomes clear then by the plain and repeated teaching of God's Word, that the Sabbath is a command to Israel under Mosaic Law as a special sign or covenant between them and God and was never commanded to Gentiles in any dispensation.

When we speak of the Sabbath, then we speak of the seventh day, Saturday, as the Old Testament command of ceremonial law to Jews.

New Testament Christians Plainly Warned Against Keeping the Sabbath

Now when we turn again to the New Testament, we find that instead of being commanded to keep the Sabbath, the keeping of the Sabbath is discouraged. In Colossians 2:14 we are told that Christ blotted out the handwriting of ordinances, since that was against us, "and took it out of the way, nailing it to His cross." Then we are plainly commanded in the verses 16 and 17:

"Let no man therefore judge you in meat, or in drink, or in respect of an holy day, or of the new moon, OR OF THE SABBATH DAYS: which are a shadow of things to come; but the body is of Christ."

Let no man judge you concerning the Sabbath days! That was a shadow which was all right until the coming of Christ, but now He is come and the shadow is fulfilled! Therefore no Seventh-Day Adventist nor Jew has the right to pass judgment on any Christian concerning the Sabbath day. The command about the Sabbath day was nailed to the cross with the commands about certain meats and with the other cere-monial laws. God does not want Christians to observe the Jewish Sabbath and plainly says so.

In Galatians 4:8–11, Paul evidently refers to the same thing. The Galatian Christians had been led away into Judaism. Paul in this letter is urging them to break the old tie of Judaism, the "weak and beggarly elements" or "bondage" of Old Testament ceremonial law. In Galatians 4:10–11 he says:

"Ye observe days, and months, and times, and years. I am afraid of you, lest I have bestowed upon you labour in vain."

The "DAYS" mentioned here were Sabbaths, part of the Old Testament ceremonial law for Jews. Paul did not want New Testament Christians to be in bondage to the Old Testament Sabbath or other days, months, times and years of the ceremonial law.

Sunday Then Is Not "The Christian Sabbath"

You can easily see then that preachers are wrong who say that Sunday is the Christian Sabbath, or who say that the Sabbath has now been changed to the first day of the week. The word *Sabbath*, speaking of one particular day of each week, the regular Sabbath, as used in the Bible, always means

Saturday, the seventh day of the week. There is not anywhere in the Bible any record where the Sabbath was changed from Saturday to Sunday. Preachers who use such an argument in explaining why they do not keep Saturday will find themselves greatly embarrassed when they cannot prove it by the Scriptures, and their congregation will be many times troubled by the Seventh-Day Adventist teaching of the Mosaic Law.

Catholics Did Not Start First Day Worship

Seventh-Day Adventists claim that Catholics changed the Sabbath from the seventh day to the first day of the week. The funny part is that some Catholic writers admit that they did! Adventist teachers ought to know however that Catholics simply mean that they claim Peter as the first pope and say that the Sabbath was changed in New Testament times by the apostles and therefore by the Catholic Church. It is true that the Catholic Church has backed some civil laws enforcing Sunday as a day of rest. Catholic popes and rulers tried to enforce by civil laws the observance of Sunday as if it were the Old Testament Sabbath, making it legalistic or ceremonial. That is an entirely different matter from starting the use of the first day as a day of worship. Acts 20:7 clearly shows that that began in New Testament times. That verse reads as follows:

"And upon the first day of the week, when the disciples came together to break bread, Paul preached unto them, ready to depart on the morrow; and continued his speech until midnight."

It is clear that New Testament disciples met on the first day of the week, and it is inferred that this group may have met regularly on this day to take the Lord's Supper.

First Corinthians 16:2 also indicates that the first day of the week had special meaning to New Testament Christians and that Sunday, as a religious day, was not an invention of Roman Catholics and the "mark of the beast," as Adventists claim.

Remember, however, that this first day of the week is never

called a "Sabbath" in the Bible, and we should not call it a Sabbath.

The First Day, the New Testament Day of Worship

The New Testament gives many records when Jesus, and later Paul, met with Jews in their synagogue on the Sabbath or seventh day and preached to them. That is just as when a preacher of today has services at such times and places as he can get a crowd. A preacher should go where the people gather and preach to them. But when it comes to the meeting of New Testament disciples for worship, we never find an account of churches using the Sabbath for that day. On the other hand, Acts 20:7 clearly states that the disciples met on the first day of the week and the context indicates that this was a regular service at a regular time to take the Lord's Supper. First Corinthians 16:2 plainly shows that "the first day of the week" had a religious significance to New Testament Christians. They were commanded to set aside on that day their gifts for the Lord's work.

It is probable that "the Lord's day" of Revelation 1:10 means the first day of the week on which the disciples were accustomed to gathering for worship. John was worshipping the Lord on this day, that is, he was "in the Spirit on the Lord's day." Certainly the Bible nowhere teaches that "the Lord's day" is the Sabbath or seventh day. The Bible does not even hint that any other day besides the first should be used as a day of worship. The Lord's Day must be our Sunday. New Testament Christians did not have a day commanded for rest, but they used the first day of the week, not the Sabbath, as a day of worship.

Jewish Sabbath Not a Day of Worship

The Sabbath, Saturday, in the Old Testament, was for physical rest alone, not a day of worship. When you read again the Old Testament commands about the Sabbath, you will notice that it was never given as a day of worship.

"But the seventh day is the sabbath of the Lord thy God: in it thou shalt not do any work, thou, nor thy son, nor thy daughter, thy man-servant, nor thy maidservant, nor thy cattle, nor thy stranger that is within thy gates."—Exod. 20:10.

The word "Sabbath" in the Hebrew language (in which the command was given), means "cessation" or "rest."

Worship went on in the tabernacle and in the temple seven days a week just the same except for certain national religious holidays when the program was somewhat varied.

We find that during the period between the Old and New Testaments the custom of meeting in the synogogue on the Sabbath arose, but not by divine command. There is no Bible command for the synagogue nor for any of the synagogue worship. The Sabbath of the Mosaic Law was purely a day of rest, not a day of worship nor church going.

We may be sure that the principle of one day's rest in seven for man and beast is a good one, and on such grounds Christians have many times advocated civil laws to provide a day of rest one day a week. Usually the day selected has been Sunday, when Christian people would want to use the day for worship. HOWEVER, NEW TESTAMENT CHRISTIANS HAVE NO COMMAND FROM GOD TO ABSTAIN FROM LABOR ON ANY CERTAIN DAY, NOR EVEN TO MEET FOR WORSHIP ON A GIVEN DAY OF THE WEEK. That is for a Christian a matter of grace and should be voluntary.

Should Christians, Then, Observe Sunday?

Since Christians are not bound by the Old Testament command to observe the Sabbath, is it right for Christians to observe Sunday? The answer is that we should not observe Sunday as a legalistic Sabbath, part of the ceremonial law; but that we do well to observe the Lord's Day voluntarily for our own good as a day of worship. The Scripture plainly says: "Not forsaking the assembling of ourselves together, as the manner of some is" (Hebrews 10:25). We are commanded to meet for worship. Since New Testament disciples in Acts 20:7 met on Sunday; and John, a lonely exile on the Island of Patmos, worshipped on the "Lord's Day" (evidently the same); and since I Corinthians 16:2 mentions Sunday as a day of religious duty, certainly we ought to give ourselves to worship on that day.

Some people object and say that if you worship on Sunday, you keep a day dedicated to the sun since Sunday was named for the sun. Well, Saturday is named for Saturn! All the days are God's days, and all should be used for Him no matter how they were named. The days of the week do not have now the same names as they had in Bible times, but we do have the same days whether we call one Sunday or the first day of the week, or another Saturday or the seventh day of the week. New Testament Christians met on the first day of the week before it was called Sunday. Jews kept Saturday as a day of rest before it was called Saturday. But what has that to do with us? We settle this by God's Word, not by history.

Christians certainly ought to make it possible for as many others as possible to worship on Sunday with them. For employers of labor to close their business on Sunday makes it possible for workmen to attend services as God commanded, and besides provides time for needful rest. We cannot put that on a basis of Jewish law and ought not to. We ought to put it on a basis of grace as Christians who seek to honor the Lord and treat our fellowman as we would be treated.

Let us not use our liberty in this matter for an occasion to the flesh (Gal. 5:13). Christians should not let their liberty concerning the Lord's Day be taken as license to do wrong. Surely Christians ought to use this day in a way which would please the Lord Jesus for whom it was named "the Lord's day." Some Christians have a legalistic idea of Sunday, calling it the Sabbath. We should not cause them to stumble and be an offense unto them by our liberty. Many things we should do for their conscience's sake and for the sake of unsaved people who might not understand our liberty. For Paul, under divine inspiration concerning meats offered to idols which were an offense to some, wrote:

"Conscience, I say, not thine own, but of the other; for why is my liberty judged of another man's conscience? For if I by grace be a partaker, why am I evil spoken of for that for which I give thanks? Whether therefore ye eat, or drink, or whatsoever ye do, do all to the glory of God. Give none offense, neither to the Jews, nor to the Gentiles, nor to the church of God: Even as I please all men in all things, not seeking mine own profit, but the profit of many, that they may be saved."—I Cor. 10:29–33.

Yes, Christians should use Sunday for their own good and the glory of Christ as a day of worship and service to God, seeking to offend none but to save all and bless all.

The Spiritual Meaning of the First Day of the Week

Six in the Bible is man's number, and seven is the divine or complete number. Six days of labor followed by the Sabbath of rest pictures man living a perfect life under the law and earning the rest, perfection and salvation pictured by the seventh day. Of course man failed under the law, and no one was ever able to keep it (Acts 15:10, Rom. 3:20, Gal. 3:11). But the New Testament Christian, worshipping God on the first day of the week, means that he already has salvation as a free gift before he did any work, and now being saved, the Christian works the rest of his life to glorify the Saviour he loves. Read Hebrews 4:9, 10.

From Mark 16:1, 9 it seems clear that Jesus rose from the dead on the first day of the week. In the twentieth chapter of John we find that when Mary and others came to the sepulchre on the first day of the week, very early while it was yet dark, Jesus appeared to her and said, "I am not yet ascended to my Father." It appears that the Saviour some time in that night which was a part of the first day of the week, had come out of the grave. Here is a great blessing for us. Jesus rising from the dead for our justification (Rom. 4:25), means that now we are counted righteous without any labor and without the deeds of the law and "have peace with God through our Lord Jesus Christ." Concerning this, Hebrews 4:10 says:

"For he that is entered into his rest, he also hath ceased from his own works, as God did from his."

Blessed is the Christian who does not depend on his own works but rests in the finished work of Christ on the cross!

From Hebrews 4:9–11 it seems that two rests or "Sabbaths" are mentioned. (The word *rest* in Hebrews 4:9 is the same word as *Sabbath* in the Greek.) That is the teaching with which all Jews were familiar.

One of the greatest feasts which God gave to the Jews, or Israel, shows this idea of the rests of a Christian, one at salvation and the other after the resurrection. The feast of unleavened bread following the passover supper, as given in Exodus 12:15, 16, lasted seven days. This week represented the complete cycle of a Christian life after conversion, which conversion is pictured by the passover lamb at the beginning of the feast. See I Corinthians 5:6–8. The unleavened bread represents, surely, our feeding on Christ, our fellowship and communion with Him. That fellowship, or peace, begins immediately at conversion as Israel ate the unleavened bread with the passover lamb. The peace and joy of a Christian life should begin immediately when one trusts Christ for salvation. The first day of that feast of unleavened bread was a day of rest when no work was to be done. That pictures a Christian resting from his own works when he has partaken of Christ.

At the close of the week was another day of rest. At the close of life's journey, Christians will enter into perfect rest, for "there remaineth therefore a rest to the people of God"! (Heb. 4:9). You can see why Israel, under the law, should keep the Sabbath just as they kept the passover supper and the feast of unleavened bread. All of them pointed toward Christ. A Christian need keep neither the passover supper nor the feast of unleavened bread nor the Sabbath since we have

Christ Himself, the fulfillment of all the shadows and types and ceremonial law.

On the other hand, the Jewish Sabbath (Saturday) is clearly a picture of a rest earned after work. Under the law, if one were perfect all his life, fulfilling all the commands, he would deserve Heaven. Since no one was ever perfect but Jesus, nor did any one besides Him keep the law, man could not be saved by the law. You can see then how the Jewish Sabbath, picturing a salvation by good works, is out of place in a dispensation of grace. We are saved by grace, freely, justified without the deeds of the law, so we worship on the first day of the week, representing peace and rest obtained without labor. The Jewish Sabbath, Saturday, is ceremonial law, and does not fit a grace dispensation. Our Lord's Day, the first day of the week, does fit every Christian.

Great Differences Between the Sabbath and the Lord's Day

1. The Sabbath was for Israelites only, under Mosaic Law. The Lord's Day is for New Testament Christians, under grace.

2. The Sabbath was law, enforced with the death penalty, by the command of God (Num. 15:32–36). The Lord's Day, or first day of the week, is grace, without command or penalty, observed voluntarily by Christians, if at all.

3. The Sabbath was a day of physical rest (Exod. 20:10). The Lord's Day is a day of worship (Acts 20:7; Rev. 1:10).

4. The Sabbath typified salvation by works; the Lord's Day typifies salvation by grace.

Christians Are Not Under the Law

Our Seventh-Day Adventist brethren, like the Galatian Christians, have tried to lead us into the yoke of bondage of the Mosaic Law. Many of them teach, and most of them believe, that salvation depends upon keeping the Mosaic Law. They not only preach the Old Testament Sabbath, but they often teach the Old Testament laws against eating certain kinds of meats. They teach the tithe as a part of the way to be saved or to stay saved. For that matter they might as well teach the rest of Jewish ceremonial laws if one must keep the law to be saved. As a matter of fact, the ceremonial laws as given to Israel were plainly fulfilled and not for us according to Colossians 2:14–17 and I Timothy 4:3–5. God plainly tells us that the law about not eating certain meats is not binding on Christians.

"For EVERY CREATURE of God is good, and NOTHING TO BE REFUSED, if it be received with thanksgiving: for it is sanctified by the word of God and prayer."—I Tim. 4:4, 5.

About circumcision, New Testament Christians are plainly told:

"Is any called in uncircumcision? Let him NOT BE CIRCUM-CISED."—I Cor. 7:18.

So about the Sabbath, the command about it was nailed to the cross and blotted out with the other ceremonial laws, as the Lord specifically says, in Colossians 2:16, 17:

"Let no man therefore judge you in meat, or in drink, or in respect of an holy day, or of the new moon, or OF THE SABBATH DAYS: which are a shadow of things to come; but the body is of Christ."

If a Christian were under the law about the Sabbath, then he should be stoned for picking up sticks on Saturday as God commanded in Numbers 15:32–36. He could not even have a fire in the house on Saturday as God commanded Israel in Exodus 35:3. Thank God, that heavy burden of ceremonial law is not for us!

The *moral* laws concerning lying, stealing, adultery, murder, etc., are repeated many times in the New Testament. These sins are inherently wrong, were wrong since before the Mosaic Law, as when Cain killed Abel. Christians ought to keep the moral law, to do right and not wrong. But it is not true that men are saved by keeping the law. They never were and never will be. People are saved by simply trusting in

Christ, and have everlasting life on that basis alone, and not by keeping either the ceremonial or moral law.

Read again these Scriptures, and have settled in your heart forever that you are not under law but under grace!

"For by grace are ye saved through faith; and that not of yourselves: it is the gift of God: not of works, lest any man should boast." —Eph. 2:8-9.

Titus 3:5 also plainly teaches that men are not saved or kept saved by acts of righteousness.

"Not by works of righteousness which we have done, but according to his mercy he saved us, by the washing of regeneration, and renewing of the Holy Ghost."

Then let us

"Stand fast therefore in the liberty wherewith Christ hath made us free, and be not entangled again with the yoke of bondage."—Gal. 5:1.

"Christ hath redeemed us from the curse of the law, being made a curse for us."—Gal. 3:13.

"Let no man therefore judge you in meat, or in drink, or in respect of an holy day, or of the new moon, or OF THE SABBATH DAYS: which are a shadow of things to come; but the body is of Christ."— Col. 2:16, 17.

(This message, with other material added, may be had from the publishers in a separate pamphlet of 24 pages for 15¢ each, seven for $1.00.)

IX

Is There Literal, Physical Fire in Hell?

"I am tormented in this flame."—Luke 16:24.
"Whosoever shall say, Thou fool, shall be in danger of hell fire."—Matt. 5:22.

"The Son of man shall send forth his angels, and they shall gather out of his kingdom all things that offend, and them which do iniquity; and shalt cast them into a furnace of fire: *there shall be wailing and gnashing of teeth."*—Matt. 13:41, 42.

"So shall it be at the end of the world; the angels shall come forth, and sever the wicked from among the just, and shall cast them into the furnace of fire: *there shall be wailing and gnashing of teeth."*—Matt. 13:49, 50.

"Then shall he say also unto them on the left hand, Depart from me, ye cursed, into everlasting fire, *prepared for the devil and his angels."*—Matt. 25:41.

"And if thy hand offend thee, cut it off: it is better for thee to enter into life maimed, than having two hands to go into hell, into the fire that never shall be quenched: *Where their worm dieth not, and the* fire is not quenched." (repeated twice over, concerning feet and eyes also).—Mark 9:43–48.

"But he will burn up the chaff with unquenchable fire."—Matt. 3:12.

"In flaming fire *taking vengeance on them that know not God, and that obey not the gospel of our Lord Jesus Christ: Who shall be punished with everlasting destruction from the presence of the Lord, and from the glory of his power.*"—II Thess. 1:8.

"*The same shall drink of the wine of the wrath of God, which is poured out without mixture into the cup of his indignation; and he shall be* tormented with fire and brimstone *in the presence of the holy angels, and in the presence of the Lamb; and the* smoke of their torment *ascendeth up for ever and ever: and they have no rest day nor night . . .*"— Rev. 14:10, 11.

"*And death and hell were cast into the* lake of fire. *This is the second death. And whosoever was not found written in the book of life was cast into the* lake of fire."—Rev. 20:14, 15.

"*But the fearful, and unbelieving, and the abominable, and murderers, and whoremongers, and sorcerers, and idolaters, and all liars, shall have their part in* the lake which burneth with fire and brimstone: *which is the second death.*"—Rev. 21:8.

Is THERE a literal, physical fire in Hell? Will lost sinners in Hell suffer literal, physical torment of body, the torment of fire?

The Bible repeatedly, from one end to the other, teaches that Hell is a place of fire. The modernists and liberalists teach that there is no Hell. Many who claim to be fundamentalists or conservatives say that the Bible passages teaching a physical Hell with literal fire are figurative in meaning. This is, I believe, because they have not studied the matter afresh for themselves in the Bible, but have simply accepted the current teachings without seeing for themselves what God has said.

But it has resulted that the whole Christian world has lost its fear of Hell, and with it has lost the soul-winning passion. To Christians all over the world, Hell has cooled. That means that Calvary means less, there is less emphasis on redemption by the blood of Christ, there is less teaching about sin, very little warning of judgment, and almost universal powerlessness and fruitlessness on the part of Christians. Our hearts are turning toward modernism while our heads still accept the letter of the Bible. At the same time, the unbelieving world tends more and more to scoffing and scorn about the things of God.

Thus it seems necessary for Christians to make a renewed study of the Bible doctrine of Hell. Oh, if there is a literal Hell of eternal torment, if it has real fire in it, and if poor lost souls will suffer eternally in physical torment as well as mental torment in this physical Hell of literal fire, then we ought to know it!

With this in mind, I call your attention to what seems to me to be the overwhelming proof that Hell is a literal lake of fire, a place of literal, physical torment for the unconverted, the Christ rejector, who dies without being born again.

I. Hell Is a Physical Place

There is abundant proof in the Bible that Hell is a literal, physical place.

First, the Bible expressly says so. In Luke 16:28, the poor rich man who cried out from Hell pled with Abraham that someone should warn his five brethren, "lest they also come into this PLACE OF TORMENT." The personal testimony of a man who went there, as recorded in the words of Jesus Christ, under the inspiration of the Holy Spirit, says that Hell is a "place of torment." Jesus certainly intended people to believe that Hell is a literal, physical place. And that was true even though the rich man's body had not yet been raised from the dead. Hell, even now, before the resurrection of the unsaved, is a literal, physical place.

Second, since Hell will be the home of people with literal, physical bodies, it must be a physical place. And the Scriptures clearly teach the resurrection of the bodies of the unsaved people. Daniel 12:2 says, "And many of them that sleep in the dust of the earth shall awake, some to everlasting life, and some to shame and everlasting contempt." Notice that Daniel refers to the body that 'sleeps in the dust of the earth,' and that the bodies of the unsaved will rise, the same as the bodies of the saved. Again Jesus said in John 5:28–29, "Marvel not at this: for the hour is coming, in the which all that are in the graves shall hear his voice, and shall come forth; they that have done good, unto the resurrection of life; and they that have done evil, unto the resurrection of damnation." There is a resurrection of damnation, and the bodies of unsaved people, in the graves, shall hear the voice of Jesus Christ and shall come forth! And the "resurrection of damnation" must be resurrection to a physical place because it is for physical bodies which will have come out of the grave. That resurrection of the bodies of the unsaved dead is pictured in Revelation 20:12–13, where we learn that the sea will deliver up the dead which are in it, and death and Hell will deliver up the dead which are in them to face the last judgment and then be cast into the lake of fire. Obviously, physical bodies demand a physical habitation. Since there are resurrected bodies, literal, physical bodies, to be in Hell, then Hell is a physical place.

Not only does the Bible expressly tell about the resurrection of the bodies of the unsaved people, but Matthew 10:28 says: "But rather fear him which is able to destroy both soul and body in hell." Bodies will go to Hell! We are told three times in the Bible that every knee shall bow to God and every tongue shall confess (Isa. 45:23, Rom. 14:11, and Phil. 2:10, 11). And that is referring to the unsaved after they are dead; so the bodies of the unsaved dead must have literal knees and literal tongues that they may bow before Christ at the last judgment and that they may confess to Him.

Third, the fact that Heaven is a place requires that Hell should be a place. Jesus said in John 14:2: "I go to prepare a PLACE for you." And if Heaven is a real, physical place with streets, walls, gates, trees, fruit, a river, mansions, and a throne, then Hell also must certainly be a real, literal, physical place.

Now, if Hell is a literal, physical place, it has a temperature. Temperature is a property of matter. Every physical body has some temperature. Every stick, every stone, every bit of earth and water and air in the universe has some temperature. So Hell, being a physical place, has a temperature. It is either cold or hot or moderate. Do you think the temperature there is seventy degrees? Do you think it is air-conditioned for comfort? Do you think that Hell was particularly designed for the happiness and perfect health and enjoyment of the Christ-rejecting sinners who go there? Do you not think that if Hell is a place of punishment, the temperature might well be a part of that punishment? Well, Hell is a physical place and has some temperature, and the Bible says it is hot. The Bible calls it a "lake of fire, burning with brimstone." The Saviour spoke of "hell-fire." He said it is a place "where the fire is not quenched." Since there must be some temperature in Hell, why not believe what the Bible says instead of guessing something else?

II. Many Bible Types of Hell Show Punishment by Fire

The Bible is exquisitely accurate in all its types and pictures, and recurring again and again in the Bible are stories of how God punished people with fire for their sins. Fire is a proper symbol of the wrath of God and is so used throughout the Bible. What more fitting than that Hell should be a lake of fire and that there should be flames of torment there?

Here are some striking examples of where God's judgment on sin came by fire.

1. In Genesis 19:24 we read, "Then the Lord rained upon Sodom and upon Gomorrah brimstone and fire from the Lord

out of heaven." And we are told that Abraham "looked toward Sodom and Gomorrah, and toward all the land of the plain, and beheld, and, lo, the smoke of the country went up as the smoke of a furnace" (Gen. 19:28). How like the Bible description of Hell that is! There was fire, there was brimstone; and Revelation 21:8 says that Hell is "the lake which burneth with fire and brimstone," while Revelation 14:10 says that the lost "shall be tormented with fire and brimstone"; and the following verse, Revelation 14:11 says, "And the smoke of their torment ascendeth up for ever and ever." Sodom was destroyed with fire and brimstone, and the smoke went up like that of a furnace. Was not that meant as a type of Hell? Was not God's wrath poured out literally, physically, on those wicked men of Sodom as it will be poured out on the lost in Hell? And we know that it was literal, physical fire that destroyed Sodom and Gomorrah. An archeological expedition, led by Dr. Melvin Grove Kyle, discovered evidences of the brimstone (sulphur) amid burned rocks around the Dead Sea which covers the ruins of ancient Sodom.

In fact, God plainly tells us, in II Peter 2:6, that the destruction of Sodom and Gomorrah is "an example unto those that after should live ungodly." That fire and brimstone was a sample of Hell!

2. Nadab and Abihu, the sons of Aaron, sinned by using strange fire on the altar. God had given heavenly fire on the altar to burn the sacrifice which Aaron had offered, but in unbelief they took, we suppose, fire from the ordinary campfire in their censers, "and put incense thereon, and offered strange fire before the Lord, which he commanded them not. And there went out fire from the Lord, and devoured them, and they died before the Lord" (Lev. 10:1, 2). Here again the wrath of God is shown and His punishment for sin is by fire on physical bodies.

3. God's punishment on the rebels of the whole nation of Israel was by fire also. In Numbers 11:1, 2 we read, "And when the people complained, it displeased the Lord: and the

Lord heard it; and his anger was kindled, and the fire of the Lord burnt among them, and consumed them that were in the uttermost parts of the camp. And the people cried unto Moses; and when Moses prayed unto the Lord, the fire was quenched." Again God's judgment on sin was by fire, physical fire on literal people. Do you believe that fire was literal fire? Then why not believe the fire in Hell is literal fire too?

4. Achan, who brought a curse on Israel when they came to the battle of Ai, was stoned and then burned with fire as punishment. Joshua 7:25 says, "And Joshua said, Why hast thou troubled us? the Lord shall trouble thee this day. And all Israel stoned him with stones, and burned them with fire, after they had stoned them with stones." Remember that this was a public punishment for a most serious sin, a warning to the whole nation; and here God expressed His wrath with fire on the sinners involved, physical fire on the physical sinners. Though Moses and the people did it, it was following the express commandment of God, who in verse 15 had said "And it shall be, that he that is taken with the accursed thing shall be burnt with fire, he and all that he hath: because he hath transgressed the covenant of the Lord, and because he hath wrought folly in Israel." So the fire was expressly commanded and intended to be more significant than the stoning. It here pictures God's judgment on the physical bodies of sinners.

5. In II Kings 1:10-12, Elijah asked that God should let fire come down from Heaven and consume the two groups of fifty soldiers with the captain in each. "And there came down fire from heaven, and consumed him and his fifty." And the second time the same thing happened. It was obviously the physical manifestation of the wrath of God on wicked, presumptuous, godless men.

6. In Revelation, chapters 8 and 9, six trumpets are said to sound as signals of great woes and afflictions that will come to wicked people on the earth during the tribulation. Those curses include water turned to blood; the star, wormwood,

which is to fall from Heaven poisoning the waters of the earth, the smiting of the sun to bring darkness, the armies of sinful men to be devil possessed, and men to be tormented with the sting of these hellish locusts, but not able to die— these are some of the terrible plagues. All of them represent the punishment and judgment of sin, but fire is prominent throughout the chapter. In chapter 9, verse 18 we are told, "By these three was the third part of men killed, by the fire, and by the smoke, and by the brimstone, which issued out of their mouths," that is, out of the mouths of horses from Hell. This is clearly a judgment of God upon the physical bodies of men and must be symbolic of the judgment of God upon physical people in Hell. It indicates that there is literal fire and brimstone and smoke in Hell!

7. In Revelation 18 we have the story of the mighty city, Babylon, the seat of the Antichrist, and how the city shall be destroyed by fire from God. Verse 8 says, "Therefore shall her plagues come in one day, death, and mourning, and famine; and she shall be utterly burned with fire: for strong is the Lord God who judgeth her." And succeeding verses tell how the kings of the earth and the merchants will "lament for her, when they shall see the smoke of her burning." But all Heaven and the holy apostles and prophets will rejoice over her, "for God hath avenged you on her" (verse 20). That is expressly said to be the judgment of God on that physical city, wicked Babylon. And does it not then picture the torments of Hell where God will judge the wicked sinners in physical bodies for their sin?

8. In fact, the valley of Hinnom, that horrible place outside Jerusalem where dead bodies were burned, a place of decaying offal and worms, and of a fire never put out, is used as a type of Hell. And in the New Testament the word *Hinnom* becomes *Gehenna*, one of the Greek words used for Hell; and Jesus, with that picture in mind, warns people that Hell is a place where "the worm dieth not and the fire is not quenched" (Mark 9:43–49). That place of stinking offal, of maggots, of

never-extinguished fire and smoke, reminded Jesus of Hell! Does not that indicate what Hell, the physical place for the confinement of wicked sinners with physical bodies, is like?

I maintain that all these examples, plus many more warnings that God is like a consuming fire, and that His wrath will burn with fury, show that God's judgment on sinners' physical bodies in Hell will include literal fire.

III. The Burnt-Offerings and All Animal Sacrifices of the Old Testament Pictured the Wrath of God Upon Sin

We know that the sacrifices of the Old Testament all pictured Jesus. The lamb pictured Christ, the Lamb of God, the innocent One who would take away the sins of the world, paying for them with His blood. The young bullock represented Christ the burden-bearing Saviour. The scapegoat represented Christ who takes our blame and carries away our sin. The mourning turtledove must picture Christ as the Man of sorrows and acquainted with grief. And the pure white pigeon must have pictured Christ the innocent One, pure and stainless, who came to save us poor wicked sinners. The passover lamb represented Christ also.

Two things stand out in our minds as we read God's Word telling about the sacrifices: *the blood and the fire!* The blood of every sacrifice was shed, showing how Christ would pour out His soul for sin and pay our debt by His death on the cross. But the fire must have pictured the wrath of God which Jesus bore for us. Jesus died as I ought to have died. He suffered the punishment of the damned. Jesus suffered the torments of Hell. We will not now argue about whether Jesus literally went to Hell or not. I think that when He said, "It is finished," the atonement was finished, that He went that day to Paradise with the dying thief, and that the Heavenly Father received His spirit. But certain it is that when Jesus suffered not only physical death for us, in some sense He suffered spiritual death, too. God turned His face away from His own Son for our sakes. And back of the bloody sweat of the garden, back of the thirst on the cross, back of the scourging, the spitting, the crown of thorns, and the nails and the spear, is the horrible fact that Christ was made sin for us and suffered a sinner's punishment. The infinite Christ, without any limit to His capacity for suffering, could have, in a moment, suffered the tortures of the damned for eternity in Hell. And when Christ "tasted death" for every man, then we may be sure He tasted the second death, too, the tortures of Hell.

There is no way for a finite, limited mind to understand all of the wrath of God and the sufferings of our Saviour. But with meticulous care throughout the whole Old Testament, the burning of sacrifices and offerings is discussed so that we might get some idea of what it really meant for Jesus to go to the cross. All of the law, all the ceremonies, all the Old Testament teachings were simply "a schoolmaster to bring us to Christ," and they pictured how He took the place of a sinner, and bore the sinner's judgment.

How strange, how striking, is the thought, then, that all these sacrifices required fire!

Leviticus 1:3–9 describes the offering of the bullock for a burnt-offering. In verse 9 it says: "And the priest shall burn all on the altar, to be a burnt-sacrifice, an offering made by fire, of a sweet savour unto the Lord." And the following verses tell how the sheep or goat which is brought for a sacrifice should also be burnt upon the altar, or how the turtle-doves and young pigeons should be burnt upon the altar.

Leviticus, chapter 2, tells how a meat-offering of fine flour may be brought. "And the priest shall burn the memorial of it upon the altar." Or how "an oblation of a meat-offering baken in the oven" is to be offered. Or of a "meat-offering baken in the frying pan." And how "the priest shall take from the meat-offering a memorial thereof, and shall burn it upon the altar: it is an offering made by fire, of a sweet savour unto the Lord." The same chapter tells how the firstfruits of green ears of corn, dried by the fire, shall be offered with frankincense, and how "the priest shall burn the memorial of it, part of the beaten corn thereof, and part of the oil thereof, with all the frankincense thereof: it is an offering made by fire unto the Lord."

Then in the book of Leviticus and elsewhere further instructions are given about sweet savour offerings, peace-offerings, sin-offerings, and how parts of these must always be burned, or all of them. *Wherever God's judgment on sin is pictured, there must be fire!*

In Exodus 12 we are told about the offering of the passover lamb down in Egypt and how that offering was to be repeated, a lamb for a family, on the same day ever year. The lamb pictured Christ; but after the blood was put upon the two sideposts and on the upper doorpost of the houses, then the lamb was to be roasted whole with fire. In Exodus 12:9 God says: "Eat not of it raw, nor sodden [boiled] at all with water, but roast with fire; his head with his legs, and with the purtenance thereof." The lamb was to be cooked without a drop of water; and what can that mean but that there is no water in Hell, just as there was no alleviation of the sufferings of Christ for sinners?

Do you think that there is any significance at all to this divinely inspired provision of sacrifices being burned with fire? Do these animals offered in sacrifice picture Christ our Saviour? Does the blood there spilt in such a river down through the centuries picture the blood of our Saviour, God's Lamb, who would take away the sins of the world? Of course you believe that that is true. Then does not the fire represent the wrath of God on sinners, the judgment of God, the physical punishment even of God's wrath upon sinners in Hell? If it does not mean that, then what else could it mean? Surely Hell must be a place of fire.

IV. The Bible Expressly States Many Times That Hell Is a Place of Real Fire

I have deliberately left the plain positive statements in the Bible, that there is fire in Hell, unto the last; but they are so plain, so often repeated, so unambiguous, that if there were never a sacrifice, never a type in the whole Bible about Hell, these plain statements would settle the matter forever for Bible believers whose attention is prayerfully directed to them.

1. First, there is the plain statement reported by the Lord Jesus of the rich man in Hell, who "cried and said, Father Abraham, have mercy on me, and send Lazarus, that he may dip the tip of his finger in water, and cool my tongue; for I am tormented in this flame." The rich man in Hell said there was real fire there and that he was *tormented in the flames*. His witness, surely, since it is authenticated by the Lord Jesus Himself, ought to be received in any court in the land. *He knew!*

2. Jesus, in Matthew 5:22, said, "But whosoever shall say, Thou fool, shall be in danger of hell fire." Here is the plain word of Jesus that fire is a condition in Hell!

3. Jesus, in Matthew 13:24–30, tells of the tares which an enemy sowed in a good man's field, and at the harvesttime the tares were gathered and burned. Jesus was asked to explain and interpret the parable, and He did. In Matthew 13:40–42 He said, "As therefore the tares are gathered and burned in the fire; so shall it be in the end of this world. The Son of man shall send forth his angels, and they shall gather out of his kingdom all things that offend, and them which do iniquity; and shall cast them into a furnace of fire: there shall be wailing and gnashing of teeth." Nothing can be plainer than this statement of Jesus Christ that the Son of man (Christ Himself), shall send forth His angels, and that these angels will cast the wicked "into a furnace of fire."

Jesus could have said the wicked would be cast into a place of *tormenting conscience*, but that is not what He said. He could have said it was a place of sorrow of which fire might be a symbol, but He did not. Then why not believe what He *did* say, that Hell is "a furnace of fire"?

4. In the same thirteenth chapter of Matthew Jesus told the story of a net cast into the sea, gathering of every kind of

fish, and how the fishermen, when it was full, drew the net to shore and sat down and gathered the good into vessels but cast the bad fish away. And then Jesus interpreted His meaning in these words given in Matthew 13:49, 50, "So shall it be at the end of the world: the angels shall come forth, and sever the wicked from among the just, and shall cast them into the furnace of fire: there shall be wailing and gnashing of teeth." Again Jesus repeats the same statement, that at the end of the world (the consummation of this age), the angels shall come forth, take the wicked from among the just "and shall cast them into the furnace of fire." And what is "the furnace of fire" but Hell itself?

5. In Matthew 25 Jesus tells of the judgment of the people who will be left alive after the battle of Armageddon when Jesus comes to sit on His throne. In verse 41, "Then shall he say also unto them on the left hand, Depart from me, ye cursed, into everlasting fire, prepared for the devil and his angels." And where is that everlasting fire, prepared for the devil and his angels? Obviously, it is Hell. Hell is a place of everlasting fire.

6. In Mark 9:43–49 Jesus gives a solemn warning of Hell, in these words: "And if thy hand offend thee, cut it off: it is better for thee to enter into life maimed, than having two hands to go into hell, into the fire that never shall be quenched: where their worm dieth not, and the fire is not quenched. And if thy foot offend thee, cut it off: it is better for thee to enter halt into life, than having two feet to be cast into hell, into the fire that never shall be quenched: where their worm dieth not, and the fire is not quenched. And if thine eye offend thee, pluck it out: it is better for thee to enter into the kingdom of God with one eye, than having two eyes to be cast into hell fire: where their worm dieth not, and the fire is not quenched. For every one shall be salted with fire, and every sacrifice shall be salted with salt."

Seven times in that brief passage Jesus mentioned fire. And He expressly says that people with hands and feet will go into Hell, people with eyes will go into Hell, and three separate times He says that we had better go into Heaven with one foot, or one hand, or one eye, than to go into Hell having two hands or feet or eyes, "where the worm dieth not, and the fire is not quenched."

Nothing could be more explicit than this plain, sober statement of Jesus Christ that Hell is a place of fire. Do you believe what He said?

7. Paul, by divine inspiration, in II Thessalonians tells us Christ will return to the earth, "In flaming fire taking vengeance on them that know not God, and that obey not the gospel of our Lord Jesus Christ; who shall be punished with everlasting destruction from the presence of the Lord, and from the glory of His power." Do you believe the vengeance of the Lord Jesus Christ is to be with "flaming fire"? Well, is that not exactly what He has promised?

8. Revelation 14:10, 11 tells of the horrible fate that awaits all those who will serve the Antichrist: they will be cast into Hell, a place burning with fire and brimstone, and be tormented forever. Read the solemn words there given:

"The same shall drink of the wine of the wrath of God, which is poured out without mixture into the cup of his indignation; and he shall be tormented with fire and brimstone in the presence of the holy angels, and in the presence of the Lamb: and the smoke of their torment ascendeth up for ever and ever: and they have no rest day nor night, who worship the beast and his image, and whosoever receiveth the mark of his name."

If the Bible can be believed, then Hell is a place of fire and brimstone and smoke; it is a place of torment "day and night"; and the smoke of their torment ascends forever, as proof that God hates sin and that sin cannot go unpunished! Does not that Scripture teach that there is a literal fire in Hell?

9. In Revelation 20:11–15 we have the story of the last judgment of the unsaved dead. We read how that the sea and

the graves give up the bodies of the unsaved dead and their spirits come out of Hell to face Jesus Christ on His great white judgment throne and how the books with their records will be opened and every one will be judged according to his works. And then all will be sent to Hell to suffer proportionately according to their deeds. Verses 14 and 15 of this twentieth chapter of Revelation read:

"And death and hell were cast into the lake of fire. This is the second death. And whosoever was not found written in the book of life was cast into the lake of fire."

This is a punishment for people with resurrected bodies. And with physical bodies these people will be cast into the lake of fire. If the resurrection is literal, then Hell is literal. If the bodies are physical bodies, then Hell is a physical Hell. If the judgment is literal, then why should not the fire and brimstone be literal? Hell is a lake of fire!

10. Revelation 21:8 again tells us that Hell is a lake of fire burning with brimstone. It says, "But the fearful, and unbelieving, and the abominable, and murderers, and whoremongers, and sorcerers, and idolaters, and all liars, shall have their part in the lake which burneth with fire and brimstone: which is the second death." This second death means to have a part in "the lake which burneth with fire and brimstone."

What can we say to all these Scriptures and many others, but that Jesus obviously intended for us to believe that Hell is a place of literal fire and brimstone, of physical torment for the unconverted who would not repent!

It is to be noted in the above Scriptures that Hell is said to have fire in it now, when only the lost souls of men and women are there without their bodies. The rich man "was buried; and in Hell he lift up his eyes, being in torments," and he said, "I am tormented in this flame" (Luke 16:22–24). Although his body was in the grave, he had all his physical senses in Hell and was tormented in the flame. His tongue was in the grave, but he felt all the horrors of a tongue parched with thirst. Even lost souls in Hell today are tormented in flames though their bodies have not been resurrected and judged and sent to Hell.

Likewise in Matthew 25:41, we are told that Jesus, when He comes to reign on earth at the beginning of the thousand years and long before the resurrection of the bodies of the unsaved dead at the close of the thousand years, as told in Revelation 20:11–15, will say to the unsaved, "Depart from me, ye cursed, into everlasting fire, prepared for the devil and his angels." So, there is a present Hell where there are only spirits and not bodies. And this is a Hell of "everlasting fire, prepared for the devil and his angels."

And then later, after the bodies of the unsaved will be brought out of the grave and out of the sea, after the last judgment is done, the poor lost sinners will depart, soul and body, into the "lake of fire," which burns with brimstone. Hell is a place of everlasting fire.

V. Accompanying Features in the Bible Description of Hell Indicate That the Fire Is Literal Fire

The Bible's accounts and descriptions of Hell are very literal, and the features which accompany these descriptions are features which seem surely to be literal.

1. For instance, the rich man in Hell prayed, "Father Abraham, have mercy on me, and send Lazarus, that he may dip the tip of his finger in water, and cool my tongue: for I am tormented in this flame" (Luke 16:24). If the fire in Hell were literal fire, then a man would crave literal water to cool his parching tongue, and quench his horrible thirst. But if the fire in Hell is only memory, or remorse of conscience, then what good would a drop of water do? And he wanted water "to cool my tongue." Now his tongue was not in Hell, to be sure, but all the physical senses of his body were in Hell. The feeling of his tongue was in Hell. The man saw, he heard, he felt, he thirsted, he cried, he prayed, he remembered! All his physical senses were in Hell. And it was a physical sense of

torment that he wanted alleviated, not a sense of moral guilt. The man was suffering physical pain and wanted physical water to cool his physical sense of heat and thirst as he was tormented in flames. Everything about the statement indicates *physical* torment in literal fire.

2. Jesus said, in Matthew 13:42, that the angels shall take the wicked, the unsaved, "And shall cast them into a furnace of fire: there shall be wailing and gnashing of teeth." The same statement, except that it is "*the* furnace of fire," is made by the Saviour in verse 50. Now if we believe there is a literal furnace of fire into which the unsaved shall be cast, it is simple to understand that the tormented ones will literally wail and will grit their teeth in physical anguish. But if the suffering is only mental, if the fire is not literal, then they would not grit their teeth. At hundreds of funerals I have seen people weep, but never saw them grit their teeth. But I have seen people gnash their teeth in pain, physical pain, with broken bones, with torn ligaments, with burns. This is a picture of physical pain in Hell, not a picture of a guilty conscience only.

3. Not only is there fire in Hell, as discussed in the Bible, but there is brimstone. If the fire in Hell were literal fire, like that which destroyed Sodom and Gomorrah, then we should not be surprised if there were literal brimstone (sulphur) like that which fell on Sodom and Gomorrah with the fire. (And the surrounding country still bears evidence to the fire and brimstone which destroyed Sodom and Gomorrah.) But if we argue that the fire in Hell is only figurative, then what is the brimstone? The people who argue that the fire in Hell means remorse of conscience never say what the brimstone means. Obviously, the brimstone is meant to be literal brimstone, and hence the fire must be literal fire.

4. Again and again in the Bible, the smoke of Hell is mentioned. Abraham saw the smoke of the destruction of Sodom and Gomorrah going up like the smoke of a furnace. And we are told that poor lost sinners in Hell will be tormented with

fire and brimstone, and that "the smoke of their torment ascendeth up for ever and ever." A literal, physical fire has smoke. But what kind of smoke does figurative fire have? If the fire only pictured memory, or conscience, then what would the smoke figure? The smoke of Hell is meaningless unless there is literal fire there.

VI. Conclusion

And my closing word is this. God says in Jude 23, "And others save with fear, pulling them out of the fire; hating even the garment spotted by the flesh." Beloved, if you get somebody saved, you are keeping them out of the fires of Hell! I think I know why Paul went about weeping, "night and day with tears" (Acts 20:31) when he so believed in a literal Hell of eternal fire and torment! I beg of you who read this, become consumed with a passion to save people from Hell! We may be fundamental in our heads, but most of us are partly infidels in our hearts, for we have no real conception of the wickedness of sin, and we have no real conception of the marvel of God's love and His infinite grace expressed at Calvary! Most of us have no sense of the awfulness of sin and the certain, horrible doom of Christ-rejecting sinners!

Oh, brother, let us win souls while we may to keep them from the lake of fire, that awful place burning with brimstone, prepared for the Devil and his angels!

X

Is the Torment in Hell Eternal?

I. One With a Simple, Childlike Faith, Taking the Scriptures at Plain Face Value Must Believe They Teach Eternal Torment for Lost Ones in Hell.

II. Reconciliation of Lost Sinners in Hell Utterly Impossible, According to the Bible.

III. No Annihilation in Hell; Tormented Sinners Cannot Cease to Be, Cannot Cease to Suffer There, According to Plain Scriptures.

"And many of them that sleep in the dust of the earth shall awake, some to everlasting life, and some to shame and everlasting contempt."—Dan. 12.2.

"And these shall go away into everlasting punishment: but the righteous into life eternal."—Matt. 25:46.

". . . into hell, into the fire that never shall be quenched: where their worm dieth not, and the fire is not quenched."—Three times by Jesus in Mark 9:43-48.

"And beside all this, between us and you there is a great gulf fixed: so that they which would pass from hence to you cannot; neither can they pass to us, that would come from thence."—Luke 16:26.

"Twice dead, plucked up by the roots; raging

waves of the sea, foaming out their own shame; wandering stars, to whom is reserved the blackness of darkness forever."—Jude 12, 13.

"The same shall drink of the wine of the wrath of God, which is poured out without mixture into the cup of his indignation; and he shall be tormented with fire and brimstone in the presence of the holy angels, and in the presence of the Lamb: and the smoke of their torment ascendeth up for ever and ever: and they have no rest day nor night, who worship the beast and his image, and whosoever receiveth the mark of his name."—Rev. 14:10, 11.

"And the devil that deceived them was cast into the lake of fire and brimstone, where the beast and the false prophet are, and shall be tormented day and night for ever and ever."—Rev. 20:10.

"Eternal damnation"—Mark 3:29.

"Eternal judgment"—Heb. 6:2.

"Vengeance of eternal fire"—Jude 7.

"Everlasting fire"—Matt. 18:8; Matt. 25:41.

WILL THE UNCONVERTED WICKED be tormented forever in an eternal Hell? Will there be no end, century after century, age after age, to their anguish and punishment? I think a man would need a heart of stone not to be moved to the depths by a serious consideration of this thought. The very idea of infinite, eternal torment, pain, anguish and hopeless suffering for any human being is so painful that even preachers rarely discuss the subject any more. The thought is so horrifying that nearly all those who are not reverent believers in the Bible vehemently deny such a thought. The thought of eternal, conscious torment of lost sinners, with never an end to their despair and pain, is so distressing that I suppose even the most reverent and believing of Bible students has sometimes searched in the Scriptures to find some hope that the torment of people in Hell would some time cease. I know that I have read every passage I could find in the entire Bible, again and again, feeling that I must not, I dare not preach such a horrible thing as eternal torment of the damned unless it were so clearly taught in the Bible as to be unmistakable. And the more I have studied the Word of God the more has become the overwhelming conviction that that is exactly what God's Word teaches. In Hell there is eternal torment.

I. One With a Simple, Childlike Faith, Taking the Scriptures at Plain Face Value Must Believe They Teach Eternal Torment for Lost Ones in Hell

Please look again at the Scriptures at the head of this article. Wouldn't any simple, childlike believer, who accepts the Word of God at face value, believe that "and some (shall awake) to shame and everlasting contempt," in Daniel 12:2 means everlasting punishment, everlasting shame and everlasting contempt? And when Jesus said, "And these shall go away into everlasting punishment" in Matthew 25:46—do you not think that a simple Spirit-filled believer who accepts the Bible at face value would be compelled to think "everlasting punishment" there meant just exactly that; punishment for ever and ever, that is, conscious eternal torment? When you, as a young Christian, read the story of the rich man in Hell, tormented in flame, did you not get the impression that Jesus meant to teach eternal punishment, eternal, conscious torment? And when Revelation 14:10, 11 tells us of certain lost people that "The same shall drink of the wine of the wrath of God, which is poured out without mixture into the cup of his indignation; and he shall be tormented with fire and brimstone in the presence of the holy angels, and in the presence of the Lamb; and the smoke of their torment ascendeth up for ever and ever: and they have no rest day nor night, who worship the beast and his image, and whosoever receiveth the mark of his name," would not any simplehearted, childlike believer in the Bible think that God meant to teach here that day after day and night after night forever sinners in Hell are tormented?

I know that that was my own impression, before I ever attended seminary, before I ever read a book on theology, before I ever read any theories about Hell. And I know that common people, earnest Bible believers all over America, all over the world, have gotten just that impression from the Bible. And what is true in this generation has been true in all generations since the Bible was written. Probably ninety-nine out of every hundred earnest Bible believers who approached the Bible with an unbiased mind, just wanting to know what God said and believing what they read, have believed that the Bible expressly and clearly teaches eternal torment for the damned souls in Hell.

Is the Bible a trustworthy book, or is it meant to deceive? Must humble Christians approach the Bible with wary caution, feeling that God in the Bible means to trap them into false teaching, that it cannot be believed and taken at simple face value? Do you believe that the Bible does not literally mean what it says, and that it cannot be taken at face value? Well, I for one believe nothing of the kind. I believe it is meant to be understood, that the Bible may be taken at honest face value. I believe that the Holy Spirit can be trusted, and that what He has had written down for us was written honestly, with frankness, with simplicity, for believing hearts, and is worthy of all acceptation. Remember that Jesus said that He spoke to the Pharisees, the hardhearted, legally-trained, haughty Pharisees, in parables, that they might not be understood. But to the disciples He said, "It is given unto you to know the mysteries of the kingdom of heaven, but to them it is not given" (Matt. 13:11). And then the parables were explained to the disciples in the clearest possible terms! Remember that Jesus said that God "hast hid these things from the wise and prudent, and hast revealed them unto babes" (Luke 10:21). Remember that Jesus said, in the very first of the Beatitudes, "Blessed are the poor in spirit: for their's is the kingdom of heaven." To humble, childlike Christians who do not think they are smart, the Bible is given; and all its mysteries are opened by the Holy Spirit to the humble and childlike heart who believes what he reads.

A humble, childlike acceptance of the Word of God at face value compels one to believe there is eternal torment for the lost souls in Hell.

If the torment in Hell will not be eternal, then the Bible was evidently meant to mislead; and Jesus, when He spoke often on Hell, must have intentionally deceived His disciples! And that is unthinkable.

False teachers have written that they would hate a God who would send a sinner to Hell to be tormented forever. And others have said that God is too good to send a sinner to Hell. Well, we know nothing about how good God is except by the Bible. I had rather have one line from Jesus Christ about what kind of a Hell sinners go to than to have all the theories in the world formulated by men as to what they think God would do or would not do. Satan hates the idea that sin must be punished. Men everywhere condone sin and shun the ideas of judgment and punishment and eternal ruin for Christ-rejecting sinners. BUT BACK TO THE BIBLE! To every believing, humblehearted person of childlike faith the Bible speaks with awful solemnity and terrible certainty about the fact of eternal torment for sinners who will not repent, will not turn from their sins to God nor trust in the Saviour God has provided. Men who go by their own theories may believe something else, but all who are willing in childlike faith to receive God's Word on the subject must believe in eternal torment in Hell.

II. Reconciliation of Lost Sinners in Hell Utterly Impossible According to the Bible

I suppose that there are only four positions possible on this question of eternal torment. First, one may be an infidel and atheist, who does not believe there is a God, does not believe man has a soul more than a beast, does not believe in rewards or punishments or a future life. Such a man would not believe the Bible nor be interested in this Bible discussion.

Second, some people hold the theory that lost sinners in Hell will eventually be reconciled to God and taken to Heaven.

Third, some people believe that sinners in Hell will be eventually annihilated, will cease to be, so of course their suffering would cease.

Fourth, the only other position possible, I think, is that there is eternal torment in Hell, that indescribable suffering through an infinite eternity is the punishment of Christ-rejecting sinners who die unsaved.

The first position, that of the atheist, is not worth our discussion here. But the Bible has a very clear teaching on the doctrine of final reconciliation of the sinners in Hell with God. And the Scripture shows that that position is utterly untenable by a Bible believer.

We believe that the following Scriptural truths are overwhelmingly convincing.

1. *The lost sinner awakes "to shame and everlasting contempt"* (Dan. 12:2). In other words, the contempt which a sinner suffers at the last judgment, and when he goes to the lake of fire is literally "everlasting contempt." That punishment, that shame and contempt last forever.

Now since the contempt that a lost sinner suffers is everlasting, he could never be reconciled to God. How could he be reconciled to God and enjoy Heaven, at the same time suffering "shame and everlasting contempt"? Even if this Scripture should not disprove the annihilation of the wicked, that they cease to be (though I think it does), it is clear that they could not be reconciled to God and have eternal blessedness at the same time they were having everlasting contempt.

Some deceitful teachers say that the word *everlasting* here simply means *age-lasting*, and after an age is completed, the contempt would be over and the sinner then might be reconciled to God and taken out of Hell into Heaven. But that contention is utterly false, as I can show you in a moment. The Hebrew word here translated "everlasting" is *olam*. In Genesis 21:33 the same Hebrew word *olam* is used in the phrase "*the everlasting God.*" In Deuteronomy 33:27 the same word is used and God's arms are "the everlasting arms." In Psalm 145:13 God's kingdom is "an everlasting kingdom." In Isaiah 26:4 the Lord Jehovah is "everlasting strength." In Isaiah 40:28 the same word *olam* is used of "the everlasting God." In Isaiah 45:17 people are invited to be saved "with an everlasting salvation" using the same word. The usage of the Hebrew word *olam* throughout the Old Testament proves beyond any shadow of doubt that the term here literally means everlasting as God is everlasting, as His arms are everlasting, as His mercy is everlasting and as His strength is everlasting and His salvation is everlasting. Thus the sinner's estrangement from God in Hell, his shame and contempt, must be everlasting. That certainly forbids the thought of reconciliation in some future age.

2. *Jesus said in Matthew* 25:46, "And these shall go away into everlasting punishment: but the righteous into life eternal." This clearly teaches that the punishment of lost people in Hell is everlasting. They could never be reconciled to God while they were enduring everlasting punishment.

Again, the Greek word used here literally means *eternal, everlasting, lasting forever.* It is the Greek word *aionios.* It is exactly the same word used in John 3:16, "but have *everlasting life.*" It is the same word used in John 3:36, "He that believeth on the Son hath *everlasting* life." It is the very word used about punishment and life, "*everlasting* punishment" and "life *eternal*" are the same Greek word! If the life eternal which the righteous have in Heaven really means eternal or everlasting life, then the punishment of the wicked is just as eternal, just as everlasting. The punishment of lost people in Hell continues the same length of time as the happiness of saved people

in Heaven. That, of course, forbids any thought of a reconciliation of lost sinners with God in some future age.

3. *The New Testament variously speaks of "eternal damnation"*
(Mark 3–29), *of "eternal judgment"* (Heb. 6:2), *of "vengeance of
eternal fire"* (Jude 7). These terms necessarily forbid reconciliation of a sinner who is in Hell, with God in some future age.

Damnation in Hell is *eternal damnation.* The judgment of lost
sinners is *eternal judgment.* Again the word for "eternal" in the
above verses is the same Greek word used continually about
eternal life or everlasting life. It is the same word used about
"the eternal Spirit" in Hebrews 9:14. So the damnation and
the judgment of lost sinners is as eternal as the Holy Spirit,
as eternal as the salvation and life that God gives Christians in
Heaven. These terms make utterly impossible a future reconciliation with God of the sinners who go to Hell.

4. *Hell is a place of "everlasting fire"* (Matt. 18:8, Matt.
25:41), *a place where the fire is never quenched and the worm never
dies* (Mark 9:43–49), *where the smoke of torment ascends up for
ever and ever* (Rev. 14:11). All these Scriptural statements
indicate that Hell itself is eternal, everlasting, unchangeable.
Small towns that never have an arrest tear down their jails.
Penitentiaries turn off the electricity from the electric chair
when it is not in use. Firing squads cease firing when there are
no more victims. In New Jersey the guard at the whipping post
does not go on flailing the air when the criminal has been
removed. Why should God maintain the fires of Hell burning
with brimstone; why should the smoke of torment ascend for
ever and ever; why should the worms never die in Hell; if the
victims will have all been taken out and carried to Heaven
and reconciled to God? To express the thing shows how silly
is such a question. The smoke keeps ascending from Hell because the fire keeps burning. The fires keep burning and the
worms keep living in Hell because lost sinners remain there
forever.

If the punishment of Hell were over, if the judgment on sin
were done, if the shame and contempt were forever ended,

then God would not maintain Hell forever. If Hell is ever-lasting, then the punishment of Hell logically would be ever-lasting.

The only way to believe in the future reconciliation of lost people in Hell and the ending of their torment by taking them to Heaven, is simply to ignore the plain statements of the Bible.

5. *Jesus said in Luke 16:26 that between Heaven and Hell "there is a great gulf fixed: so that they which would pass from hence to you cannot; neither can they pass to us, that would come from thence."* There is a great gulf fixed between Heaven and Hell; no one ever crosses it going either way. Lazarus could not leave Heaven to go down to Hell to comfort the rich man. The rich man in Hell could never cross that gulf to ascend to Heaven.

Notice the statement has two aspects. First there is a "great gulf" between Heaven and Hell. An enormous, unpassable distance separates the two, a barrier that cannot be crossed. And second, notice that this gulf is *fixed*. It is established. It is permanent. The gulf between Heaven and Hell will forever remain. Hence, of course, those who are in Hell can never go to Heaven. This is the plain meaning of Luke 16:26.

6. *In the particular case of Judas Iscariot Jesus said, "It had been good for that man if he had not been born"* (Matt. 26:24). *That meant, certainly, that Judas could never get out of Hell to enjoy eternal blessing in Heaven.*

If Judas should stay in Hell two thousand years or five thousand years, and then at last be reconciled to God, and enter into all the joys of Heaven, he would enjoy the blessings of Heaven for millions of years, and yet those joys would be only beginning. For certainly the blessings of Heaven are eternal blessings, never ending. And no matter how long it measured, if it were a limited time one should spend in Hell, then if he were going to spend eternity, billions of years, in Heaven with perfect peace and joy and happiness, it could not be said of him that it would be better if he had not been born. Dr. H. A. Ironside used this argument the first time I ever met with it, and I believe it is absolutely unanswerable. It proves that for Judas Iscariot there could never be any reconciliation with God. Oh, how he must have wished a million times, in Hell, that he had never been born! For there he knows that his case is utterly hopeless, and he can never get out of Hell. And if there is no reconciliation for Judas Iscariot in Hell, then why should there be for other sinners?

Before you read further, I hope you will go back and review these points, proving surely to Bible believers that the doctrine of a future reconciliation of the wicked in Hell, the doctrine that they will be taken out of Hell and reconciled to God and then will spend eternity in Heaven, is an unscriptural doctrine that the Bible never teaches. It gives a false hope to sinners that has not a single basis in the Bible.

Men, looking for an excuse to say that eventually sinners in Hell will be reconciled to God, have sometimes used Colossians 1:19, 20 which says, "For it pleased the Father that in him should all fullness dwell; and, having made peace through the blood of his cross, by him to reconcile all things unto himself; by him, I say, whether they be things in earth, or things in heaven." But that Scripture does not refer to the reconciliation of *man* to God but *things*, "to reconcile all things unto himself." In the same passage it is made clear what things are meant. In verses 16 and 17 preceding we read, "By him were all things created, that are in heaven, and that are in earth, visible and invisible, whether they be thrones, or dominions, or principalities, or powers: all things were created by him, and for him: and he is before all things, and by him all things consist." There is a dominion and rule in Heaven. There are thrones, dominions, principalities and powers on earth. Christ created them all. He will reconcile all of them to Himself. Christ will reign on earth from David's throne, and all the kingdoms of the earth will become subject to Him one day. Thus through Christ all things in earth and Heaven will be reconciled to God.

But notice clearly in Colossians 1:20 where these things are;

they are in *earth and in Heaven, but not in Hell.* Colossians 1:20 says, "Having made peace through the blood of his cross, by him to reconcile all things unto himself; by him, I say, whether they be things in earth, or things in heaven." The reconciliation which Colossians 1:20 mentions is the reconciliation of things in earth and things in Heaven unto God through Christ. No reference is made here to the reconciliation of things in Hell to God.

So many times, as I have shown in the Scriptures discussed above, God has declared that the punishment of sinners, the damnation of sinners, the shame and contempt for sinners in Hell is eternal and everlasting and as God is everlasting and as salvation is everlasting, that it is a perversion of Scripture to try to make any Scripture mean that sinners will one day be rescued from this eternal damnation. If you find any Scripture that, to you, seems to teach that God will reconcile lost sinners in Hell to Himself one day, then you are perverting that Scripture, because you are making it contradict the plain and emphatic statement of passage after passage scattered throughout the whole Bible. And the Bible, God's Word, never contradicts itself. When it appears to do so, it is because the Scripture is misinterpreted by men who have twisted Scripture to try to make it prove what it does not mean.

Surely, surely, there is no reconciliation to God for a sinner who dies without Christ. His separation from God is eternal, and without hope.

III. No Annihilation in Hell; Tormented Sinners Cannot Cease to Be, Cannot Cease to Suffer There; According to Plain Scriptures

In the preceding divisions of this message, I have been proving that there is no future reconciliation with God for lost sinners who go to Hell, that sinners can never get out of Hell and go to Heaven. If you have had an earnest heart, anxious to know what God's Word really said on the subject, you have that matter settled, I feel sure.

In that preceding division we have not been primarily trying to answer the theory that sinners in Hell will be annihilated, burned up, will cease to be and cease to suffer, simply passing out of existence. I say we have not been primarily trying to answer that theory. We were first answering the theory that sinners in Hell will be eventually saved and taken to Heaven. But at the same time we believe we have given overwhelming proof to the simple Christian of childlike faith, to those who have not been perverted by false doctrine, that Hell is really eternal, conscious torment. While we were proving no reconciliation of sinners in Hell, I believe we have also proved no annihilation for sinners in Hell for all those simplehearted, Bible-believing Christians who are unbiased and who are anxious to take the Bible at simple face value in childlike faith. For most Christians it would not be necessary to go further.

But the Bible has far more overwhelming proof than that given. Even if you are prejudiced, even if you have had false teaching, even if you do not want to believe in eternal torment, yet if you will prayerfully examine the Bible proof I will now give, you will see that poor sinners in Hell can never quit suffering but must be tormented day and night forever. Oh, may God help us to see that we must keep people from going to that place of torment!

Will you consider, with an open mind and an open Bible, these positive proofs that sinners in Hell are not annihilated but continue to suffer forever?

1. *Nowhere in the Bible is the annihilation of the wicked stated.*

Remember that death is not annihilation. Death of the body does not mean that the body disappears, it does not even mean the soul ceases to be, else there could be no judgment. Spiritual death, likewise, cannot mean annihilation, for God said to Adam and Eve in the Garden of Eden, "In the day that thou eatest thereof thou shalt surely die" (Gen. 2:17). They ate of that forbidden fruit and they did spiritually die; but they were not annihilated. They simply became lost sinners, separated, alienated from God. And so the *second death* is not annihilation. We are plainly told that the rich man who died and in Hell lifted up his eyes being in torments, saw, heard, felt, was tormented, remembered, called for help. Death *never* means annihilation.

Not a single statement in the Bible is to the effect that lost people in Hell will pass out of existence and cease to suffer. Why then should Christians who believe the Bible try to found a new doctrine which has no Bible support?

Some people who would teach soul sleeping, and others who would teach annihilation of the wicked, quote Ecclesiastes 9:5. That verse says, "For the living know that they shall die: but the dead know not any thing, neither have they any more a reward; for the memory of them is forgotten."

What a strange verse! At first glance it seems to teach that "the dead know not any thing." But if you take that literally as true, then you must take the rest of the verse as true, "neither have they any more a reward." If that means annihilation for people in Hell, it also means annihilation for people in Heaven! If it proves anything there, it proves too much. To take that verse at face value, without looking further into the context, would lead one to believe that man is only a brute beast after all with no soul, no resurrection, no Heaven, no Hell, no reward, no punishment. In fact, that is what the verse plainly says! So we must look into the connecting passages and see that it is a book written by Solomon telling what he had learned by his own experience, and *not by divine revelation*. It is a book written out of human wisdom. The key phrase in the book, often repeated, is "under the sun," that is, things seen and learned by human experience on this earth alone. The *record* of this man's reasonings is divinely inspired, just as the Bible gives a divinely inspired record of what Satan said to God about Job, and to Jesus in the temptation; just as what many other men have said is recorded for us by the Holy Spirit, though God does not endorse all they say. If you will read the book of Ecclesiastes carefully you will see that it never claims that the reasonings of Solomon recorded therein are inspired. Solomon, in writing the book, never said, "Thus saith the Lord," nor "The word of the Lord came unto me saying," as occurs so many times in other parts of the Bible. No, Ecclesiastes 9:5 simply says that as far as human intellect can see, apart from divine revelation, that "the dead know not any thing, neither have they any more a reward." As far as a man can see, unaided, going only by his own experience and vision, his own wisdom, there is no Heaven, no Hell, no punishment for sin hereafter, no reward for the saints, no eternal life, no eternal death. *All these things must be received by divine inspiration!*

So God does not say that "the dead know not any thing." God simply tells us that Solomon said that, in his human wisdom. But God repeatedly tells us differently throughout the Bible.

Annihilation of the wicked is not one time taught within the pages of this holy book, God's Word!

2. *Eternal torment is always inferred, even when not stated.*

In Daniel 12:2 we are told of the two resurrections, with people being raised, "some to everlasting life, and some to shame and everlasting contempt." The inference clearly is that the shame and contempt last as long as the everlasting life. In the history of the rich man and Lazarus given by the Saviour in Luke 16:19–31, Lazarus is said to have gone directly to Heaven and the rich man directly to Hell. Abraham, talking to the rich man about Lazarus, said, "But now he is comforted and thou art tormented." The plain inference is that the eternal comfort of Lazarus in Heaven was matched by the eternal torment of the rich man in Hell. There was a great gulf between the two which could not be crossed, and the inference is that the rich man would remain in Hell as long as Lazarus would remain in Heaven.

In Revelation 21:1–8 the same contrast is given. We are told about a Heaven where God would wipe away all tears, where there would be no more death, nor sorrow, nor crying, nor pain, where all the thirsty should drink of the water of life freely, and the overcomers should inherit all things. But then it is said, in verse 8, that all the wicked "shall have their part in the lake which burneth with fire and brimstone: which is the second death." The saved have an eternal, blessed part in Heaven. The wicked have their part in the lake of fire. Since God did not say otherwise, we must infer He intended for us to believe that Hell will last as long as Heaven; that the part of the unbeliever in torment will last as long as the part of the believer in happiness.

The Bible says the wicked "shall have their *part*" in Hell. It did not say they should have annihilation. The rich man in Hell called it "this place of torment" (Luke 16:28). He did not call it the place of annihilation. The inference throughout the Bible is that Hell is a place of eternal torment.

Revelation 14:10, 11 plainly infers, yea, it almost proclaims that the torments of the doomed last forever. "And the smoke of their torment ascendeth up for ever and ever: and they have no rest day nor night," says the Word of God. In Hell there are days of torment. In Hell there are nights of despair. The torments of the lost continue and the smoke of their torment forever ascends! How wicked it is to brush aside such plain statements. Statements that infer eternal torment in Hell are so many that childlike faith must accept them; and only those who choose, because of some heresy hugged to their hearts, can deny that there is eternal torment, unending, for the sinner in Hell.

3. *All the unsaved must remain in Hell till the last judgment following their resurrection.*

"It is appointed unto men once to die, but after this the judgment" says Hebrews 9:27. God commands all men everywhere to repent "because he hath appointed a day, in the which he will judge the world in righteousness by that man [Jesus] whom he hath ordained" (Acts 17:31). It is repeatedly stated in the Bible that every knee must bow to Christ and every tongue confess to Him (Rom. 14:11, Phil.

2:10). That judgment of the unsaved dead will come after the resurrection of their bodies as is clearly taught (Dan. 12:2, John 5:28, 29). A careful description of this judgment of the unsaved is given in Revelation 20:11–15. You will note that it is after the thousand year reign of Christ on earth. There death and Hell will deliver up the dead that are in them, and the bodies of those buried at sea will come out of the sea when "the dead, small and great, stand before God." THERE-FORE ALL THE UNSAVED IN HELL CANNOT CEASE TO BE TILL AFTER THIS JUDGMENT! The coming judgment proves that the wicked in Hell cannot be annihilated for many centuries.

Now consider that the Scripture plainly teaches that the unsaved dead go immediately into torment. "The rich man also died, and was buried; and in hell he lift up his eyes, being in torments," said Jesus in Luke 16:23. Jesus said to the dying thief, "To day shalt thou be with me in paradise" (Luke 23:43). Paul said that he had a desire "to depart, and to be with Christ" (Phil. 1:23) and said that "to be absent from the body was to be present with the Lord" (II Cor. 5:8). There can be no soul sleeping, then. The lost man who dies goes immediately to Hell; the saved man who dies goes immediately to Heaven.

Consider also that Hell is now, already, a place of torment in flame, as Jesus said in Luke 16:24.

All this means that lost souls now in Hell must stay there, tormented in flame, at least until the judgment. If Cain died unsaved, as we suppose he did, then he has already been in Hell, tormented in flame for about six thousand years. Judas Iscariot has already been there for more than nineteen hundred years. And any lost man that should die today must remain in Hell, tormented in flame, until Jesus comes to take away His bride, all the saved; must stay there then through the great tribulation time until Jesus returns to reign on the earth; then must remain in Hell still through the thousand years of the millennium. Then he must be brought out to face

Christ at the last judgment and be returned again to the lake of fire!

All this shows certainly that there can be no immediate annihilation of the wicked in Hell. And if Cain, for example, has remained in Hell about six thousand years, and must remain at least another thousand years in Hell, without ceasing to be, without losing consciousness, without coming to an end of his torments, what reason is there for any sensible man to believe that he will cease to be afterward?

4. *The coming world dictator, called "the Beast," and his False Prophet, will remain in Hell alive with physical bodies a thousand years and beyond.*

In Revelation 19:11–21 we have a wonderful account of how the Lord Jesus will return from Heaven to reign on the earth. John saw it all pass before his eyes, as a vision, and it is written in the past tense, though it is yet future. We are told how the battle of Armageddon will take place and all the armies of the Antichrist or "Beast" will be slain. And then we are told John's vision of a remarkable thing will take place. "And the beast was taken, and with him the false prophet that wrought miracles before him, with which he deceived them that had received the mark of the beast, and them that worshipped his image. These both were cast alive into a lake of fire burning with brimstone" (Rev. 19:20). Here by divine revelation John was allowed to look into the future and see this future event. And he saw two men, a world dictator and his false prophet, "cast alive into a lake of fire burning with brimstone."

Now read straight on through into the twentieth chapter of Revelation. The thousand years' reign of Christ on earth begins and runs to its close. "And when the thousand years are expired" we are told that Satan will be loosed, will deceive many, and at last will be cast into Hell forever. So Revelation 20:10 says, "And the devil that deceived them was cast into the lake of fire and brimstone, *where the beast and the false prophet are*, and shall be tormented day and night for

ever and ever." AFTER A THOUSAND YEARS, THE
BEAST AND HIS FALSE PROPHET WILL STILL BE
IN HELL! This is all the more important since we are expressly told that they were cast ALIVE into the lake of fire
that burns with brimstone (Rev. 19:20). They will go to Hell
without dying. They will enter into the second death without
going through the first death. And in the second death, that
is, in Hell, they live on and on and on, tormented in that lake
of fire. And when occasion comes to mention that place
again, and when Satan will be cast into it a thousand years
later, we find that those two men are still alive, tormented,
living in their bodies in Hell! That clearly shows that even
men with resurrected bodies, after the last judgment, will remain in Hell without annihilation. They will never cease to
be. Their torment will never end.

5. *The last judgment will find all sinners in Hell still impenitent,
with none of their sins atoned for, and so must remain in Hell for ad-
ditional punishment.*

In Revelation 20:11–15 is given this account of the last
judgment of the unsaved dead:

"And I saw a great white throne, and him that sat on it,
from whose face the earth and the heaven fled away; and
there was found no place for them. And I saw the dead, small
and great, stand before God; and the books were opened:
and another book was opened, which is the book of life: and
the dead were judged out of those things which were written
in the books, according to their works. And the sea gave up
the dead which were in it; and death and hell delivered up
the dead which were in them: and they were judged every
man according to their works. And death and hell were cast
into the lake of fire. This is the second death. And whosoever
was not found written in the book of life was cast into the
lake of fire."

Here we have the striking word that the dead will be
"judged out of those things which were written in the books,

according to their works" (verse 12) and again that "they were judged (as John saw it ahead of time) every man according to their works." When Cain is dragged out of Hell, after seven thousand years, he is still to be judged "according to his works." That means his punishments will be in proportion to his sin. There are degrees of punishment in Hell. When Judas Iscariot comes to stand before God after three thousand or more years in Hell, he will still have to face all of his sins. God will open the record book and he will be judged out of the things written in his record book according to his works. This means that when a sinner comes to the judgment after long years of torment, his sins are still not paid for. He is still no nearer peace with God. He is still condemned, and all the sins he ever committed are still held against him. In the very nature of the case, that proves that sinners must remain in Hell after the judgment, to be punished according to their works.

State and national prisons are sometimes called "penitentiaries." The intention was that prison should be a place of penitence, of sorrow for sin and of reformation and repentance. If prison really should lead a man to repent, then of course he would be a better man when he came out than when he went in. But the truth is that many hardened sinners spend years in a prison without repentance. They are not penitent in heart. They do not confess their sins. They do not sorrow over them. They do not turn to God in righteousness. In such cases they continue in crime and must be returned to prison.

So it is with sinners in Hell. After centuries tormented in flames they are still impenitent rebels against God. Their hearts have not been changed. Their love for sin is the same. They have not taken a single step to make peace with God. They have not atoned for a particle of their sin. And this proves that all the punishment for sins must continue after the judgment of sinners, after their bodies are raised up to bow before Jesus, and after they are returned, both soul and body, to the lake of fire. There can be no annihilation, no passing out of existence, even after the last judgment of the unsaved dead.

In this connection we must see that since there are degrees of punishment in Hell after the resurrection of the unsaved dead, and after their judgment, then they must remain alive in a living death, in Hell. If all were simply annihilated, their punishment would be equal. But if they continue in the living death, suffering each one according to his own works, according to his own deserts, then their suffering will fit their sins.

How can punishment stop, even by annihilation, as long as sinners are still enemies of God with their sins unatoned for?

6. *We are expressly told that Satan "shall be tormented day and night for ever." This proves eternal punishment.*

Revelation 20:10 says, "And the devil that deceived them was cast into the lake of fire and brimstone, where the beast and the false prophet are, and shall be tormented day and night for ever and ever." A bit ago we discussed the part of this verse that refers to the Beast and the false prophet. Now I call your attention to the fact that it expressly says that "the devil . . . shall be tormented day and night for ever and ever." And that punishment is in "the lake of fire and brimstone," the same Hell where all lost sinners are cast. That Hell is not a place of annihilation. It is a place of eternal torment.

Every logical inference of the verse is that the Beast and the false prophet continue in the same Hell, tormented in the same flame, even along with Satan. There may be differing degrees in their punishment, but they are in the same place, and the punishment of one would naturally be expected to be as long as the other. The lake of fire and brimstone is really a place of literal, conscious, eternal torment for lost men. Who can doubt it in the face of such Scriptures?

I hope you will carefully review this chapter proving that there is no annihilation in Hell, no end to the torment in

Hell. I earnestly plead with you to consider that you cannot master in one casual reading these studies upon which I have spent months, even years of prayer and preparation, searching the Word of God. Please read this part again and remember: 1. The Bible nowhere promises, not once, that the wicked will cease to be, cease to feel, cease to suffer or will pass out of existence in Hell. 2. *Eternal* torment is always inferred where not expressly stated. 3. All sinners in Hell must remain there, tormented, until the judgment after their bodily resurrection. 4. Two particular men, the Beast or world ruler and his false prophet are plainly said to remain alive in their physical bodies in Hell for a thousand years and more. 5. When God's record books are opened at the last judgment, no sin will have been paid for, but all must, *after this judgment*, be punished "according to their works." 6. Satan "shall be tormented day and night for ever and ever"; so Hell is not a place of annihilation but of eternal torment.

Oh, brother, sister, I beg you, accept this awful fact that torment in Hell is eternal, and let us set out to save people from going to Hell!

XI

"Churches" and "The Church"

Local Congregations; When Israel Was a Church; the Mob That Was a Church; Who Is in the True Church; Why It Cannot Be Denomination. Does It Include Old Testament Saints? Was It Begun at Pentecost?

IN MODERN ENGLISH the word *church* is sometimes used about a local congregation, sometimes is used about a church house, and very, very often is used about a denomination, as "the Roman Catholic Church." In the Bible the word does not have this variety of meanings but is very simple. The New Testament was written in Greek and the Greek word for church is *ekklesia*. Always in the Bible the word *church* means "a called-out assembly" or "called-out ones." The word is used in the Bible for many different called-out assemblies, sometimes Christians, sometimes not; sometimes on earth, sometimes in Heaven. But it always means a called-out group. The word *church* in the Bible never refers to a denomination. The Catholic denomination is not a church, nor the Baptist denomination, nor any other. The word *church* never means a group of churches. In the Bible the word *church* is used in the following ways: (1) It is used of Israel in the wilderness before Mount Sinai. (2) It is used to designate a mob of idolaters at Ephesus. (3) It is used for local assemblies of Christians, or congregations. (4) The word *church* in the Bible sometimes refers to that great assembly of Christians to be called out at the second coming to meet Christ in the air and to be assembled in Heaven.

I. Israel at Mount Sinai Was a Church

The word *church* is used of Israel in the wilderness before Mount Sinai. Acts 7:38 says:

"This is he, that was in the church in the wilderness with the angel which spake to him in the Mount Sina, and with our fathers: who received the lively oracles to give unto us."

Israel was really a called-out group, called out of Egypt and assembled in the wilderness, and was literally a church. The same Greek word *ekklesia* is used as it is used everywhere else in the Bible. This called-out assembly, most of them quite certainly unbelievers since practically all of them died in the wilderness for their sins, was yet a church. The word translated "church" throughout the Bible simply means a called-out assembly.

We call attention to this verse of Scripture to help you get the Bible meaning of the word *church*. Do not be afraid of anything that is in the Bible. Israel at Mount Sinai: saved, lost, grown folks, young people and babies, were all called a church by the Word of God. That was not a Christian church, but it was a church, a called-out assembly.

II. The Mob of Idolaters at Ephesus

The Greek word *ekklesia*, translated "church" everywhere else in the Bible, is also used to designate a mob of idolaters at Ephesus. In Acts 19, verses 32, 39 and 41, the word *assembly* is really a translation of the Greek word *ekklesia*, usually used for *church*. That mob, called out by Demetrius to do away with Paul, Gaius and Aristarchus, was a called-out assembly and therefore a church. Check up in Young's Analytical Concordance, or the Greek New Testament, and see that the word *assembly* in these verses is translated from *ekklesia*, the Greek word everywhere used for *church*. A called-out assembly is a church.

This mob at Ephesus was not a church of believers in Christ, not a church of Christians, but nevertheless, in the language of the Bible, it was a church. In the English translation the word is *assembly*, but it should have been translated *church*, as the same word is so translated *in every other single case in the Bible except these three times* in Acts 19:32–41. If we read into the word *church* more than the Bible means by the word, then we fail to understand the Bible teaching on the subject. It is interesting that in the same chapter is the only case in the Bible where any word is wrongly translated church. "Robbers of churches" in verse 37 is a single word in the Greek language, meaning, "robbers of temples" and has no connection with the word *church* whatever. The translators had already begun to use the word *church* for a church building and so made this mistake. In the Bible the word *church* never means a building but simply *a called-out assembly*.

III. Local Congregations of Christians Are Churches

The most common use of the word *church* in the New Testament is of local assemblies of Christians or congregations. We are told about "the churches of Galatia" (Gal. 1:2), "the seven churches which are in Asia" (Rev. 1:4), etc. Every local congregation of Christians was a called-out assembly. About ninety times in the New Testament the word *church* means a local congregation of Christians. It is important to note that a called-out assembly of Christians was a church whether they had pastors or deacons or not, whether there was any church roll or not, having church covenant or articles of faith or not having them. The word *church* means a called-out assembly. Many times it referred to called-out assemblies of Christians.

"Church" Means One Congregation, Not Many

Be sure to notice that a local congregation of Christians was never called *a part* of the church. Speaking of different congregations of Christians, the Bible always uses the plural term *churches,* not the singular term *the church.* The Holy Spirit did not speak of "the church" in the province of Galatia, but of "the churches of Galatia." He did not speak of "the church" in the cities of Asia, but of the seven "churches" of Asia. Every local congregation is a separate church, and these congregations are never put together to form one body called a church in Bible terminology. A group of churches forming a denomination does not make one large church. They are still churches. In Bible times they did have local churches, but they did not have a denomination. The local assemblies were churches. Had there been a denomination, it would NOT have been a church in the Bible sense, a called-out assembly.

For example, it is thoroughly unscriptural to say, "I joined the Baptist church." There are many Baptist churches but no such thing as "THE BAPTIST CHURCH," referring to the whole group of Baptists. One joins a particular Baptist church, not a whole system or denomination of Baptists. A church is a called-out assembly, not a denomination.

Of course one may join a denomination. If so, it would be proper to say, "I joined the Methodist denomination." Or it would be proper to say of a local congregation, "I joined Grace Methodist Church." A denomination is not a church and a church is not a denomination, in the Bible sense. Our modern use of the term in this matter is not Scriptural.

A local assembly of Christians is a church in the Bible use of the term, irrespective of its doctrine or organization. The Bible clearly gives the doctrines that New Testament churches ought to teach and the practices they ought to follow. But New Testament churches which were wrong in doctrine and practice were still called churches. For instance, the church at Corinth had the tongues heresy, some of the members got drunk at the Lord's Supper, and they were guilty of many hurtful divisions. Yet they were called "the church of God which is at Corinth." The local congregations or called-out assemblies of Christians in the province of Galatia went far wrong in doctrine and were very much like Seventh Day Adventists, teaching salvation by the law instead of by grace. Yet they were called "the churches of Galatia." For that reason it is foolish to claim that only the congregations of your own denomination are churches. Some Baptists say that Methodist congregations are not churches. Others with the same denominational vanity are sometimes guilty of the same sin. But if Israel at Mount Sinai was a church, if the mob at Ephesus was a church, and if the Christian congregations of the New Testament were churches, in spite of their false doctrine, then any congregation of Christians is a church in the Bible sense.

IV. The Body of Christ, Including All Christians, Is a Church

The word *church* in the Bible sometimes refers to that great assembly of Christians to be called out at the second coming to meet Christ in the air and to be assembled in Heaven. Hebrews 12:22, 23, plainly says that this great assembly of the spirits of just men made perfect, who will be gathered in the presence of an innumerable company of angels and of Christ, is a church. It will be a called-out assembly and therefore literally a church in the Bible sense. This certainly does not refer to any human denomination but refers to all the saved.

Hebrews 12:22, 23 says:

"But ye are come unto mount Sion, and unto the city of the living God, the heavenly Jerusalem, and to an innumerable company of angels, TO THE GENERAL ASSEMBLY AND CHURCH OF THE FIRSTBORN, which are written in heaven, and to God the Judge of all, and to the spirits of just men made perfect."

Here the inspired apostle tells Christians that they must face now, not Mount Sinai and the whole assemblage of Israel gathered there when the law was given, but a far greater assemblage in Heaven. That Heavenly assembly of "the spirits of just men made perfect," the "general assembly and church of the firstborn, which are written in heaven," will be a church. It will be a called-out assembly, will be made up of all the saved called out of the world to meet Jesus in the air and then assembled in Heaven.

First Thessalonians 4:16, 17 tells about how this assembly will be called out to meet Christ in the air and that it will include both the Christian dead and Christians then living.

"For the Lord himself shall descend from heaven with a shout, with the voice of the archangel, and with the trump of God: and the dead in Christ shall rise first: then we which are alive and remain shall be caught up together with them in the clouds, to meet the Lord in the air: and so shall we ever be with the Lord."

First Corinthians 15:51, 52 tells in different words part of the same story:

"Behold, I shew you a mystery; we shall not all sleep, but we shall all be changed, in a moment, in the twinkling of an eye, at the last trump: for the trumpet shall sound, and the dead shall be raised incorruptible, and we shall be changed."

Old Testament Saints, With All Other Christians, in This Church

Taking the passages quoted above at face value, we can see that all the saved will be in the rapture at the second coming of Christ. First Thessalonians 4:16 says that "the dead in Christ shall rise first." Not part of the Christian dead but all the dead in Christ will be in that rapture. Verse 17 adds, "Then we which are alive and remain shall be caught up together with them . . ." Not part of the Christians who remain alive, but all of them who remain alive, will be caught up to meet Christ in the air and will be in this called-out group which will be assembled in Heaven.

First Corinthians 15:51, 52, is even more positive in stating that every Christian will be changed, glorified, with resurrection bodies, at this time. Notice two statements given there, "We shall not all sleep, but we shall ALL be changed," and "the dead shall be raised incorruptible, and we shall be changed." Every person who has ever been saved will be changed and given a resurrection body when Christ comes for

His saints; first the Christian dead and then the Christian living. Then all together will be caught up in the air to meet Christ and will be assembled at the heavenly Jerusalem.

That heavenly assembly, then, is called in Hebrews 12:23, quoted above, "the general assembly and church of the first-born, which are written in heaven." That great gathering is properly called by the Scriptures a church since it is a called-out assembly.

Remember that this assembly is not made up of local congregations of Christians. The unit here is the individual Christian. For example, Judas Iscariot was a member of a local congregation, but being unsaved he certainly will not be in this assembly in Heaven. On the other hand, Abraham was not a member of any local congregation of Christians, but since he is one of the dead in Christ, and the Scriptures tell us that "the dead in Christ shall rise first," then Abraham will be in that heavenly assembly, that church of the firstborn, as will every other Christian saved up to that time. That church or heavenly assembly will not be made up of any one denomination nor of all the denominations, but of individual saved souls, without respect as to whether they were members of any local congregation or church. No denomination is that church, though many claim to be. No denomination is a branch of that church. No local congregation is a branch of that church. Every saved person is counted a member of that church which will be assembled in Heaven at the second coming of Christ.

That "General Assembly and Church" Now Being Formed as the Body of Christ

To distinguish between that Heavenly assembly and other churches, Ephesians 1:22, 23 calls it "the church, which is his body." Colossians 1:18 says that Christ "is the head of the body, the church." As you read the Bible with an open mind, it becomes clear that Christ is now forming or building that body which will be called out at His second coming. Although this body is not yet assembled in Heaven, called out physically from this earth, yet they are all a part of the same "body of Christ." And God's Word, looking forward to the rapture, calls this body a church.

In Matthew 16:18 Jesus said, "Upon this rock I will build my church; and the gates of hell shall not prevail against it." The term "will build" would be more clearly translated "will be building." Jesus did not say that at a particular date He would "organize" or "institute" or "found" or "begin" His church. Local congregations are founded, organized, instituted or begun; but that is not what Jesus was talking about here. His apostles were already called out and assembled with Him in a local congregation, and He did not here refer to that or any other local congregation, but to that body, the church, which will be called out at the rapture. Jesus said here in effect that He would be building or forming this body or church until the time it was called out. If you will keep clearly in mind that the word *church* never means denomination or group of congregations, then it will not be hard to see what Jesus meant here.

Jesus is building that church today. First Corinthians 12:12, 13 tells us that every Christian has been baptized (buried) into this body.

"For as the body is one, and hath many members, and all the members of that one body, being many, are one body: so also is Christ. For by one Spirit are we all baptized into one body, whether we be Jews or Gentiles, whether we be bond or free; and have been all made to drink into one Spirit."

When the Holy Spirit regenerates a sinner so that he is "born of the Spirit," the same Holy Spirit then buries this newborn Christian into the body of Christ. Baptism is a burial. When people are baptized in water, we expect them to come out of the water. But when the Christian is baptized into this body of Christ, he is sealed in there by the Holy Spirit and becomes a part of that body. Thus Christ is building His church by the addition of new converts as "lively stones."

First Peter 2:4, 5, tells how people come to Christ, the living Stone, and are built up as lively stones into a spiritual house:

"To whom coming, as unto a living stone, disallowed indeed of men, but chosen of God, and precious, ye, also, as lively stones, are built up a spiritual house."

This spiritual house is the church or body which Christ is building now and the gates of Hell shall not prevail against it. Ephesians 2:19–22 tells us how the saints at Ephesus are built into this "spiritual house," "household of God," "building" and "holy temple."

"Now therefore ye are no more strangers and foreigners, but fellow citizens with the saints, and of the household of God; and are built upon the foundation of the apostles and prophets, Jesus Christ himself being the chief corner stone; in whom all the building fitly framed together groweth unto an holy temple in the Lord: in whom ye also are builded together for an habitation of God through the Spirit."

Notice that the same language is used here as in Matthew 16:18. Jesus said there, "I will build my church." Here we are told that the saints "are built," and then we are told that the "building" "groweth unto an holy temple." Christ is now building this church or body which will be called out at the rapture and assembled in Heaven. Every saved person is a member of this body. This is a precious truth. It does not pander to denominational pride and vanity but tends toward Christian love and fellowship for all the children of God.

Only One Body, Not Two

Some people believe that that heavenly assembly will include two different groups of people, two separate bodies, one body to be the bride of Christ, and another body to be guests at the wedding. Such people usually believe that those of their own denomination and name will be the "bride" and that saved people of other faiths will be "guests" but not equal to the bride. This is a vain and hurtful teaching which is not anywhere taught in the Word of God but is born of denominational pride.

The Scripture expressly states that there is only one body. Ephesians 4:4 says:

"There is one body, and one Spirit, even as ye are called in one hope of your calling."

That body is mentioned many, many times in the Scripture but always in the singular. There is but one "body of Christ." There will be just one assembly of the saved in Heaven when Christ comes and receives His saints. Do not think there will be a line between your denomination and others at that time. There will not. Do not think there will be a separation between you and Old Testament saints at that time. There will not! There is one body and only one and that includes all the saved.

Sometimes the rapture of the saints, caught up to meet Christ in the air, is illustrated in the Scripture by a wedding. But when the wedding guests are mentioned, the bride is never mentioned (Matt. 22:1–14). When the bridesmaids are mentioned, no bride is mentioned (Matt. 25:1–13). In Ephesians 5:23–33 the relation of husband and wife is likened unto the relation between Christ and His church, but there no other group is mentioned. It takes many illustrations to picture the glory that will be ours when we see Jesus. But these illustrations do not mean that we will be divided into separate bodies as a bride, bridesmaids, guests and servants. For example, Jesus is mentioned as "the Lamb of God," "the Lion of the tribe of Juda," "the bright and morning star," "the root and the offspring of David," etc. But all these refer to the same Christ, not different Christs. So all the illustrations of Christians at the rapture refer to one body.

"When Was the Church Founded?"

Many people are greatly concerned over the question of when the church was founded, organized, instituted, originated, or begun. They argue much about it, and yet the Bible never says one word on the subject of the date! All the trouble is caused by misunderstanding the word *church*. If you mean this body of Christ which Jesus is now building, then it was never founded or organized. It did not begin at Pentecost. It is not a human organization, so it never needed to be organized. Jesus is building it and that is enough. He does not even tell us in the Bible when He began building it. Since Adam will be in it, if he was saved outside the Garden of Eden, then we suppose that Jesus began building this body when He saved the first man. But since the Bible does not set a time as the birthday of the church and makes no issue about it whatever, we will do well to follow the Bible example. The date of "the founding of the church" is unimportant anyway, unless you are seeking to prove that the church Jesus mentioned is your own particular human denomination. It is enough to believe what Jesus expressly stated, that He is building that body and it will be complete at the rapture of the saints. After that, people saved on earth during the tribulation period, and Jews saved after we return with Christ to reign on the earth, will be saved and on an equal basis with others saved before, but they will not be called out to meet Christ in the air and so will not be a part of the church.

Notice carefully that the Bible never refers to the church as a body after the assembly in Heaven. When we come back to reign on the earth, we will no more be a called-out assembly, a church. Then we will be a kingdom, not a church.

I hope it has become clear from this study that, scripturally, local congregations are churches and that all the saved who will meet Christ in the air form an entirely separate body, the church and body of Christ. Denominations are not churches in any Bible sense.

Never use the word *church*, then, about a denomination. If you say "the Roman Catholic church," or "the Methodist church," you should remember that you use the term as an accommodation to modern usage and not at all in the Bible sense. Actually, there are many local churches, but no denomination is that; and in the Bible the word *church* is never used about denominations.

The world has been cursed by the example and teaching of Roman Catholicism in many ways. The Roman Catholic idea of a great human denomination and organization which is to be the bride of Christ, is an utterly false idea. They claim that their human organization, heading up in the Pope, is the bride and body of Christ. Episcopalians, copying them, claim their denomination is the bride of Christ, the true church. Churches of Christ, or Disciples, sometimes make the same claim. Baptists sometimes very foolishly claim that the Baptist denomination, made up of Baptist churches, is the bride of Christ. That is using the word *church* as Roman Catholics do in a wholly unscriptural sense. Remember that the Bible teaches that Roman Catholicism would be the mother of religious abominations in the earth (Rev. 17:5). To teach that some denomination is the church of Christ appeals to human vanity and pride, but it is utterly untrue to the Scriptures.

The Church, the Body of Christ, Was Not Born at Pentecost

Smith's Bible Dictionary sums up the belief of many when it says, "Just as the appearance of God on Mount Sinai was the birthday of the Jewish nation, so was Pentecost the birthday of the Christian Church" (article "Pentecost"). But in this case *Smith's Bible Dictionary* is mistaken, as I think I can show. Dr. Smith had in mind that the church, the body of Christ, was an organization, which it is not. That viewpoint is natural for a Church of England man, but is not Scriptural.

The notes in the Scofield Bible seem to take for granted that the church was founded at Pentecost; but that view is based upon a false conception of what the church is. For instance, Dr. Scofield's note on I Timothy 3:15 says, "Church (visible), Summary: The passages under this head (I Cor. 10:32; I Tim. 3:15), refer to that visible body of professed believers called, collectively, 'the Church,' of which history takes account as such, though it exists under many names and divisions based upon differences in doctrine or in government."

This idea that denominations are branches of the church

and that "that visible body of professed believers," or any other visible group is called "the church" in the Bible is utterly wrong. What popes and bishops and denominational leaders down through the centuries have organized and called historically "the church," is never called the church in the Bible.

Where did the idea start that the church was born at Pentecost? It grew out of this unscriptural conception of the church. If there was a denomination, it had to be organized. If the church and body and bride of Christ is what Catholics mean by those terms, then of course it would have to have an origin and its birth would be a public matter, a historical matter.

But the word *ekklesia* literally means a called-out assembly. It does not mean an "organized" assembly. That word translated "church" in Acts 7:38, "the church in the wilderness," referring to Israel in the wilderness, pictured an unorganized and motley group. Israel was a "called-out assembly" as soon as they gathered outside of Egypt. It did not take Mount Sinai nor the Mosaic law, nor consecration nor ceremony to make them into a called-out assembly. So Israel in the wilderness is called in the Bible, a church.

In Acts 19, verses 32, 39, and 41, that idolatrous mob, called together by Demetrius, the silversmith, to murder Paul, is called an "assembly," in both the King James and Revised versions. But in the Greek it is really the word for church, *ekklesia*. That mob, called out against the preaching of the gospel, was a called-out assembly, a church in literal Bible language. For in every other chapter in the New Testament but this one, the word *ekklesia* is always translated "church."

That shows that a church does not need to be organized or founded or born in order to be a church. It is simply a called-out assembly.

A local congregation of Christians called together is a church.

Israel in the wilderness, called out of Egypt, is a church.

A howling mob called together at Ephesus is a church.

And so all the saints of God, all those who were ever born again, whose names are written in Heaven, will at the rapture constitute a church. Literally then, the saints of God will be a called-out assembly, meeting in the heavenly Jerusalem.

Note these reasons why the church could not have been founded at Pentecost, as many people believe.

1. In all the discussions in the New Testament about Pentecost and what happened then, not a single word is said about the church being born then. Such an idea is not mentioned in the twenty-fourth chapter of Luke where Jesus commanded the disciples to "Tarry ye in the city of Jerusalem, until ye be endued with power from on high." The idea of the birth or origin of a church is not mentioned in the first chapter of Acts where Jesus "commanded them that they should not depart from Jerusalem, but wait for the promise of the Father, which, saith he, ye have heard of me . . . ye shall be baptized with the Holy Ghost not many days hence" (Acts 1:4, 5).

The second chapter of Acts, which tells in such glowing detail the happenings of that glorious day when the Holy Spirit came upon the people and they were all filled with the Holy Ghost and three thousand people were added to the church— that chapter does not even hint at the origin of a church.

References to Pentecost in Acts 11:15–17 and in Hebrews 2:4 do not hint that the church was founded at Pentecost.

2. The instructions of Jesus to His disciples long before Pentecost, that if the erring brother would not hear two or three who come to reprove and intreat, that they should "tell it unto the church: but if he neglect to hear the church, let him be unto thee as an heathen man and a publican" (Matt. 18:17), indicate that the local group of called-out disciples was recognized as a church long before Pentecost. If there was a church at Pentecost, it was, of course, a local group, but it was not the *first* time the group was called a church. Even the local church at Jerusalem was not founded at Pentecost.

3. The universal church, composed of all believers, the

body and bride of Christ, could not have been born at Pentecost because of its very nature. First, that body of Christ is slowly building. It "groweth unto an holy temple," the Scripture says (Eph. 2:21). Christ in the Greek text said literally, "I will be building my church." Every new convert is like a stone laid upon a wall, covered with mortar and with other stones, and so buried or baptized into the body. "Ye also, as lively stones, are built up a spiritual house, an holy priesthood, to offer up spiritual sacrifices, acceptable to God by Jesus Christ" (I Pet. 2:5). A house is not born; it is builded. And Christ is building His church. What is the origin of a house? Is it when the first stone is laid or when the house is finished? If it is when the first stone is prepared, then the first soul ever saved in the world was the origin of the church. If it is when the house is finished, then it will be at the rapture when all the saints of God are called out "unto the city of the living God, the heavenly Jerusalem, and to an innumerable company of angels, to the general assembly and church of the firstborn, which are written in heaven . . ." (Heb. 12:22, 23). The material for this called-out assembly began to be prepared with the first soul saved, whether Adam or Abel. (I think it was Adam.) But the church will not be literally called out until the rapture. To put artificially a birth date for the body and bride of Christ anywhere between the beginning and the end is unscriptural. Pentecost was not the birth date of the church.

4. The fourth proof that the church was not born at Pentecost is the serious misapplication of Scripture which people must make in trying to prove it. Note the weakness of the proof. First, they think of the church, the body of Christ, as a human, visible, earthly organization, with the denominations as "branches of the church." This is a wholly unscriptural idea, which was adopted from the Catholic position thoughtlessly. But with that idea of an organization with human officers, people try to find a starting place. Peter preached at Pentecost; and Catholics say that Peter was given

the keys of Heaven and could let people in or keep them out, that Peter is the first pope of the Catholic church and that their church, which they call the *true* church, so began at Pentecost. Then other denominations which sprang from the Catholics claim to be branches of the true church, so they also claim that the church began at Pentecost. With that background, they look for Scripture to prove it. And all they find is I Corinthians 12:13 which says, "For by one Spirit are we all baptized into one body, whether we be Jews or Gentiles, whether we be bond or free; and have been all made to drink into one Spirit." Jesus promised that at Pentecost the disciples would be baptized with the Holy Spirit (Acts 1:5). This verse (I Cor. 12:13) says that "By one Spirit are we all baptized into one body." So people who already want an earthly organization founded at Pentecost, teach that this means that at Pentecost everybody who would ever be saved, was "symbolically" or "legally" or "potentially" baptized into the body of Christ.

How foolish is this interpretation! Actually, I Corinthians 12:13 has no reference whatever to Pentecost or to what happened there. This interpretation confuses two entirely separate things. At Pentecost, Jesus Himself poured out the Holy Spirit to cover (and so baptize), and fill the disciples with soul-winning power. That was the meaning of Pentecost (Luke 24:49; Acts 1:8). But when souls are saved, the Holy Spirit takes new converts and buries them into this body like stones built into a wall, and they become a part of the body of Christ. Christ baptizing one already saved in the Holy Spirit for soul-winning power, is an entirely different thing from the Holy Spirit placing new converts into the body of Christ.

Paul wrote to the church at Corinth and said in effect, "All of us have been placed by the Holy Spirit in the body of Christ when we were saved, and the Holy Spirit has come into our bodies to stay." He was speaking of the time when each one was saved and he had no reference to Pentecost.

Nor is there a single verse in the Bible that teaches that the church was formed at Pentecost.

After the doctrine is formed, then people find, they think, a symbolical meaning in the wave-loaves of the Jewish Old Testament Pentecost, which seems to them to picture the church, though the Scripture never gives it that meaning.

The artificial division between New Testament saints and Old Testament saints which is made by so many modern Bible teachers is contrary to the Scriptures. Salvation has been the same in all ages. People were saved by exactly the same gospel in the Old Testament times, then under the preaching of John the Baptist, then in the personal ministry of Christ, and later in the book of Acts and in the times after Pentecost. And when Jesus comes for His bride, to call out all of the redeemed, He will get all His church. The called-out assembly, the *ekklesia*, will include every person who ever trusted Christ in any age.

How important that we remember, then, that we are blood brothers to every born-again one, every child of God. Denominational differences may be matters of sincere and honest conviction. But they must never keep us from feeling that every born-again child of God is a brother or sister beloved, a fellow member with us of the body of Christ and to be lovingly regarded as a member of the household of faith.

Dear reader, if you are a converted, born-again Christian, I hope you are a member of a congregation of Christians, a local church which is true to the Bible and true to Christ, "Not forsaking the assembling of ourselves together, as the manner of some is" (Heb. 10:25). But oh, I beg you, make sure you are born again and so, having trusted Christ alone for salvation, are a member of His body, that "church of the firstborn" which will be assembled in Heaven. I will be there because I have trusted Christ as my own Saviour. Can you say you too will be there?

XII

Jesus May Come Today!

"*Watch therefore: for ye know not what hour your Lord doth come.*"—Matt. 24:42.

"*Therefore be ye also ready: for in such an hour as ye think not the Son of man cometh.*"—Matt. 24:44.

"*Watch therefore, for ye know neither the day nor the hour wherein the Son of man cometh.*"—Matt. 25:13.

"*Take ye heed, watch and pray: for ye know not when the time is.*"—Mark 13:33.

"*Watch ye therefore: for ye know not when the master of the house cometh, at even, or at midnight, or at the cockcrowing, or in the morning: lest coming suddenly he find you sleeping. And what I say unto you I say unto all, Watch.*"—Mark 13:35-37.

"*Be ye therefore ready also: for the Son of man cometh at an hour when ye think not.*"—Luke 12:40.

"*Behold, the judge standeth before the door.*"— James 5:9.

"*Behold, I come quickly.*"—Rev. 22:7.

"*The time is at hand.*"—Rev. 22:10.

"*And, behold, I come quickly.*"—Rev. 22:12.

"*He which testifieth these things saith, Surely I come quickly. Amen. Even so, come, Lord Jesus.*"— Rev. 22:20.

YES, JESUS may come today! The coming of Christ to the earth is imminent: it may occur any moment, day or night!

There is not a single event prophesied in the Bible which must come to pass before the Saviour returns. As far as we can know, no event, either political, economic or spiritual, need occur before Jesus comes. Not another war need be declared, not another gospel sermon preached, not another soul be saved, as far as can be told from the Scriptures, before the Saviour comes to catch up His saints into the air for the marriage supper in Heaven.

And I do not mean that signs of the Saviour's coming show that it is likely to be soon. Some say that Jesus must come soon because the little modern nation Israel is established in Palestine. I do not believe that is the restoration of Israel promised in the Bible. I do not believe one can tell from that even approximately when Jesus will come. I do not believe that wars, earthquakes, dictatorships, communism, or modernism are signs that Christ will come at any predictable time or within any given generation. My conviction is that we should look for Christ's coming simply because He said to look for His coming.

We should not look for Christ's coming because of meteor shower or because of numerals found in the Bible and mistakenly applied to reckon when Christ will return. The Millerites went wrong on that in 1842. We should not presume that with a tape measure we can measure a passage in the great pyramid in Egypt and, making an inch mean a year, find when Jesus will come. British-Israelites were made a laughing stock by that false premise nearly twenty years ago. I know one who thus set a date for Christ's return and is now a scoffing infidel. No, let us stop looking in the newspapers for signs of Christ's coming and simply believe Christ may come at any moment because He said so.

At any moment we may expect Christians to be caught up

into the air to meet Christ in the first promised phase of His second coming. We do not know when. We bring reproach on the blessed hope by speculations, but we can watch because Jesus said we should.

The Scriptures quoted above do not discuss any signs that might precede the coming of Christ but rather the fact that He may come at any moment. The Scriptures teach that *Jesus might have come at any moment since He went away!* Jesus Himself taught the apostles and all the Christians then living that He might return in their lifetime. They were commanded and entreated earnestly to watch and pray since they knew not the day nor the hour when the Son of man should return. At Pentecost the promised pouring out of the Holy Spirit upon the apostles took place and they began their witness for Christ. Since that day there has never been a moment but what Christians ought to have expected Jesus to return as He most certainly might have done.

All these Scriptures quoted above show that the coming of the Lord *might have been at any time* from Pentecost on until now. There is not one single sign for which Christians have needed to wait before they should expect the return of the Saviour. And not one single event has occurred or will occur definitely enough that any person can know the day or hour of His return.

I. Christ's Imminent Return Clearly Stated By Christ Himself

The Bible is full of teaching about the second coming of Christ and related events. Those of us who take the Bible literally and believe it all and are therefore premillennialists, expecting the literal, bodily, physical return of Christ and His reign upon earth as foretold in the Scriptures, have much to preach. We have the great themes of the resurrection; the rapture or meeting Christ in the air; the judgment seat of Christ; the great tribulation; the man of sin, or Antichrist; the glorious return of Christ with saints and angels; the battle

of Armageddon; the restoration of the Jews to Palestine; the
judgment of the living nations; the millennial reign of Christ
on David's throne, etc. All these matters ought to be preached
for they are clearly taught in the Bible. But, very strangely,
we often neglect the greatest theme in connection with the
Saviour's coming, and that is that His coming is imminent,
and that every Christian is commanded to watch! watch!
watch! for no man knows the day nor hour when He shall
come.

Whatever Jesus taught about His second coming, the point
of His message was always this: that His coming is to be sudden, unexpected, and surprising so that every Christian should
be ready for His coming at any moment.

In the twenty-fourth chapter of Matthew, after thirty-five
verses concerned with the second coming, then Jesus said,
"But of that day and hour knoweth no man, no, not the angels
of heaven, but my Father only."

From verses 36 to 51, the last sixteen verses of the same
chapter, Jesus earnestly urges the unexpectedness and imminence of His coming. In verse 42 He says, "Watch therefore: for ye know not what hour your Lord doth come."
And in verse 44 He says, "Therefore be ye also ready: for in
such an hour as ye think not the Son of man cometh."

The angels do not know when Jesus will return. Jesus Himself, while in the flesh, did not know when He would return
as He Himself said in Mark 13:32.

Then in Mark 13:33 He said, "Take ye heed, watch and
pray: for ye know not when the time is."

And in Mark 13:37 He repeats again His warning, saying:
"And what I say unto you I say unto all, Watch."

In Matthew 25:13 Jesus closes the parable of the ten virgins,
saying: "Watch therefore, for ye know neither the day nor
the hour wherein the Son of man cometh."

In Luke 12:40, after warning Christians that they should be
"like unto men that wait for their Lord," telling them "And
if he shall come in the second watch, or come in the third

watch, and find them so, blessed are those servants" (Luke 12:38), and next reminding them how a man should be constantly watching lest the thief should break in and steal (vs. 39), then Jesus said, "Be ye therefore ready also: for the Son of man cometh at an hour when ye think not."

Only one honest meaning is possible in these Scriptures: Jesus may come today!

If the Bible is a trustworthy book, then Jesus might have returned even in the lifetime of these New Testament Christians, He might have returned any time during the centuries since then, or He may return now at any moment. If the Father Himself has set the time, then He has not revealed it even to the angels and certainly not to any man. He may come today. There is no other possible meaning to these Scriptures.

He has put no promised event before the Saviour's coming. There are no Scriptures yet to be fulfilled before Jesus comes, and we are commanded plainly, repeatedly, insistently to watch for His coming.

If you do not believe that the coming of Christ is imminent, then you make Christ Himself a deceiver. It would have been cruel and insincere for Jesus to have all the apostles and New Testament Christians earnestly watching for His return if it were already a settled fact that He could not return for thousands of years. No, the words of Jesus were true words, and they are as good today for us as they were the day they were uttered to the apostles. Jesus may come this very day, yea, this very hour. We may hear the sound of the trumpet and may feel ourselves suddenly changed and caught up to meet the Lord in the air where we will be gathered with the saints of all ages and carried to the Father's house of many mansions while the unsaved are left on a wicked world, turned over to sin and to the man of sin until we shall return with Christ to reign. Today I may see Jesus! Today I may see my mother, my father, my baby brothers! Today I may enter into the reward of my labors. Today I may lay down my burdens, lay down my sorrows, lay down my weaknesses, lay down my disappointments, lay down my frail, sinful body! Today I may be clothed upon with a glorious body like that of our Saviour! Oh! today I may see Jesus and report and bring in my sheaves rejoicing, and kiss His dear feet! May God grant that I will not be ashamed before Him at His coming but that I may be watching with my lamp trimmed and burning when I hear the great shout, "Behold, the bridegroom cometh; go ye out to meet him!" Jesus may come this very day! Hallelujah!

II. His Imminent Second Coming Illustrated By Jesus

How precious this doctrine is to the Saviour and how important to His disciples we can see by the way He repeated it and illustrated it. Notice the illustrations the Saviour gave.

1. The second coming will be like the flood in the days of Noah. Jesus said:

"*But as the days of Noe were, so shall also the coming of the Son of man be. For as in the days that were before the flood they were eating and drinking, marrying and giving in marriage, until the day that Noe entered into the ark, and knew not until the flood came, and took them all away; so shall also the coming of the Son of man be.*"—Matt. 24:37-39.

The fact of the coming flood had been clearly foretold. For one hundred years Noah had been building an ark and preparing for the flood. You may be sure that everybody in the inhabited portion of the earth knew of God's warning. You could no more keep the ark a secret than if in the Panhandle of Texas or in the mountains of Arkansas men should work for a hundred years building a ship like the Titanic or the Queen Mary! Noah's preaching "got over." Yet the people did not know *when* the flood would come. They did not believe it. Noah himself did not know when. The Lord gave no definite date. Noah went into the ark when he was commanded, and God shut the door. Even then the flood did not come for seven days. There were no preceding signs by which they could be sure of the exact date of the threatened deluge, even if they had believed it was coming, so the men of that age "were eating and drinking, marrying and giving in marriage, until the day that Noe entered into the ark." That is the way it will be, the Saviour says, when He comes. People will be as unprepared and His coming will be as sudden and unexpected.

2. The Saviour's coming is likened to the coming of the bridegroom whose bridesmaids have been waiting until far into the night (Matt. 25:1-13). Some of the bridesmaids had no oil and expected their dry wicks to burn until he came, but their lamps went out. All of them, the wise and the foolish, those with the oil of salvation and those with only the lamps of profession, "slumbered and slept." And then at midnight His coming was so sudden and unexpected that those who had no oil did not have time to secure it but were left without and missed the wedding.

And so there could be no doubt of His meaning, for the closing verse of the parable says,

"*Watch therefore, for ye know neither the day nor the hour wherein the Son of man cometh.*"

The point of the parable of the ten virgins is this, that the coming of Jesus is imminent. He may come today, so therefore be ready.

The virgins knew the bridegroom was coming, but just when, they did not know. He might have returned at once. They ought to have been ready at any moment.

It is strange that people would so pervert the Scriptures as to miss the very heart of the Saviour's teaching here. Yet a few years ago the story of the ten virgins was given in the International Sunday School Lessons but only the first twelve verses were printed. The thirteenth verse where Jesus gives the conclusion and lesson of the parable was omitted entirely in the Sunday School quarterlies that I saw. The Saviour's second coming was not even mentioned! The parable of the ten virgins is not simply a lesson on preparedness. It is a lesson on preparedness—not for usefulness, not even for death primarily—*but preparedness for the second coming of Christ.* The lesson is that Jesus may come at any moment, so watch and be ready!

3. The second coming is as imminent as a master returning to his home after a long journey. Jesus used this illustration more than once. In Matthew 24:45–47 Jesus said:

"Who then is a faithful and wise servant, whom his lord hath made ruler over his household, to give them meat in due season? Blessed is that servant, whom his lord when he cometh shall find so doing. Verily I say unto you, That he shall make him ruler over all his goods."

The return of such a master is imminent. That is, he ought to be expected at any moment, and it is a faithful and wise servant who earnestly does his duty day by day looking forward to his master's return.

But there are those who say that "my Lord delayeth His coming," and that we ought not to expect Him momentarily now. For such the Saviour continued the same parable in verses 48–51 as follows:

"But and if that evil servant shall say in his heart, My lord delayeth his coming; and shall begin to smite his fellowservants, and to eat and drink with the drunken; the lord of that servant shall come in a day when he looketh not for him, and in an hour that he is not aware of, and shall cut him asunder, and appoint him his portion with the hypocrites: there shall be weeping and gnashing of teeth."

This is a picture, perhaps, of an unsaved one. But the unsaved are as much accountable to Jesus as the saved. All a sinner has he gets from God, and he must give an account to the Lord Jesus Christ whether he loves Him or not. This world belongs to Jesus Christ and one day He is going to claim it. Meantime, all who read this had better be ready for Jesus to come for they shall certainly have to give an account for their stewardship even if they have not been converted.

And what a sad teaching this is! Don't you see that one who says in his heart, "My lord delayeth his coming," is not right in his heart? He is not anxious for Jesus to come, perhaps is not willing for Jesus to come, and therefore does not watch. This Scripture indicates that it is always unbelief and sin that keeps one from eagerly watching for Jesus to come.

Jesus taught the same matter in Mark 13:34 37, and verse 35 says, "Watch ye therefore: for ye know not when the master of the house cometh, at even, or at midnight, or at the cockcrowing, or in the morning." Surely the coming of Jesus may be today, may be any moment.

The imminence of the Saviour's coming He illustrated by the unexpected thief.

In Matthew 24:43, 44, Jesus said:

"But know this, that if the goodman of the house had known in what watch the thief would come, he would have watched, and would not have suffered his house to be broken up. Therefore be ye also ready: for in such an hour as ye think not the Son of man cometh."

In Luke 12:39, 40, Jesus said:

"And this know, that if the goodman of the house had known what hour the thief would come, he would have watched, and not have suffered his house to be broken through. Be ye therefore ready also: for the Son of man cometh at an hour when ye think not."

The coming of a thief to break in and steal is a matter that people ought always to be forewarned and forearmed about. There is no set time for the thief to come. He may come at any moment. Therefore every householder ought to be prepared and constantly watching. Just so the coming of the Saviour may be at any moment, and the only way for us to be safe from embarrassment and shame when He comes is to be watching and ready. The saved who slumber and have their lamps smoky will be embarrassed; the lost who have no oil of salvation will not only be ashamed but will be left behind and will miss the wedding.

III. Sinner, Take Warning!

Let the unsaved readers observe the note of solemn warning in all these passages where Jesus spoke of His coming. Every time He mentions that we should watch because He might return any hour of any day there is a thrill of joy for the Christian, and yet there is a solemn and fearful thought for the unsaved.

"As the days of Noe were, so shall also the coming of the Son of man be," Jesus said. And remember that all the world, except eight souls, perished in that terrible flood because of their wickedness of which they did not repent!

And when Jesus spoke of the return of a master to call his servants to account after a long absence, He warned of the fearful punishment that would befall the unfaithful servant who began to eat and drink with the drunken and to beat the other servants, etc. The coming of Christ for His saints will be a sad day for every unsaved soul.

His coming is likened unto a thief in the night, and like the householder who, being not ready, has his home broken up and his goods stolen, so every sinner who has not trusted Christ will find himself bereft of the most precious things in this world—his loved ones who are Christians. Many a man will have mother, father, wife, babies or dear friends taken away in an instant, and he be left to face a world gone mad in sin with every single Christian removed at one stroke!

Some few will be saved during the great tribulation, but even then they cannot miss the tribulation. Some of the virgins who had no oil in their lamps may go back and get oil, but when they come to knock at the door where the wedding is, they will find the door is shut and they are left outside. Some will be saved, I say, during the great tribulation, but at what terrible cost! With churches closed, preachers gone, loved ones gone, they will be left as poor, crying babes in a wilderness of sin without a single man of God to teach them, without an older Christian to comfort them or give them strength.

And saddest of all is this fact: when Christ comes and takes away all His saints, then most of the good influences will be taken out of this world and most of those who reject Christ will then plunge headlong into such sin as they never before dreamed of. The Antichrist will be so deceptive and his power so terrible that few will oppose him. None can buy or sell without taking his mark, and those who take his mark will never be saved. Many of those who are saved will endure the fiercest persecution, hunted like wild beasts and put to death for the cause of Christ. Those who are unsaved when Jesus comes for His saints, will be left behind and most of them then will never, never, never turn to Christ for salvation.

You who read these lines, then, make sure that you are saved now for Jesus may come today. It is terribly dangerous for any unsaved sinner to live one day without Christ. It will be a thousandfold more dangerous to go into the great tribulation without Jesus when all the saints have been taken out at the coming of the Saviour.

IV. Objections Answered

Here I can imagine that some reader says, "I know that the words of Jesus seem to teach that He may return at any time. But certain other Scriptures appear to contradict that." Some good Christian people do not understand certain passages of Scripture relating to the Second Coming, and so stumble at this blessed teaching that the Saviour may return at any moment. Therefore they do not constantly watch as He commanded. They miss the joy of "the blessed hope."

However, since the Bible never contradicts itself, it will not be difficult to reconcile these Scriptures, and that I will try to do and show that there is no prophesied event to come before the return of Christ.

(1). It is sometimes said that the gospel must first be preached to all the world before Jesus comes; that He cannot return for His saints until the evangelization of the world is completed.

The Scripture quoted for this is Matthew 24:14:

"And this gospel of the kingdom shall be preached in all the world for a witness unto all nations; and then shall the end come."

The mistake here is in supposing that "the end" is the coming of Christ to take away His saints. Rather, "the end" is the end of the tribulation time. In the same passage, verse 8 tells about "the beginning of sorrows," which I believe is the time just after the rapture of the saints. Verse 21 in the same passage says: "For then shall be great tribulation, such as was not since the beginning of the world to this time, no, nor ever shall be."

Remember that there are two phases of the coming of Christ. First, He will come into the air and call out His saints to meet Him. This is the first part of His coming, the part always referred to by Jesus when He said, "Watch, therefore, for ye know neither the day nor the hour wherein the Son of man cometh" and made similar statements. Then on the earth there will intervene the seventieth or last "week" of Daniel's prophecy (Dan. 9:24–27). On the earth then there will be "the beginning of sorrows," and in the last half of the "week," three and one half years of great tribulation while the Antichrist rules the world. Then Christ will return from Heaven, coming literally in the clouds with the saints and angels to fight the battle of Armageddon, destroy the kingdoms of the Antichrist, and reign upon earth. During the great tribulation this gospel of the kingdom will be preached to all the world and then will come the end of the tribulation in the battle of Armageddon when Christ comes to set up His kingdom. That is what Matthew 24:14 means. The gospel or good news of the coming reign of Christ will be preached by a newly converted remnant in all the world after Christ comes and takes away His saints.

But in any case, the gospel has already been preached "in all the world for a witness unto all nations." At Pentecost we are told that "there were dwelling at Jerusalem Jews, devout men, out of every nation under heaven," that is, those who had come to abide there temporarily during the feast, probably from the time of the Passover through Pentecost. We are told that these heard the gospel by the Spirit-filled Christians and they were "out of every nation under heaven."

At a Bible Conference where I answered many Bible questions, came a full-blooded Indian from Oklahoma who asked for an interview. He had heard me on the radio and was sent by his tribe from northern Oklahoma to ask me this question. Opening his Bible to this verse, Acts 2:5, he said, "My people want to know if any of those devout Jews were from America, among the Indians and prehistoric races in America at that time." His question certainly astonished me, and for a time I did not know what to answer. He continued to tell me how traditions had come down through the years from father to son among his people about God, the creation, the flood, and even some faint glimmer of ideas about the Christ. All I could tell him was that I believed the statement of the Scriptures, though I did not know whether the Scripture meant that there were Jews present who had lived among the American Indians or not. In any case, the gospel was preached to representatives in all the world when it was preached at Pentecost.

Again we are told about the church at Rome that "your faith is spoken of *throughout the whole world*" (Rom. 1:8), and Paul wrote to the Colossians about "The gospel; which is come unto you, as it *is in all the world*" (Col. 1:5, 6). So the gospel has already been preached in all the world. Even if Matthew 24:14 referred to this age, then it has already been fulfilled. We ought to do all we can to get the gospel to every creature, but the second coming of Christ need not be delayed awaiting evangelization of the world. Jesus may come at any moment. No prophesied event is to intervene before the coming of Christ to take away His saints.

(2). Some people believe that the coming of the man of sin, the son of perdition, or Antichrist, must precede the coming of Christ. They have in mind the warning of II Thessalonians 2:1–3 as follows:

"*Now we beseech you, brethren, by the coming of our Lord Jesus Christ, and by our gathering together unto him, that ye be not soon shaken in mind, or be troubled, neither by spirit, nor by word, nor by letter as from us, as that the day of Christ is at hand. Let no man deceive you by any means: for that day shall not come, except there come a falling away first, and that man of sin be revealed, the son of perdition."*

The above Scripture plainly warns that "the day of Christ" is not "at hand." Some had evidently written in Paul's name, and others had evidently quoted Paul as saying that the day of Christ was at hand, that is, impending soon. Paul urged them not to be deceived since this day of Christ cannot come until there comes a great falling away and the man of sin or son of perdition (the Antichrist) be revealed.

But we must not confuse "the day of Christ" and the coming of Christ for His saints. The day of Christ here means the same as "the day of the Lord," a term used many, many times throughout the Bible. That term refers always to that future time when Christ will visibly, bodily, personally and literally return to the earth, destroy the armies of the Antichrist at the battle of Armageddon and set up His throne at Jerusalem and there begin His millennial reign. "The day of Christ" or "the day of the Lord" includes all the millennial reign of Christ until He shall turn the kingdom over to His Father. The day or period of Christ means the time of His rule. But the term, "the day of the Lord," or of Christ, never refers to Christ's coming into the air as a Bridegroom for His bride when the Christian dead will be raised and living Christians will be changed and all caught out together to meet Christ in the air. The rapture, the hope of the church when we will be caught out with Jesus for a honeymoon in our Father's house of many mansions which Jesus is now preparing for us, comes *before* "the day of Christ" or "the day of the Lord." After Christ takes out His saints, and the Holy Spirit who makes His abode in the bodies of the saints is taken away, then the man of sin will be revealed and will run his short and terrible course. The Holy Spirit who dwells in Christians now hinders the man of sin so that he does not appear and is not revealed to the world as yet. But as soon as we are taken out, then the man of sin will be revealed. Fol-

lowing him then will come the day of the Lord or the day of
Christ.

The coming of Christ to the earth when His feet shall stand
on the Mount of Olives, when He shall fight the battle of
Armageddon and sit on His throne at Jerusalem is NOT imminent. The coming of Christ into the air to call out His
saints, both living and dead, to meet Him, IS imminent. With
this in mind, you can see that this passage of Scripture does
not contradict the many plain passages where the Saviour
warns us that His coming will be like a thief in the night or
like the flood on the unsuspecting wicked in Noah's day, or
like the unexpected return of the master to judge his servants
after a long absence.

After the rapture of the saints, then there is a well-defined
train of events foretold in the Bible, and those on the earth
may know if they will read the Word of God about when the
Saviour will return to destroy the man of sin and set up His
kingdom. They may know about when the day of the Lord
will come. But before that is the sudden coming of Jesus into
the air for which all of us are to watch earnestly since no one
knows that day nor the hour and since He may come at any
moment.

After studying the Scriptures which prove the imminence
of Christ's coming, it becomes evident that the saints must be
called out of this world before the great tribulation. In order
that the rapture may be the great surprise which is foretold
in the Scripture, then the rapture of the saints must be the
next event prophesied in the Bible. It must come before the
battle of Armageddon, come before the reign of the man of
sin, or the great tribulation time. The thing that every Christian should watch for next is not the appearing of the Antichrist, not the restoration of the Roman Empire, not the
mark of the Beast, not the great tribulation, not the last great
war and the battle of Armageddon, and not the reign
of Christ at Jerusalem; but the coming of Christ for His
saints.

V. New Testament Christians Expected Christ to Come in Their Lifetime

We have given above many of the plain statements of Jesus in the gospels concerning His imminent coming, but the rest of the New Testament is equally clear. New Testament Christians expected Jesus to come at any moment.

The people at Corinth were "waiting for the coming of our Lord Jesus Christ" as the Apostle Paul wrote by divine inspiration (I Cor. 1:7). The people of Thessalonica "turned to God from idols to serve the living and true God; *and to wait for His Son from heaven,* whom he raised from the dead, even Jesus, which delivered us from the wrath to come" (I Thess. 1:9, 10). After people were saved in New Testament times, Paul properly taught them to be looking for and waiting for the coming of the Saviour! They knew His coming might be at any moment.

Writing to the Philippians, Paul said, "For our conversation is in heaven; *from whence also we look for the Saviour,* the Lord Jesus Christ: who shall change our vile body, that it may be fashioned like unto his glorious body . . ." (Phil. 3:20, 21). Paul himself was continually looking for the coming of the Saviour. He had in mind here the time of the rapture when he would have a changed body, caught out to meet Christ.

To Paul was given the highest revelations in New Testament times, we suppose. He wrote fourteen books of the Bible (if we include as his the book of Hebrews, which I think we should). He was not only a great teacher, but was himself so filled with the Spirit that he was caught up into the third Heaven and received revelations that were not lawful to utter. He was the most used of God of any New Testament character, and will meet more souls whom he won to Christ than any other apostle. And it was constantly in the mind of Paul that Jesus would come, possibly in his lifetime, so he looked for Him steadily.

When Paul wrote about the rapture of the saints, that event

when Christ comes into the air to receive His own, he wrote of himself as being among the living. In I Thessalonians 4:15 he said, "We which are alive and remain unto the coming of the Lord shall not prevent them which are asleep."

"We which are alive and remain"! Paul expected to be alive and remain until Jesus came. Again in the seventeenth verse of the same passage he said, "Then we which are alive and remain shall be caught up together with them in the clouds, to meet the Lord in the air." The Christian dead are mentioned in the third person, but the living are mentioned in the plural, first person. It was Paul's confident hope, nay, his expectation, that he should be living when Jesus should come. That is how clearly were the apostles were taught the imminency of Christ's return. They knew that He might return any moment.

Likewise, in I Corinthians 15:51, 52, Paul says:

"Behold, I shew you a mystery; We shall not all sleep, but WE shall all be changed, in a moment, in the twinkling of an eye, at the last trump: for the trumpet shall sound, and the dead shall be raised incorruptible, and WE shall be changed."

Again Paul spoke of the dead in the third person, "The dead shall be raised," but he spoke of himself with all the living, saying, "And we shall be changed." Again you notice that this is the time of the rapture when Christ calls His saints out to meet Him in the air. He is not speaking of the day of the Lord, a little later when Christ returns with all the saints to destroy the Antichrist and reign on the earth.

In James, the fifth chapter, are several references to the coming of Jesus as if He might come at any moment. To Jewish Christians scattered abroad, the inspired writer says, "Be patient therefore, brethren, unto the coming of the Lord" (verse 7). In verse 8 he says, "The coming of the Lord draweth nigh." In verse 9 he says, "Behold, the judge standeth before the door." These statements would only be true for that generation (or for any other generation, for that matter), if Jesus might be expected at any moment. It is the clear testimony of all the New Testament that we should expect Him at that hour or any time since the time of the apostles.

The imminency of the coming of the Saviour, and of course of the things that follow, are clearly taught by the Apostle Peter. In I Peter 4:7, we are told, "But the end of all things is at hand: be ye therefore sober, and watch unto prayer." We are reminded of the exhortation of Jesus to "watch therefore, for ye know neither the day nor the hour wherein the Son of man cometh." The coming of the Saviour was at hand in the sense that He might come at any moment; and in the same sense His coming is still at hand.

The book of Second Peter was written primarily with this in mind to stir up the people, reminding them of the promises of the apostles and prophets concerning the coming of the Saviour. Here is what that book says:

"*This second epistle, beloved, I now write unto you; in both which I stir up your pure minds by way of remembrance: that ye may be mindful of the words which were spoken before by the holy prophets, and of the commandment of us the apostles of the Lord and Saviour: knowing this first, that there shall come in the last days scoffers, walking after their own lusts, and saying, Where is the promise of his coming? for since the fathers fell asleep, all things continue as they were from the beginning of the creation*"—II Pet. 3:1–4.

And then follows in verse 9 the inspired explanation of why the coming of Christ has been postponed.

"*The Lord is not slack concerning his promise, as some men count slackness; but is longsuffering to us-ward, not willing that any should perish, but that all should come to repentance.*"

The coming of the Lord is at hand: it is only God's mercy that delays His coming so that others may be saved!

One should notice, too, that it is scoffers and unbelievers who will not believe that the Saviour is likely to come soon. These scoffers and unbelievers walk after their own lusts (verse 3) and do not believe in direct creation and other miracles of God (verse 5). Dear reader, do not put yourself among these scoffers! Believe the Word of God that Jesus is coming. We believe He is coming very soon; we know that He may come at any moment.

VI. The Closing Testimony of the Bible

Today I have been greatly impressed with the powerful exhortation given us in the last chapter of the Bible concerning the coming of the Saviour. Here God's revelation to man is finished; the canon of Scripture is closed. And in the last chapter of Revelation at least five times we are warned that the Saviour is likely to come at any moment. Verse 6 says, "These sayings are faithful and true: and the Lord God of the holy prophets sent his angel to shew unto his servants the things WHICH MUST SHORTLY BE DONE."

Any honest interpretation of that verse must agree that it means the events pictured in Revelation must shortly be fulfilled, that is, every reader should look forward and expect Him soon. And remember that the next thing on God's calendar is the coming of the Saviour to take away His saints.

And then in verse 7 the Saviour said, "BEHOLD, I COME QUICKLY: blessed is he that keepeth the sayings of the prophecy of this book."

Jesus is coming *quickly*. Is not that meant for a warning that you must be ready? Does not that mean that Jesus is likely to come at any moment? Unless this Bible is a fraud we must understand it so. The time is not named, but we are warned to be on our guard, to watch and be ready.

Again, in verse 10 the Lord said, "Seal not the sayings of the prophecy of this book: for THE TIME IS AT HAND."

"The time is at hand"! That is what Peter said (I Pet. 4:7). The coming of the Saviour is at hand.

Then in verse 12 we are warned again, "AND, BEHOLD, I COME QUICKLY; and my reward is with me, to give every man according as his work shall be."

And then the last verse in the Bible besides the closing benediction is verse 20 which says, "He which testifieth these things saith, SURELY I COME QUICKLY. Amen. Even so, come, Lord Jesus."

Conclusion: Are You Ready?

Quickly! *Quickly! QUICKLY!* Jesus is coming quickly! He may come at any moment; it seems certain that He will come soon. Brother, are you ready?

I beg every Christian to lay aside the cares and covetousness and pleasure of this world that would prevent you from being happy if Jesus should come today. Here we must return to the words of the Saviour in Luke 21:34–36.

"And take heed to yourselves, lest at any time your hearts be overcharged with surfeiting, and drunkenness, and cares of this life, and so that day come upon you unawares. For as a snare shall it come on all them that dwell on the face of the whole earth. Watch ye therefore, and pray always, that ye may be accounted worthy to escape all these things that shall come to pass, and to stand before the Son of man."

Notice these commands, "Take heed to yourselves." 'Your heart will be overcharged with eating and drinking, and the cares of this life, and so that day will come upon you unawares,' the Saviour said, 'if you do not beware.' "Watch ye therefore, and pray always" is the next command of Jesus. Christians are to take heed about their lives. They are to watch hopefully, expectantly for the Saviour's coming, and they are to pray often for His coming. Jesus gave it in the model prayer, "Thy kingdom come. Thy will be done in earth, as it is in heaven." That prayer asks for the return of Jesus and for His kingdom and all the related events. And John, the beloved disciple, was allowed to use the impassioned and Spirit-directed prayer of his heart when he cried out, "Even so, come, Lord Jesus" (Rev. 22:20). So, Christians, take heed, watch and pray. Do not lose your testimony. Do not be too busy about making money. Do not get too absorbed in pleasure. Do not eat too much or drink too much. God will destroy both the belly and the meats, Paul says. Rather, look for Jesus and live a pure life and win souls so you will not be ashamed before Him at His coming.

And, sinner, are you ready for Jesus to come? If not, only one thing will make you ready, and that is for you to trust Him today to forgive you, surrender your whole heart to Him, claim Him as your Saviour! Do it today! Make sure of it while you can, and then you, too, can join in the happy watching for the coming of the Saviour.

One night at the close of a service I went down a darkened aisle to prepare for a baptizing while the people waited. A woman seized my sleeve and stopped me. With quivering lips and broken voice she said, "Brother Rice, do you believe Jesus is coming soon?"

I answered back, "Yes, I believe that Jesus is coming soon: I ought to believe it much more than I do. There are many people who think so. Certainly the Bible teaches He may come at any moment."

"Oh! I am afraid He is! I am afraid He is!" she said. I was startled and asked her the reason why she, a Christian, should talk this way. I said, "Don't you know you are saved? Haven't you trusted Jesus for forgiveness?"

"Oh, yes," she said, "but my husband is not saved. I am afraid that Jesus will come and leave him behind. What will I do if Jesus comes and my husband isn't saved and I have to go away and leave him?" I earnestly urged her to put the salvation of her husband's soul before everything else.

Do you believe that Jesus is coming? Then the way to prove it is to win souls, separate yourself from the wickedness of this world and let your light shine while you can.

When I used to play college football, the referee would call to the captains of the opposing teams,

"Are you ready, Decatur?"

"Are you ready, Denton?"

And then the whistle would blow. So with an earnest heart I call today to every reader,

"Are you ready, Christian?"

"Are you ready, sinner?"

"Watch therefore, for ye know neither the day nor the hour wherein the Son of man cometh."

Other Books by Dr. Rice

PRAYER: Asking and Receiving

The most popular book on prayer in America—160,000 copies in print.

Full of Scriptures, heart-warming exposition, concrete examples from Dr. Rice's own life, it cultivates a believing, expectant attitude to receive from God. Twenty-one chapters on every phase of prayer—hindrances to prayer, praying through, healing, miracles, the sin of prayerlessness, praying in the will of God, praying for everything you need and want. Will transform your prayer life!

328 pages, cloth, $2.50

THE HOME: Courtship, Marriage, and Children

A practical Bible manual on the home. Answers the problems of young people anticipating marriage, discusses carefully and Scripturally the relationships of husbands and wives, discipline, teaching and winning children, family worship, divorce, etc. Dr. Rice writes from a wealth of experience as pastor and counsellor—and father of six. He speaks with authority, because he teaches straight from the Bible.

Sunday School Times recommends, "One of the best and most complete discussions of these topics from the Bible viewpoint." Cloth, 381 pages, 22 chapters, $2.50

The Power of Pentecost

This book will transform the lives—literally—of many Christians who desperately need power. Fifteen thrilling chapters including: The Lost Secret; The Usual Work of the Spirit; Jesus, Filled with the Spirit; Misunderstood Pentecost; Empowered Witnessing; Bible Terminology; Ministry Gifts in Old Testament and New; Speaking with Tongues, Power for Every Christian; How to Be Filled; Prayer a Condition; Why Persistent Praying Is Necessary; Do You Really Want to Be Filled?; How Great Soul Winners Were Filled; Claim Your Blessing!

441 pages, cloth binding, $3.00

15¢ each   *Life-Changing*

These pamphlets by Dr. John R. Rice have been a tremendous help to thousands of people. Nearly two million copies have been printed. Each is 5½ x 8, has 24 to 40 pages, attractive pictured covers. Buy them to settle your own questions. Give them to needy friends with real assurance. 15¢ each, set of 30 only . . . $4.00.

FOR THE UNSAVED:

Hell—What the Bible Says About It. Plain, simple, compelling Bible teaching. 190,000 copies in print, 40 pages.

Sermon from a Catholic Bible. What the Catholic Bible says about the Bible, the Mass, the sinner's mediator, and how to be saved. Reverent, and kindly. Ideal for Catholic friends.

Neglect the Shortest Way to Hell. A powerful message to the unsaved.

All Have Sinned. Corners the sinner with overwhelming, convicting proof of his sin. Shows how vilest may repent, be saved.

The Last Judgment of the Unsaved Dead. A clear, evangelistic exposition of Revelation, chapter 20, shows sinners dragged out of hell to face their records.

A Good Man Lost and a Bad Man Saved. Shows how the most moral people in the world will be lost without heart repentance—how a crooked tax collector was saved.

Infidels—Answered by Three Immortals. Compiled by Dr. Rice. "My Infidelity and What Became of It," by B. H. Carroll; "How I Know There Is a God," by R. A. Torrey; and "D. L. Moody and the Free Thinkers."

Trailed by a Wild Beast. Sermon on, "Be Sure Your Sin Will Find You Out!" Also sermon "Come Unto Me."

Religious But Lost. Proof from the Bible that millions of moral religious people who expect to go to Heaven will never get there, and why.

Crossing the Deadline. The unpardonable sin, what it is, who commits it, how to know it.

DOCTRINAL TEACHING:

Eight Gospel Absurdities If a Born Again Soul Ever Loses Salvation. Kindly, convincing.

Healing in Answer to Prayer. Sane, Scriptural; recognizes God's power to heal; shows it is sometimes God's will to use doctors. Many actual healings.

Verbal Inspiration of the Bible. Proof from the Bible that the original manuscripts are direct, divine revelation. Proves Bible to be infallibly correct.

Can a Saved Person Ever Be Lost? Discusses many Scriptures sometimes presented to teach that a saved person can be lost, then positive proof they cannot.

Christs Literal Reign on Earth, from David's throne at Jerusalem. Brief Scriptural introduction to Bible prophecy and premillenial truth.

Sunday or Sabbath. Which should Christians observe? Why Sunday is not the Sabbath.